WE
ADOPTED FIVE
SPECIAL-NEEDS
FOSTER KIDS

WE ADOPTED FIVE SPECIAL-NEEDS FOSTER KIDS

THE INSPIRING TRUE STORY OF HOW AN ABSOLUTELY CRAZY IDEA LED TO ONE VERY BIG, HAPPY FAMILY

Ann Ellsworth

Skyhorse Publishing

Skyhorse Publishing books may be purchased in bulk at special discounts for sales promotion, corporate gifts, fund-raising, or educational purposes. Special editions can also be created to specifications. For details, contact the Special Sales Department, Skyhorse Publishing, 307 West 36th Street, 11th Floor, New York, NY 10018 or info@skyhorsepublishing.com.

Skyhorse® and Skyhorse Publishing® are registered trademarks of Skyhorse Publishing, Inc.®, a Delaware corporation.

Visit our website at www.skyhorsepublishing.com.

10 9 8 7 6 5 4 3 2 1

Library of Congress Cataloging-in-Publication Data is available on file.

Cover design by Paul Qualcom
Cover photo credit: iStockphoto

Print ISBN: 978-1-5107-4529-2
Ebook ISBN: 978-1-5107-4530-8

Printed in the United States of America.

To My Amazing Children

CONTENTS

PROLOGUE

*I*n the spring of 2008, my husband and I adopted five high-risk children through the foster care system in New York City. At the time, Dan was forty-five and I was forty-three. I was childless, excited, and unprepared. Our children, aged five to ten years old, had been neglected and abused, and diagnosed with behavioral, cognitive, physical, and psychiatric conditions, none of which could be treated medically.

I read a lot of books about adoption before becoming a parent, but none came close to describing what we went through when adopting a large sibling group of older, special-needs children through foster care. I wish there was a book that could have shared some of the systems that worked, given me a heads-up on a few issues I had not seen coming, and put some faces to the devastating effects of early trauma, abuse, and neglect on developing brains.

Maybe this memoir can be a remembrance for my children of our first years together, a baby book of sorts, a mark in pencil on our kitchen door frame to show them how little they were, and how far they have come.

Maybe this story can reach out to someone like myself,

someone in a position to act and make a difference, but who had never considered special-needs adoption. Before I started this journey, I had been completely unaware of foster care; I'd never known anyone who had gone through the system and had no idea of the enormous need for permanent homes. I didn't know that I, as an adult, could make all the difference in the world to a child. I could be a parent to someone who didn't have parents. I could make a family for children who didn't have a family.

Love can make a family, but a family is not love. It is a container for love. It is a secondary womb where love can do its slow work of growing and nurturing a child's heart and brain. And it doesn't end when you grow up and are ready to leave. A family misses you, waves from the porch until you're out of sight, then waits and hopes for your return. It loves you when you feel unlovable, accepts you when the world turns away, and hugs you even when you don't hug back.

I always had it. But not until I loved my own children did I understand what it means not to have parents, a family, a home. Not everybody has a family—but every human deserves one and every child needs one.

Author Note: Please be advised that this book speaks candidly about violence and severe mental and physical abuse.

1

CONCEPTION

*J*ake lay staring up at me by the river, lying there, grinning ear to ear like a boy with a secret. "Hey cousin," I said, "what's buzzin?" Jake yelled back at me, his voice distorted and strained. He stiffened his arms and legs and yelled again. My first cousin Melanie had adopted Jake as an infant. She was sitting ten feet upstream and I looked over at her for help: "He's hard to understand," she said, "but if you listen carefully, he has a lot to say." I knelt on the smooth rocks and put my ear near his mouth.

He spoke again, arching his back. It sounded like, "I have to pee." I pulled my head back, "You have to pee?" Jake rocked his body side to side, excited. "All right then," I said. I called to my husband, knee deep in the river, "Dan! Jake needs to pee!" I smiled down at my cousin, "I don't see you for five years and the first thing you say to me is 'I have to pee'?" He laughed, rocking back and forth. Dan splashed to the shore, "I gotcha, buddy." Dan rolled Jake onto his arm and, lifting him up, pointed him towards the reeds. Jake yelled something at me. His mother translated, "Jake says no peeking!" I yelled back at Jake, "Not peeking!"

At nine years old Jake was maybe three feet long, and very thin, with stiff blond hair and lazy blue eyes. His body was limp from cerebral palsy; he couldn't stand or hold up his head. His speech was thick, but consistent, like a dialect. Once I caught onto his speech patterns, he was chatty and engaging. "My mom is trying to get me to use the bathroom," he said. "She gives me a quarter every time I don't pee my pants. But it's hard for me, so she gives me a nickel if I can get most of it in the toilet and just have a little spot on my pants."

"That sounds like a money maker right there."

I love my family. I have fifty-two first cousins, each with an average of six kids. It's hard to foster family tensions with so many bodies looking alike, so many humans growing so fast. We come from the Intermountain West, Mormon Country: wide streets and narrow paths. I am no longer active in the church, but with a last name like Ellsworth, I enjoy a cultural affiliation with my religion; faith and family are synonymous and my worldview remains awash with that hallmark Mormon optimism.

My life, however, was taking a very different path. I was thirty-seven, childless, enjoying a career as a classical musician, and the first ever in my family to get divorced in her twenties. I considered myself a pioneer in this regard. I was recently remarried to a lapsed Lutheran from South Dakota. He loved and accepted my family as his own and, except for our wildly differing doctrines, I felt at home in Dan's congregation, sitting in his hometown church, watching him sing in the choir.

Dan and I were hosting my family reunion at our lodge in the Adirondacks, an old YMCA camp with a big field stone fireplace, bunk rooms, and a twenty-three-foot dining room table. It was rare for my family to gather so far east, but the lodge was big enough to hold everyone and in close proximity to the Mormon Mecca: Palmyra, New York, the birthplace of our faith. Jake and I were enjoying some quality time with our loved ones. We lay on our backs, watching the clouds while Jake shared with me his adoption story. "When I was born, I had cerebral palsy and my birth mom couldn't take care of me, so one of the doctors in the hospital called my Dad, and my Dad says he knew right then I was his son. He told my Mom, 'Our son is lying in a hospital in Seattle and I am going to get him.' He got in the car right then and drove six hundred miles to pick me up." There was pride in Jake's voice. He belonged to someone.

Jake was four the first time we met. I was on a road trip and stopped to visit Melanie and her family on their little farm in Idaho. The kids were outside chasing chickens when I pulled up, Jake screaming with excitement. I had to smile as Melanie's husband, Max, grabbed his tiny son by the waist and dove with him head-first under a bush after a chicken, just like any other kid. These are good people. I wasn't like them, but I was proud to belong to them.

* * *

I had met Dan two years earlier on an online dating service. My brother helped me with my profile: solidly non-smoker but not particular about age, race, religion, or income. Dan and I spoke on the phone and he told me he was an FBI agent. I said, "Well, that's hot. Are you sure you want to go with that? Have you tried race car driver or astronaut?" He laughed, "I'm going with it." I met him the next night for dinner. He was serious-looking and clean shaven, with a military buzz cut. I stared at him, trying to reconcile his strange appearance with the fact that he seemed so familiar. I felt like saying, "Oh, it's you! Thank god!" But we'd never met. He asked me about my family and what it was like growing up in Northern California. He asked about my big life choices, what my music career meant to me and, after dessert, he asked if I would walk with him through Times Square. I said, "Sure, I'll show you where I work." I took him through the stage door of the broadway show I was currently playing. I showed him the orchestra pit and costume rooms. It was Sunday night, so we had the place to ourselves, talking as we walked, the acoustic of our voices changing as we walked onto the stage. We stood there for a few minutes looking out into the dark, empty seats. Taking my hand, he gently kissed me. It was wonderful. I closed my eyes and my head dropped slowly onto his shoulder. I rested there, surrounded, feeling quietly terrified, lost and happy in the middle of our embrace. His slow breathing brought me back and I took his arm as he walked me home.

For our next outing, Dan invited me to a sentencing. *What does one wear to a sentencing?* "It's not the most conventional date, but," he said, "you might find it interesting." *Why not?*

Dan sat in front with the prosecution and I sat behind him, staring at his shoulders beneath his wrinkled grey suit. Dan was living on a boat in the Hudson River at the time, directly across from my apartment in Hell's Kitchen, so his dress clothes were all a little wrinkled and had a sort of musty boat smell. The case involved a child kidnapping, and the judge spoke harshly and at length to the convict before pronouncing the sentence. The court adjourned and the mother came up to Dan, crying, hugging and thanking him for saving her child. I had never seen a mother's look like that before. I got chills.

After, I invited him for a ride up the Palisades on my motorbike. He climbed on behind me, put his arms around my waist, his helmet tipping slightly right of mine. I accelerated out of the rest area, shifting fast, and was in fourth by the time we merged with traffic. Dan was hiding his weight, leaning when I leaned, turning when I turned, bracing his feet on the pegs when I braked so there was no pressure from him as the front shock compressed. His face shield clicked against the back of my helmet and I started blushing. *Oh, Ann, really?*

* * *

But the moment of truth soon arrived, the moment when my partner wanted to hang out with me, but I wanted to practice without being interrupted. Dan invited me to come over to the boat. I said, "I wish I could but I have some work to do, maybe another time." He said, "Come practice out here, I promise I won't bother you." I went out and set up in the forward cabin. I could see him on the dock working on a project, walking back and forth, sawing and drilling things. For two and a half hours he did not speak or look at me. No solicitous waves, winks, or annoying, "Can I get you anything?" When I was done, I packed up and walked out onto the dock. He put his drill down and smiled, "How was it for you?" I laughed, blushing, "I like it." He pulled me to him, "Me, too." We made out in the afterglow of our compatibility.

Around that time, I was traveling to Austria for a week on a study grant and Dan invited himself to come with me. This was huge for me, to travel together to Vienna, my musical Mecca. But he came with me and he stayed with me. He listened with me, watched with me, and gasped with me in the thin air of high art. Ears to Mahler, eyes to Klimt, we dressed in duvets for days and days, the horizontal, sideways view. "You are my choice," said the moist lower lip of his kisses. "I choose you."

Communication under these circumstances is the stuff of life: nonverbal, rich in meaning, short on specifics and ripe with promises never made. I lay there with him, still with love, unable to discern my feet from his, two now four, nesting alone in their own close meeting. I was floating in the thought that there might be nothing else to life but this moment when a shadow flicked across my conscience, and I heard myself whisper aloud, "If I get pregnant, I'm keeping the baby." *Wait, what?*

Is this you trying to be responsible? Because as family planning goes, it's a little short on planning. Oh my God! It was your mother voice! You're mothering! Dan interrupted my self-talk with a compelling, nonverbal confirmation that not only was he was fine with me getting pregnant, he thought it was an awesome idea. I did not get pregnant but for the first time in my life, I conceived of myself as a mother. It was huge for me and an opening into imagining having children.

We got engaged shortly after our trip. My brother was concerned: "He's a great guy, Ann, but I just don't see it." Nobody could see it; everybody thought it was going too fast. "Where's the magic? Why him?" I said, "He makes me feel like a woman." My brother, bearded, 6'3" and 200 pounds, laughed and said, "He makes ME feel like a woman. Not good enough!" I sighed, "I'll tell you but you can't tell anyone. Promise!" John held up his pinky for pinky swear. I blushed, ". . . he sings to me." John's jaw hit the floor. "No way." I nodded, "He sings to me. Country music songs." My brother took a deep breath and sat back in his chair. "Marry him." I do.

Dan and I bought the lodge and invited our families to the Adirondacks for a week of canoeing, barbecue, and roof repair. Then one day after breakfast, Dan told everyone to leave their plates on the table. "We're going to the waterfall." And with all our loved ones near, Dan and I eloped, right there at the edge of the falls. His sister, a Lutheran minister, made it legal.

Flying back to the city, I thought to myself, *It doesn't get any better than this.* And I was right. It didn't. It was September 9, 2001.

* * *

After 9/11, Dan's work went into overdrive. Months of twenty-hour work days, relocations, and just as things finally started settling down, the Marine Corps called wanting Dan to come back in. He was an officer before joining the Bureau, and an expert in the coordination of close air support for ground troops.

* * *

We were separated for almost two years. When Dan finally came home we had to get to know each other again. We held hands a lot, didn't talk about the past and spoke softly about the future. These things take time. Three years passed.

* * *

The 2005 reunion was held at Fish Lake in southern Utah. Dan and I had started talking, still softly, about starting a family. Ours was a second marriage for both of us and we were both heavily into our careers. I had never felt strongly about having kids and certainly not my own—with such a large family, there were certainly enough Ann molecules on the planet. Independent of the reproductive imperative, we asked ourselves what having children was really about. In the end we agreed: having a family was about giving something to someone else.

Jake was twelve now and handsome, giving rides to his cousins on the back of his new bright red electric wheelchair. "Jake!" I called out, "Sweet ride, cousin!" He motored over to me, spinning around, showing off his wheelies, talking me through the specs. I asked Jake about his trip to Ecuador, where his parents, Melanie and Max, ran a program organizing college students to volunteer in the orphanages. Jake struggled as he spoke, "Ecuador was fun but also intense. I love the kids but it makes me sad. I mean, I have the one thing they really want: parents. I don't think we can really know what it's like not to have parents." I turned away from him and pretended I was looking at something far away, blinking to keep my tears back. I nodded, "That's a tough one." Jake was quiet.

That night after the barbecue, Dan and I sat on a bluff overlooking the picnic area. I told Dan about my talk with Jake. "He can't sit or stand, can't feed himself, and he's watching these kids out there playing soccer feeling sorry for them because he has parents and they don't." Dan took my hand and we sat for a while. Above us the sky was turning pink and grey, that southwestern sky, so big it rounds the horizon. Below us, a water balloon fight was in high gear. "We should step up," Dan said. "The need is there." I felt a chill. My head tipped back and, looking up, I felt I might slip off this earth and fall into the vacuous universe. And in that moment, on that quiet bluff, an adoption was conceived.

2

THE ADOPTIVE INDUSTRIAL COMPLEX

*D*an and I flew back to New York, quiet and expectant.
I didn't want to tell anyone we were going to adopt. I
wanted to keep it inside, this strange, slow calm I felt
in the days after our decision. This was new for me, feeling
ready. I had always feared having children: the change, the loss
of control, the loss of self. I'd had scares before, times I thought
I might be pregnant. Gripped and panicky, all my emotions
firing at once: hope, fear, ecstasy, despair, until my fate in a
pale pastel would surface on the pregnancy test and release me,
exhausted and childless, into a pile of sadness and relief. Our
decision to adopt was not that. I wanted this. I felt grounded
and strong, as right as rain.

I called my cousin. "Melanie! Dan and I have decided to
adopt!" She was excited for me. "That's wonderful, tell everyone
you know." I wanted to ask her about special needs. "What's it
like raising Jake?" Melanie paused. "It's very physical," she said.
"Very physical and very spiritual." I could hear the weight in
her voice. "Jake has been an enormous gift to our family, especially to the other kids. Huge lessons there. If you are open to
adopting special needs, be sure you know what you are signing

up for. It's a great service if you can do it. Those kids are hard to place."

Her husband Max got on the phone, "Wow, Ann, it's great news! I wished I'd known a week ago. I got a call about a two-year-old South American who needs heart surgery. You guys have health insurance, right?" We did indeed. "And you've got your home study done, right?" Hmm. I cringed a little, "Nope, never heard of it." Max paused. "Well, you have to have a home study and get approved. You might want to get on that. You'll need it for domestic or foreign adoption. Best bet is to get in touch with an agency." I was writing this down. "Home study. Agency. Thanks, Max. I'll let you know when we're all set."

I called my social worker cousin at Columbia and she recommended an agency on the Upper East Side. I made an appointment for Dan and me. The social worker was all smart and businesslike in her red, rectangular glasses. "It says here you are open to special needs, micro-preemies, cystic fibrosis, etc. What do you know about these conditions?" We gave her an overview, throwing in a few personal stories that would make us seem more credible, personable.

She was not impressed. "No religious affiliation . . . would you consider yourselves religious or spiritual, just not attached to an institution?" Neither. She was not encouraging. She shuffled our papers and shrugged, "I don't get it. You don't fit the profile. Both professionals, double income, no kids, no religious affiliation . . . it doesn't make sense. Why special needs?" There was a pause. Dan said, "I grew up in South Dakota." I jumped in, "I was raised Mormon!" She leaned back in her chair and nodded slowly. "So you're both from out west. That's where most of our special-needs kids get placed: big religious families with cultures that value life." *Value life?* Her choice of words seemed out of place on the Upper East Side of New York City. "You're going to need a lot more information," she said. "Read these," and handed us a list of books. She stood up and thanked us for coming. We were being shown the door! I couldn't believe it!

"Can you recommend someone to do our home study?" I asked as she walked us into the hallway. She handed me a list of names and numbers. "Anyone in particular?" I asked as she shook our hands. "Anyone of them would be fine." The elevator closed. I was incredulous. "That's not at all how I thought this was going to go! I thought she was going to hug us, have us sign something, and walk us down to the nursery." I felt dismissed. Why was I being dismissed?

Brushing my teeth that night, I gave myself a good stare in the mirror. The real question was, why would anyone want to give me a baby? I had no experience: Hell, my biggest parenting cred to date was being Melanie's cousin. Why would anyone want to give me a child to raise? The answer was easy and sad: money.

*   *   *

Armed with a checkbook and high-hopes, Dan and I entered what we called "The Adoptive Industrial Complex." Many of the agencies that make up this enormous infrastructure were, like us, well-intended. Nonetheless, they were businesses and most of the meetings I attended were an uncomfortable mix of high emotion and enormous fees. The persons who ran these meetings wanted to know what we were looking for: color of hair, curly or straight, race, color of skin and eyes, age and disposition. I could buy a photograph, a video, get a list of a child's characteristics on the Down syndrome rubric or a deluxe examination by a physician. "Would you like a boy or a girl?" I was concerned that we were getting off track. The process was overtaking the product. "Would you like more than one? There is a rebate if you get two and of course you save on airfare!" What do I want? I want to give! They were selling me a noun and I wanted a verb.

Like nausea, the paperwork came in waves: personal essays, fingerprints, references, every address since 1970, finances, and medical histories on both sides of both families. This was so different from a pregnancy. There was no weight gain, no sonograms, no life force driving its miracle through your body. With adoption, it is all on you. You have to manually grow your baby every day, call by call, check by check.

Four months into our adoption process, which I tried not to think of as the first month of our second trimester, we chose a foundation that facilitates adoptions from Eastern Europe as an arm of its child advocacy work. They had a reputation for being both ethical and politically connected. *Wait, is that possible?* At one point, they told us that a man holding a sign would meet us at the airport, "and you will need to give him five-thousand dollars in cash which we suggest you carry in your shoes." Dan was already in bed when I got home from the meeting. "I just keep thinking how that five-thousand dollars would be better spent on, oh, I don't know, maybe raising a kid?"

There was no easy answer. We'd been warned against domestic adoption, the potential that it held for heartbreak is enormous: biological relatives can appear years into your family life and take your child. Or you finally find someone who wants to give you their child and at the last minute, they change their mind. It's devastating. Nobody wants to go through that.

I started hashing over our remaining options when Dan looked at me and said, "Foster care." *WHAT?* I froze. We had never spoken of foster care. He said, "I checked it out." I gulped. The only stories I'd heard about foster care adoption were disastrous.

"Dan! That is so hard core!"

"That's where the need is."

"But the horror stories . . ."

"Horror? A horror for the adults or the kids?"

"Did you say 'kids'? Plural?" I was almost yelling.

"Sibling groups are considered special needs."

I felt a chill. "It would be really, really hard."

"It's harder for them."

He was right. I called my sister, Michelle. Michelle had agreed to be our backup, the person to take our kids should anything happen to us. "So, we've decided to adopt through the foster care system," I told her. Silence ". . . Michelle? Are you there?" Silence. She sounded stressed when she finally answered, "I'm out. I can't take that on. Oh my God, Ann! I've heard terrible stories. I have my own children to consider. I have a friend who adopted a foster kid, it was horrible!"

I called my brother John, my kid brother, my best bud. "Dude, you have to sign this form." John said, "Ann, I can't raise your kids, my life is not set up for that." I assured him, "You don't have to raise them, you just have to decide what to do with them if we both die at the same time. Come on." Silence. Then finally: "Fine. I'll sign."

We were back on track.

3

ARE YOU MY MOTHER?

"*T*hey want to know if we would be okay with the behaviors listed here below, please mark in pen the boxes yes or no." Dan and I were lying in bed filling out forms for foster-to-adopt parents. I read aloud:

Masturbation, masturbation of other children, masturbation of other children of the same sex. Yes? Check.

Lighting matches, lighting matches to start fires, starting fires. Check yes.

Defecating in public, defecating in his or her clothes, smearing his or her own feces on bathroom walls and environment. "Wow," I said, "it kind of makes you wonder what the hell happened to these kids."

"I'm okay with it," said Dan.

"Good. Check. Schizophrenia? I didn't know you could diagnose a child with schizophrenia. Down syndrome? Fetal alcohol syndrome? Autistic? I'm going to say no. I think we could further a child who is not topped off intellectually, maybe go with emotionally disturbed, but not mentally ill. ADHD, ADD, check, check, all good."

"I agree."

Cystic fibrosis, multiple sclerosis, cerebral palsy, muscular dystrophy, birth defects. Check.

"Copy."

"Blind, check yes. Here's one: Deaf. I don't know if I could do that. I don't know how I would communicate. Sign language of course, but in terms of relating to the child, it would be difficult for me. I don't know if I could do it."

"I feel that way about sight."

"You could do deaf, but not blind?"

"You're a musician, I'm a pilot."

"I never thought of us that way. You perceive the world visually whereas I can imagine a world without sight but not without sound."

"We can learn."

"Right. Check. Sibling groups."

Dan was interested. "What do you think?"

"Well, it would be hard in our apartment but we could definitely go more than one."

"How many?"

"Let me think. Two? I would have the laundry sent out. Three, I would need the groceries delivered and part-time help. Four? All of the above, plus live-in help. We'd have to move."

"We could do it."

"Sounds good. And just to reiterate, I will be the primary caregiver, but I am not a stay-at-home mom. Just something to keep in mind."

"Copy."

We were in agreement then.

* * *

Through our research, we'd discovered that there is an online database of children all over the country, legally freed for adoption and awaiting a permanent home. There were over 2,500 children waiting in New York City alone. We typed in our preferences for children six years and younger, twelve years and younger, and then eighteen years and younger. There was an exponential rise in numbers as the kids timed out of their formative years. And I thought online dating was ageist and cruel. Preadolescent? Teenager? Good luck with that. Do teenagers need a family? Yes. Is it fair? No.

There are laws limiting what an agency can reveal about a minor online, so main interests were often listed. But really? Eighty-five percent of all foster children like the Yankees, watching television, and eating pizza? The real information is between the lines. "This child should be placed in a caring home with no other children," or "This child needs a loving home with no pets." Profiles can mention a disability but not what the disability is, or the need for medication but not what the medication is. Flag words are, "challenged," "special," "potential," and "winning smile."

When searching, Dan and I both found kids we instantly fell in love with. If we could have adopted them in that moment, we would have. I bet a lot of people would have. But it doesn't work that way. We had a long way to go.

* * *

Before adopting through foster care, we first had to become foster parents. We needed thirty hours of instruction through a city-sponsored program for foster-to-adopt parents and then, with adoption as the goal, we would match with children whose biological parents no longer had parental rights. The kids would be placed with us as foster children and then six to eight months later, we would legally adopt them. Our class, consisting of four other couples and two single women, met Tuesday nights in a building on West 39th Street.

The instruction involved group discussions, class participation, and role playing. In one exercise I was assigned the role of a mother in a scenario showing how children get taken into foster care. My character had two daughters, ages ten and two, and she and her husband had recently moved to a new city where he had a job in a factory. They lived in a small house about five miles out of town, far away from family and friends.

In this story, my husband of ten years loses his job, we run out of savings, tensions mount, and we begin to argue. The baby starts screaming, my husband starts yelling, and I tell the ten year old to take her sister outside. I push her towards the door, she trips and hits her head on the coffee table and goes to school the next morning with a black eye. She gets flagged by social services. My husband, depressed, drives drunk and crashes the car, punches the cop who arrives on the scene, and spends thirty days in prison.

I have no money, no car, and no one to help with the two year old during the day. So I take a night shift at the convenience store, walking into town after the girls are asleep and walking back before they wake up. One night the baby wakes up crying and the pre-teen older sister doesn't know what to do. She walks to the neighbor's house, they call social services, and the children are gone before I get home.

This was the example they chose for the class? I could not believe it. These children didn't need our help, the parents did. They hit a rough patch and needed a hand. They needed support. I broke with my character and spoke out in class, "Hey, here's an idea! What if our social safety net had sent someone to help this woman with the kids for a week or so? Brought some food in, asked her what she needed? It would have cost what? $500? $1,000? That's still less than the $580 per month per kid stipend we give the foster parents. Now we've got trauma to two children, a stressed marriage bent to the breaking point." I looked over at Dan and he dropped his eyes as if to say, "Shh."

I sat down. "Sorry." Our teacher observed a moment of silence and continued. After class, she took me aside. "You're right. This system is broken. I've seen kids taken for less than that."

I laid low for the rest of the classes. Our instructor was talking about how to deal with some of the behaviors of children who have been traumatized. "They may not be able to appreciate what you are doing for them. They may not trust you right away, and even lash out as they deal with feelings of loss and helplessness." One of our classmates, a young man in his thirties, said, "So let's say we turn my office into a kid's bedroom, paint it, fix it up, and buy him a bed. And you're saying he may not thank us for that? How does that make us feel?"

Dan responded quietly, "Don't expect gratitude." Silence.

"He's right," said our teacher. She went on. "If a child is hitting and kicking, you may want to get him a punching bag or karate lessons, something to help him focus and channel his anger."

The same man answered, "But if a kid is hitting, why would you give him karate lessons? It would just make him stronger." Well, that was one way to look at it,

On the walk home I said to Dan, "I guess foster care isn't for everyone."

"It can be for anyone who wants it."

"That couple is going to be eaten alive."

"They can learn."

"Do you think they will?"

"No."

The guest speaker at our training graduation was Andrea, a young woman in her twenties, a foster care success story, a survivor of the system and a triumph of the human spirit. Articulate and poised, Andrea spoke candidly about her experiences in foster care, never making a burden of her emotion as she described being bumped around with her sisters before landing in the home of a preacher. "At church he held us up before the community as an example of his charity, but at home we were treated like servants, cooking and cleaning for his biological family with no possessions of our own. At fourteen, I ran away. It was a hard to leave my sisters, but I could no longer stay."

"Did something happen that made you leave?" Andrea answered the question from the audience, "I was sexually abused for four years by the foster father. I documented the abuse but the social workers wouldn't believe me. When he started abusing one of my sisters, I told the foster mother and she beat me. Then the foster father beat me and I ran away. I was placed alone with a single mother who had three of her own children. Back then you could no longer be adopted after you were fourteen, but this woman said, 'I don't care. From now on you're my daughter.' She introduced me to everyone as her daughter. She paid attention to me, did what she could for me. She loved me, even though I couldn't see it at the time."

After some trials, Andrea turned her life around, got her grades up, and went to college. She was currently working on her second master's degree and serving as a spokesperson for the foster care system. "I have been back to my old neighborhood where I used to live with my biological parents. I see the kids I used to play with still living there, and I realized that foster care gave me the chance to break out of that cycle. Not all my experiences were positive but even the homes I was in for a short time showed me there were different ways to live, other paths I could take away from the violence and poverty that defined my childhood."

Dan and I slipped away from the party. As the doors of the elevator were closing, Andrea caught it and rode with us to the lobby. I thanked her for sharing her story—I was moved by it. She smiled, tired, "Thanks, but I've got a long way to go." Her voice was about a third lower than it had been during the ceremony. There was a small oxygen tank with a mask in her large purse. Health issues? She seemed fragile, exhausted. "I'm doing it, you know, but I have issues. I haven't even begun to deal with some of the things that happened to me." The elevator slowed. "Good luck, Andrea," Dan said, and we got off.

* * *

There are thirty institutions in New York City that oversee the foster care of some 16,000 kids. Members from each of these agencies are mandated to attend monthly meetings with potential adoptive parents to find permanent homes for the children in care. These meetings are held in the morning, when adoptive parents are supposed to be working at the gainful employment required to qualify them as such, and begin with ten to twelve hopeful parents introducing themselves, passing out copies of their one page profile and stating briefly what they were looking for.

"Hello, my name is Ann, and my husband and I are looking for a sibling group. We live here in midtown in a two bedroom apartment and have been married for seven years. My husband is in law enforcement and I am a music teacher." I thought "music teacher" sounded more maternal than "musician."

The agency reps took turns introducing their children to the group for placement, speaking in loving tones and passing around photos. "This is Sarah. She's seventeen, her favorite food is pizza, and when she grows up she wants to be on *American Idol*. This is Robert. He is fifteen and I can tell you he is a really special kid. He has a brother who has some aggression issues but can be adopted separately." I looked at the picture of Robert, a handsome young man with curly hair and linebacker shoulders, about a hundred and eighty pounds. "Robert is doing well in school, he is at grade level, and wants to be a professional athlete."

The next representative introduced Lucy. "She's nine and

has some major medical issues. She's very sweet, nonverbal, but has a great sense of humor and a wonderful smile. She can operate her electric wheelchair but she would definitely need a family in an elevator building." Lucy was the only one that agency presented. Five more agencies presented a total of twelve more children and one five year old who was celebrated for being "under six." The formal part of the meeting ended, coffee and butter cookies were served, and the conversation between interested agencies and parents began.

I turned to the woman sitting next to me, Nina, a single, African American investment banker about my age. "I don't get this," I said, frustrated, "they tell us there are 2,500 children waiting to be adopted and show us fifteen photos. Where are they? Where are the children?"

Nina nodded, "I know. I've been coming to these meetings for months and there's nothing. I'm looking into interstate adoptions at this point." We ate butter cookies and watched a gay couple clearly getting blown off by the representative from the Catholic agency.

Nina and I sat together month after month while the same agencies talked to the same adoptive parents about the same children. I told Dan about Robert, the fifteen year old with the problematic older brother. Dan said, "Give it a shot." I approached the agency representing Robert and his brother Brian. The woman looked at me, surprised. "Really? You would take a fifteen-year-old male?" I nodded. "My husband is a former Marine officer." She said, "Oh, I see. Well, actually, Robert is in the matching process right now with a family in Long Island. It's really wonderful, he is so deserving of a forever family." *What the hell?* I gave a weak smile. "I see. Thank you."

Over four months, I was introduced to twenty-five photographs of children, all but three well over the magic age of six, and the only child in a sibling group was already in the matching process.

I caught up with my advocate. "We need to talk." She led me into her office and sat down. "I need to know. How does this work?" I felt I was being played. "The short answer?" she said, "It doesn't. Our organization is here trying to get these kids to parents, and the agencies won't give them up." If a child becomes free for adoption, the current foster parents can choose to adopt them, but in most cases, once a child is adopted, the state no longer provides a subsidy once the foster parents become adoptive parents. Losing that income can be a deterrent to adoption. "If it gets as far as arranging a meeting with potential adoptive parents, I've seen foster parents deliberately bring the kids in dirty and sick looking because if the kid is adopted, the foster parents lose the subsidy." I sat back in my chair. "It's about money." Our advocate nodded. "Yep. And the agencies get paid by the city of New York based on the number of kids they have." I asked her what we should do. "Hang in there."

At the next meeting, a woman from a different agency approached me. She said she'd overheard me asking about Enrique. "You're looking for a sibling group, is that right?" She smiled, "I think we have a sibling group that would be a perfect match for you guys, eight and ten years old. Let's set up a meeting." I called Dan. "Finally!"

* * *

Jimmy and Ruby were waiting for us in a large room at the end of a long hallway. The social worker introduced us, "Hi guys! I have two people here who want to meet you! This is Ann and Dan!" Eight-year-old Jimmy stood playing with some action figures at a toy cupboard in the corner, and pretended to ignore us, an oversized T-shirt hanging over his thin broad shoulders. Ruby, his older sister, was ten years old and extremely nervous, running back and forth along the walls of the room, her back hunched over, like a little fly buzzing along a windowsill trying to get out. I felt for them. I am sure they knew why we were there and had even less idea than we did what was going to happen next.

After the brief introduction, the social worker left the room. Dan and I sat down at one of the low tables. I caught Ruby's eye and smiled. She shrieked and giggled in response. She was beautiful, with almond-shaped eyes, dark skin, long arms and legs, her hair pulled back in loose cornrows. I waved at her. She shrieked again. Dan and I smiled at each other. Dan walked over to Jimmy with his digital camera and took Jimmy's picture. He held up the image so Jimmy could see it. Jimmy sneaked a look and quickly turned away. In response, Dan handed his camera to Jimmy, pointed to the button, and Jimmy pushed it. *Click.*

Ruby was watching from the other side of the room. I am a French horn player and had brought a little miniature horn to play for them. I pulled it out from a bag, shiny and reflective in the low fluorescent lights. It caught her eye and I quickly put it back in the bag, making a face as if I'd been caught. She came over. I made a sound on it, and she laughed. I handed it to her and she took it. Jimmy took pictures of Ruby playing the tiny horn, scaring herself every time she made a noise. Then Dan showed Ruby how to use the camera, while I taught Jimmy to make loud sounds. We broke out the Rice Krispies treats, while Dan showed them pictures of our dog, Charlie. "Would you like to come visit us sometime? We have a playground nearby." The kids seemed interested. We left for the day, encouraged by the initial positive first visit. It seemed like things were finally starting to happen.

* * *

On September 9, 2007, we began our matching period, meeting with the kids every weekend for four months. Most of our days were spent swinging and playing basketball. Dan built loft bunks for the kids in preparation for our first sleepover. We bought desks and dressers, each new furnishing meeting with great interest. Dan made Jimmy a slot car race track on a piece of plywood for his birthday.

Winter approached and we set up a Christmas tree in the apartment, with shiny presents proliferating between visits and eagerly inspected each weekend. Books were everywhere and never more than an arm's length away from any point in their new home; we even had a bookshelf in the bathroom. Picture books, chapter books, classic, comic, children's books, fiction books, how-to books, bright, shiny covers begging to be judged, and candy-colored Christmas books, all shouting "Read me! Read me!"

On December 19, three months into our matching period, Jimmy and Ruby moved in with us permanently. We taped a giant heart made of gold wrapping paper on the door and threw our children a welcome home Christmas party. Our friends turned out in droves, bearing gifts, hugs, happy wishes, and exclamations: "Wow! I love slot cars! Ruby, you painted this yourself? Jimmy, you made that? Awesome!" We sang carols around the piano and got all sugared up on candy. As the party wound down, a friend looking for a lost glove heard Jimmy talking to himself in his room, snuggled up in his bunk, unawares, "This is my bed. This is my Lego. This is my blanket. This is my book. . . ." Merry Christmas, Jimmy.

As the party ended, the house quieted, then fell asleep. I cleaned up to the glow of the Christmas tree lights. Dan was snoring, and Charlie the dog was curled up at the entrance to the children's room. My breathing was shallow, high in my chest, as if I worried someone might hear me and wake suddenly. I was lightheaded, anxious but happy; I was floating, weightless, looking down from my dizziness, "This is my son. This is my daughter. This is my family. This is my life. . . ." Merry Christmas, Ann.

4

JIMMY

"You wet the bed? Don't worry, Jimmy. I also used to wet the bed." He stared at me. I smiled and winked. "I was ten before I stopped and you have a cousin Spencer who wet the bed until he was eleven, maybe twelve." Jimmy stared at me. "My cousin wet the bed?" I smiled, "Of course he did! It's a sign of intelligence! We have more important things to think about than using the bathroom." Jimmy smiled.

"Now climb up there and toss me down those sheets." He stripped the bed and handed me the pile of strong smelling sheets and blankets. He had been hiding it for a few days. I swallowed hard not to choke on the smell of ammonia. "Nothing to be embarrassed about, Jimmy. We bedwetters stick together."

Jimmy was having a hard time transitioning. Of course he was. He'd been in one foster home for almost six years, probably the only home he could really remember. Just days before we had helped Jimmy and his sister unpack their black garbage bags full of clothes and meager playthings, and put them into their new dressers and toy boxes. We still had eight months to go before we could legally adopt them but Dan told them, "You aren't foster kids anymore, we're your parents now. As far as we're concerned you are our kids, we are your parents and this is your home." We wanted them to feel permanent and welcomed. To feel loved.

Jimmy was a quiet boy, afraid to be alone. He refused to use the bathroom unless Dan or I stood outside the bathroom door and talked to him; he didn't feel safe unless he knew we were close by. He was eight when we met him, though he'd been told he was nine. "I'm eight? I'm eight?" He couldn't believe it.

We set up a routine for our kids, one that was predictable and consistent. At the end of every night, we'd get the kids into their pajamas and then I would tuck them into bed. I taught Jimmy the Eskimo kiss, where we rub noses, and the butterfly kiss, where we take turns blinking and brushing our eyelids on each other's cheeks. He would put his head next to mine on the pillow when we read together after school, Ruby's head on my other shoulder. We swam together, sang together, and rode the swings at the playground.

But despite these little moments of joy, things weren't easy. Mornings were especially hard. Jimmy and Ruby had trouble getting up and ready for school, not used to the routine. I tried to make a game out of it. I put a chart on the fridge, one star for every day we were on time, ten stars and we'd go to the toy store. Our nemesis, "Evil Mr. Time Man," was a sinister force bent on making us cranky, late, and above all, divided. Sticking together and helping each other was our only hope. I would hold my analog watch up to their little ears, "Hear that? That faint click . . . click . . . click? That's him laughing his evil laugh." The kids totally went with it, pitting us against him instead of them against me. Evil Mr. Time Man was mean and relentless, but we as a family would rally, fall back, and scramble to regroup behind a hot breakfast, the kind worth fighting for, "if only we have enough time!"

Jimmy struggled with school: he was bright but had trouble learning. He was good at math and enjoyed it until he got a problem wrong. When that happened, he would slump over the desk and slide slowly to the floor, defeated. He would lie there crying, motionless and unresponsive. We would encourage, cajole, tease, and bribe. "I can't do it," he'd whine, lying on the floor. We'd take a break and I'd make him read to me from a joke book. "How do you make time fly?" I'd look puzzled, "Um . . . I give up." Jimmy would smile. "Throw the clock out the window!" But Jimmy was stressed about failing. I'd tell him, "It's okay, Jimmy, you can't know what you don't know."

Jimmy's anxieties about school seemed to unleash other issues. He opened up about the bedwetting over dinner one night. "They would punish me if I wet the bed at the foster home." Ruby interrupted him, "They'd put him in the bathtub and pour cold water on him and then take his covers." Jimmy looked at his sister, "Then she'd hit me on my hands with a metal spoon." Ruby added, "Ten times on each hand." I looked down at my plate. "Would you all excuse me for a minute? I forgot something. I'll be right back."

I ran down the five flights of stairs and out onto the street. My sobs turned to steam in the freezing January cold. "Dammit," I said, "Dammit." I felt sick inside. I was not giving Jimmy a line when I told him I was a bedwetter. I knew what he was going through; so I knew that you don't need to punish a child for wetting the bed; it is punishment enough. When I wet the bed, I would help my mom strip the sheets and we would move on with the day. My siblings were not allowed to tease me and it was not spoken of outside of the house. It was not my favorite part of growing up, but I was never made to feel it was my fault.

Crying in front of a child about something bad that happened to them was warned against in the adoption books. The child would perceive the parent as weak and unable to protect them. In addition, the books suggested the parent show controlled anger towards the child's perpetrator following a disclosure of an abuse. So, I breathed in the cold air, got my game face on, and went back upstairs. "Thanks, guys, sorry about that," I said, taking my seat at the table. They were still talking about the foster home. I said, "I'll tell you one thing, Mr. Jimmy. Nobody's ever going to hit you again, not on my watch." Jimmy and Ruby stared at me. "That woman made a bad choice. That's not how you help someone who wets the bed." Dan smiled at me. We had dessert.

Especially after that episode, I wanted the children to know this was a safe place to show their emotions and cry if they needed to. I chose *Where the Red Fern Grows* for our after-school read-aloud book; I remembered reading it aloud on a family road trip and everyone, even my parents, were bawling. The kids and I had been reading for a week before we got to the sad part. Jimmy and Ruby lay on either side of me, the three of us snuggling on the daybed, light streaming in the windows. Sure enough, I started crying, tears running down my cheeks as I struggled to keep reading. I stopped and smiled at the kids. They stared at me, not moving, stiff and still. "It's okay, guys, I'm just sad. It's okay to cry when you're sad." They nodded, still staring. I smiled and said, "It's a part of living. Is it strange to see me cry?" Ruby smiled, "Yeah, it's kind of weird." I stroked her hair, "It's alright, nothing's wrong. It's what we do when we're sad. It helps get it out." I winked. "You guys okay?" They seemed fine with it.

"If I have to keep reading through this sad part, we're going to be here all day. Jimmy? Would you mind?" Jimmy took the book and finished reading. Ruby said, "It's alright, Mom." She stroked my hair. I winked at her, "Thanks, Sweetie." When it was over I dried my eyes, "Just a part of living." It was a family moment.

They talked about it, over and over. "Remember when you cried, Mom, about Big Dan?" I would smile, "I sure do. That Big Dan was a good dog." Ruby went on, "You couldn't keep reading because you were crying. Jimmy had to finish reading." I said, "That's right. That sad part always gets me."

The next afternoon, Jimmy put his head on my lap while I read aloud. I stroked his head, stopping only to turn the page. Half way through our reading time, he sat up and looked at me, then went silently to his room and shut the door. I wondered if something was up with him, but he seemed okay and I wanted to respect his space.

That night on my desk I found a drawing on an index card of an inky, blotched, knife impaled heart with red marker drops oozing from a jagged cut. Around the heart in thick, permanent marker were the angry words, "Ann is the worst mom ever!" I picked it up, touched and excited. I took it back to our bedroom and showed Dan. "Look, Dan! He feels vulnerable! We're winning!" Despite seeming bad, it was actually a positive response. It was textbook reactive attachment behavior: the child feels close to you, it makes him feel vulnerable, and he tries to push you away before you can abandon him. You don't abandon him, the cycle repeats, and over time he comes to trust you and attaches. This was a huge victory for me. Jimmy was telling me he felt close to me. And thank God for textbooks! I might have thought he was telling me I was the worst mom ever. I put the card with my most precious possessions. That week we celebrated our one-month anniversary as a family.

* * *

I waited for Jimmy on the sidewalk with the other parents outside his school. The bell rang, the children ran out, but not Jimmy. He finally appeared with his fourth grade teacher, who wanted to talk with me. "Jimmy's not paying attention in class. He's playing during our reading time and has not turned in any homework. I just thought you should know." I smiled weakly, surprised. "Well, thank you. I appreciate you keeping me up on things. We'll follow through at home." We shook hands.

I was devastated. I'd failed him. Jimmy and I started walking home. After a block he said, "Are you going to punish me now?" I put my hand on his shoulder, "No, Jimmy, I'm not going to punish you. You just need more support. We'll get it going, don't worry."

Jimmy said, "You're going to punish me." He started to cry, shrugged my hand off his shoulder and started walking ahead of me.

"No one's going to punish you, Jimmy. We just need to spend more time on homework." I ran to keep up with him.

Once inside the apartment, Jimmy dropped his book bag on the floor, took off his belt, and held it out for me to take. "You can punish me now." I tried to hide my surprise. "Jimmy, I'm not going to punish you, Sweetie. Put that belt down, let's have a snack." Jimmy sat at the table, his face tight and strained. He took off his shoes, crossed his legs and resting one foot on his knee started to whip at the sole of his foot with his leather belt. I took his hand and wrestled the belt from him, "Not on my watch, Jimmy. No one hits my kids, not even my kids." He was agitated. He tried to grab the belt back, stood up and pushed me. "Nobody's going to hurt you, buddy." He pushed me again, "I hate you! I hate you!" his breathing fast and shallow, hands clenched.

He was looking for a fight, growling, panting, his arms stiff and shaking with tension. I ran ahead into his room and pulled his pillow down from his bed. "Come and get it, Jimmy! Hit the pillow! Work it out!" He came into the room swinging. I held the pillow in front of me and let him have at it. "That's good, Jimmy, get it out! Hit hard, it's okay. I can see you are mad." He punched and punched. I held tight. His eyes looked wild, mouth open, his lips curled back away from his teeth. My heart started racing and I felt like crying. I could feel his distress; he was enraged, frightened, and fighting for his life.

He grabbed the pillow and tried to pull it away. "Punch it, Jimmy, keep punching." He wouldn't let go, he kept pulling and then charging, growling, breathing hard. He tripped and fell, pulling the pillow down with him. I held on and let him wrestle it on the ground. He was tearing at it. *Do something!* Like what? Should I stop him? *How are you going to that?* I knelt beside him, holding the pillow to him, providing resistance in his struggle. After twenty minutes, exhausted, he let go of the pillow and began to sob. I stroked his head, "It's okay, buddy, you're going to be fine. I love you, Jimmy." He sobbed and sobbed and then suddenly fell asleep. "Jimmy?" He was out.

I looked at my watch. Ruby's bus was due any minute. "Jimmy?" Nothing. He was sound asleep. I left the apartment door open behind me as I ran down the five flights to the street and propped open both entrance doors to the building. If Jimmy called out I would hear him and more importantly, he would hear me answer.

I could see Ruby's bus stuck in afternoon traffic halfway down the block and ran towards it, waving at the driver to let Ruby off. "Hi, Sweetie! How was school?" I helped her with her pack. "Good! Ms. Priscilla let me sit at her desk during independent study. . . ." I pretended to listen as I rushed her back to the apartment, worried Jimmy might wake to find that I'd left him, rejected him. That would be terrible for a boy with abandonment issues who was also afraid to be alone. "That's awesome! Sounds like a great day."

Once inside the apartment I could see a sleeping lump on the floor down the hall. Jimmy hadn't moved. "Shh, let's be super quiet. Jimmy is taking a nap." Ruby and I had a snack, and got her homework done. Jimmy slept for two and a half hours. Sweet boy. Sweet stressed-out boy. But under the calm, I was flying blind. I had held it together during his tantrum, but was worried he had sensed my lack of composure. I had felt a chemical reaction to his violence that left me unsure of myself, uncalibrated, like shooting baskets after lifting weights.

The next morning Jimmy wouldn't speak. When he got home from school, he tried to provoke me; picking things up, pretending to drop them and staring at me angrily as he shoved piles of mail and papers off my desk. "Take it easy, Jimmy." I said, using my crisis line voice, "Come sit down, let's get a snack." He ignored me and walked into his room, slammed the door, and started punching at the frosted glass window with his fist, harder and harder. *He's going to break it.* What should I do? *He is going to put his fist through the glass and cut his hands!* Right. He is now a danger to himself. It is appropriate to intervene and neglectful not to. *Go!*

I threw open the door, ran past him and grabbed his pillow, "Okay, Jimmy. Work it out." He just stood there, glaring at me. I started shifting my weight like a boxer, ducking, smiling, "Come on, Jimmy, show me what you got." I had no idea what to do. He started throwing stuff on the floor, kicking toys, shoving Ruby's things off her desk. "Come on, Jimmy. Let's do this!" I moved towards him and shoved the pillow at him. "Hit it, Buddy! Hit it!" I taunted him, trying to direct his anger at the pillow. He wasn't having it. He screamed and ran at me, swinging with everything he had. He was after me, not the pillow. "Take it easy, Jimmy." Swinging wildly, he hit my chin with his head, grabbed one of his heavy new dress shoes, and brought it down as hard as he could on the bridge of my nose.

My head exploded in pain. I actually saw stars. I had never been hit before. Sure, I had bumped my nose on things, been injured while playing sports or rough housing with a sibling, but no one had ever hit me with the intent to hurt. I was in shock. We were both on the floor at this point and I rolled Jimmy over onto his stomach and lay across his back. I just lay there a minute, trying to take all this in. He was struggling and crying. "It's okay, Jimmy," I said, "I'm not going to hurt you but I can't let you behave like this. Safety first, my man, safety first." I was shaking, my nose throbbing, the pressure in my sinuses spreading like fire to my cheekbones and forehead.

I called my brother, who lived in the apartment below mine. "I need you to meet Ruby's bus and bring her up here, I'm having a situation." I could hear him running down the stairs in the hallway as he answered, "Can do!" I was still holding Jimmy down when John and Ruby walked into the back room. I didn't get up.

"Hi, Babe," I said to Ruby while still on the ground. "Thanks, Uncle John, for bringing her up. How was school, Sweetie? Do you want a snack? Jimmy's having some issues, I'm not hurting him but I can't let him up right now. Can you grab an apple and then come on back? Let's get started on that homework." Jimmy kept struggling. I just lay there across his back, smiling as if everything were normal. Ruby was a face watcher and she was taking her cue from me. Was everything okay? I winked at her. Ruby sat down next to me and we did her homework. "Good, now don't forget to carry the one. Excellent. Next one." Jimmy struggled for maybe thirty minutes before exhausting himself and falling asleep.

Ruby and I got up, went into the kitchen and sat down. "How are you?" She nodded.

"It's alright if you have feelings about what just happened." She shrugged.

I tried to explain. "I love you and Jimmy. I'm not going to let anyone hurt him and I'm not going to let him hurt anyone else, including himself." Ruby smiled. "It's fine, Mom. I'm okay." I was pretty sure she wasn't okay, but she was coping. Jimmy slept until dinner.

That night I filled Dan in on the day. I admitted, "That was the first time anyone has ever hit me." He responded, "Imagine how Jimmy felt the first time he was hit." Damn.

I closed my eyes and imagined Jimmy, tiny and frightened. He's too small to hit back. No one comforts him, no one defends him, one hundred times more visceral, one thousand times more damaging.

* * *

Every morning on our way to school, Jimmy and I passed an old limo driver sitting in his black town car parked watching us. On my walk back home, I could see his eyes following me in his rearview mirror. He never said anything, never smiled or waved, just watched me daily failing over and over to connect with my new son. One day, the driver rolled down his window and waved me over. *Here we go.* New Yorkers love giving advice. I've been told how to lock my bike, how to parallel park, how to vote, walk a dog, and how to fuck myself. And now, it appeared, I was going to be told how to parent.

"Excuse me, Ma'am." I stopped and stood back a safe distance from his window. I was in a defensive stance and already close to tears. "I've been watching you work with that boy for over two months now. I don't know who you are or what your relationship is to him but this morning, God told me to tell you, 'Never give up on that boy. Keep working with him.'" I started crying. "Thank you, sir." He nodded. "My name's Aaron." I nodded. "Thank you, Aaron. The boy's name is Jimmy. I'm Ann, his adoptive mother."

I don't believe in God, but I could believe Aaron. He set a bar for me I could meet; I just had to keep working and never give up.

But as the weeks went on, Jimmy's episodes were becoming more frequent and violent. One day he started hitting me and I just stood there, trying to see if I could talk him down. He was

raging, circling me, "It's okay, Jimmy. I'm not going to hurt you."
He lunged at me, reaching up to grab my neck, his hands tight
around my throat. I looked down at him, my arms by my side,
and said softly, "You've got the wrong person, Jimmy. I want to
help you." We stared at each other for a minute, he released my
throat, dropped his hands to his side and started sobbing. His
little body was shaking. I caught him as he dropped to the floor
and held him until he fell asleep.

A few days later, Jimmy starting throwing things in the
apartment. I told Ruby to go into my room with the dog and
shut the door. Jimmy was not safe, high on rage and more
aggressive than usual. He hit me. I grabbed him and wrestled
him, the two of us thrashing and struggling to the floor. He
let out a whimper, a tiny little cry, like a two year old and his
body relaxed. He looked up at me, strangely calm and childlike.
"Mommy," he whispered, "Mommy, Mommy." I was still holding him. He reached up and touched my hair, playing with it in
his fingers, "Mommy, Mommy . . ." He quickly fell asleep.

And while Jimmy struggled to adjust to his new family, I
was trying to manage the effects of mothering a violent child
on my performance career.

During the intermission at a recital, a friend came back-
stage to say, "You have a smudge under your chin, it looks like
charcoal or grease." I lifted my chin to the truth of the dressing
room mirror, its surround-sound bulbs revealing a bruise on
the bottom of my chin. "Thanks," I said, "I wonder what it is." I
pretended to wipe it off, knowing full well it was a bruise from
one of Jimmy's head butts. My worlds were literally colliding. I
put concealer on it and walked out for the second half.

Later that week I played on another recital down at NYU.
Dan was home with Ruby and Jimmy. I was standing back-
stage listening to the performer before me. I was in pre-game
mode. My phone rang on vibrate. It was Dan. He wouldn't call
unless it was important. I whispered, "Hi." His voice was quick,

"Jimmy's freaking out, come home as soon as you can." I could hear struggling and crying in the background. I put my phone down, walked out, and performed. The audience clapped, I bowed and walked off stage. I packed quickly and ran to grab a cab on West 4th Street.

It was dark outside. I stared out the window as we flew up the West Side Highway in that eerily quiet traffic lull when the Broadway shows have started and the crowds, parked and fed, are finally sitting in their seats. We hit the timed traffic lights up 10th Avenue and rode a wave of green, the Red Sea parting before us. I felt numb and hollow on the inside. Something enormous was happening to my life. I closed my eyes and thought of Jimmy and imagined what he must be feeling. I was an adult. I chose this change. Jimmy was a child. No one had asked Jimmy what he wanted.

*   *   *

When I got home, Dan was sitting on the floor cradling Jimmy. He looked tiny, biting and scratching at Dan's massive arms. Ruby was in her bed looking at a book. I waved up at her and smiled. She waved back. Dan said, "We need to have a family meeting." I nodded and climbed up next to Ruby in her loft bunk and gave her a hug. Dan said, "Okay, Jimmy. I'm going to let you go. You are going to stand up and climb up into your bunk. We are going to have a family meeting." Jimmy did as instructed. I was amazed. *How did Dan get him to do that?* The curtain between the beds was open and Ruby and I sat side-by-side facing Dan and Jimmy, our heads almost touching the ceiling.

Dan began our meeting by asking Jimmy, "Did anyone ever hit you, bud? It seems like you're looking for a fight. Did anyone ever fight you?" Jimmy nodded. "Yeah," he said. Ruby started talking, slowly at first, then faster and faster. Jimmy joined in.

The stories they told were chilling and sad. I was speechless. Ruby sat on my lap while she talked. Dan sat with his arm around Jimmy.

The social workers had told us that theirs was the perfect foster home, a dream home; no complaints, no trouble what-soever. Monthly visits were predictable and stable, the children quiet and polite. It turns out the foster kids were beaten regu-larly but the foster mother, a nurse, would sew up the kids her-self. There were no reports or hospital visits because there was no evidence. The kids lied to teachers and social workers about the cuts and bruises, threatened with more beatings if they told.

As the children talked, Dan would ask a follow up question, then ask it again in a slightly different way. He was interrogating them, gently. He is a mandated reporter of child abuse. The kids were consistent. Scars were revealed and details fleshed out, all of it holding up. Then, a round of nervous laughter, shaky and relieved. Dan assured them they were safe here. There would be no retribution and no one would ever hurt them again. Jimmy and Ruby worried aloud about the other foster kids still living there: Jason, Susie, and Anthony. I couldn't help but share their worry.

After that first family meeting, the kids would break into stories about the foster home spontaneously; at the dinner table, on the way to swim, after reading aloud. Dan made a report to social services and was told there would be an inves-tigation on the foster home.

A woman from social services came to visit us. She sat with Dan and me, while Jimmy and Ruby played nearby. The woman turned to Ruby. "How is school going, Ruby? Do you like your teacher?" Ruby popped up and sat on the edge of Dan's knee to answer. The woman looked at Dan with Ruby sitting there listening and said, "I would suggest not letting her straddle your leg like that. You don't know what these foster children are capable of, she may accuse you of sexual abuse. These kids know the system and they know how to work it." Dan stood up, "Ruby and Jimmy, I need you to play in your room now, head on back." He turned to the woman, "The suggestion is not appreciated. Please finish your questions." The woman dismissed our concerns about abuse in the foster home, explaining that the children's perception of abuse was actually discipline and we needed to allow for cultural differences.

Hitting is hitting. As a foster parent, that woman had signed the same form we did saying we would not hit.

After that visit, it seemed like the Administration for Children's Services was investigating us instead of the foster home. Social workers were talking to the kids' current teachers, meeting with the kids at school, calling me with questions and talking to our neighbors. We learned through the grapevine that the investigator was a friend of the foster mom and that she'd done an investigation on her home before. As the investigation continued, I could feel our credibility as parents begin to erode in the eyes of our children.

*   *   *

We needed a break. Two months into our parenting, we flew with Jimmy and Ruby to the West Coast to meet their new grandparents, new aunts, and new cousins. Jimmy met his cousin, Spencer, another intelligent bedwetter. Spencer wrestled in high school and kept Jimmy laughing and in a headlock, half nelson, or some other wrestling move for the entire visit. I had never seen Jimmy so happy. The kids jumped on the trampoline, dropped from the rope swing into my parents' pond, caught frogs, and let them go. We picnicked at the beach and lay on quilts on my parents' fresh cut grass and watched the clouds. It was blissful.

Back home in the city, we built an even firmer routine around the playground, reading together, and homework. Saturdays we went to our favorite diner for breakfast, then to the piers to ride bikes. Sunday was basketball in the park, swimming, then library. Breakfast at 7:00, snack after school, dinner at 6:00. Reading was encouraged, aloud, alone, and together in silence. There was no television, just books. Jimmy and Ruby would carry them around, rearrange them in the bookshelves, lay them out in stacks or in a circle on the carpet in their room and play school with them. Ruby carried around a score of a Brahms symphony for three days in a row, giving me the heads up that they weren't necessarily reading them.

We kept a very predictable schedule so Jimmy and Ruby could anticipate rather than worry about what was going to happen next. They were more relaxed and in the present.

On school nights, the kids were in bed by 8 p.m. and had thirty minutes to read before lights out. A few nights a week we would have a guest reader come to the house. To create suspense, we would turn the lights out at 8 p.m., open the curtain dividing the room and sit the guest in the middle of the room and then, ta da, turn the lights on. Who was it? Uncle John? A neighbor? Maybe the lady from the Christmas party or the guy who plays trumpet in Mom's band? The guest would read aloud from the current read-aloud book: *A Wrinkle in Time, James and the Giant Peach, The Lion, the Witch and the Wardrobe.* Then, lights out.

At the playground, Jimmy made friends with a kid named Booker. His mom and I would visit while they played, toughing it out together in the miserable February cold. I asked Jimmy if he would like to invite Booker and his mom over to our apartment for hot chocolate. Jimmy nodded, wide-eyed and excited. This was a big deal for him, his first time having a friend over to his house. Our guests accepted and we started walking together towards the apartment. *Shit!* Jimmy had overslept that morning and we hadn't stripped bed! "Guys," I said, "let me run ahead and get the water on, just ring the bell, and I will buzz you up."

I ran like the wind, two stairs at a time, put a pot of water on the stove, and made a sheet change worthy of the America's Cup. The buzzer rang as I stuffed the wad of stinkies in the hamper. "Hi guys, come on in!" Jimmy was animated, giving Booker a tour of our tiny apartment. They walked into the kids' room and Booker saw Jimmy's loft, "COOL!" and started up the ladder. Jimmy tensed and looked back at me in horror, remembering the sheets. I was ready for him, smiling, winking, and giving him every "I got it" hand gesture I could think of. He turned and climbed up anxiously after Booker. As Jimmy's eyes met the freshly made bed, he turned back and looked at me. Booker was talking to him, asking him questions, but Jimmy just stood on his ladder, staring back at me. I held his gaze and smiled reassuringly. He smiled back and turned quickly to Booker, "That's my Lego alien ninja spaceship, it can also fly underwater. . . ."

A few days later, Jimmy and I waited outside with Ruby for her school bus. We waved goodbye to her as she boarded and I turned stiffly to Jimmy, "Son, you've got a giant booger in your nose." Jimmy smiled under his scarf. We were freezing; I would have preferred giving him one of my kidneys over taking my glove off. "If I get that booger out for you, our relationship is going to be at a whole new level, do you understand that?" Jimmy was grinning. He nodded. "Only a mother would take her glove off in this cold to get a booger out. Do you want me to get it out?" Jimmy chuckled and nodded. I took my glove off and made a very big deal of cleaning out his nose. Once out, I pretended to wipe the booger on his coat. He laughed and tried to jump away. I grabbed him and we play wrestled. He broke free and I chased him around the corner. I chased him with the booger for three blocks.

We stopped to catch our breath, bent over, our hands on our knees, the vapor from our gasps making clouds of mist around our heads. We stood up and sighed. As we walked the last half block to school, I put my arm around his shoulder. He didn't say anything, but he didn't pull away. Parents and kids were around, nannies dropping off, everyone would see him with my arm around him. I said, "Hey Jimmy, how do you feel about me having my arm around you?" He said, "It's okay. A lot of parents put their arms around their children." I got a thumbs up from Aaron.

As time went on, Jimmy's meltdowns grew less intense, fewer and farther between. He still slid to the floor when math was hard and wet the bed every night, but the violence stopped and we were able to get back to building our family. One afternoon I was in the hallway, deep in thought, standing perfectly still and staring at nothing. Jimmy popped his head out from around his door. "I know what you're thinking," he said. I turned to him, surprised. He was smiling. "Really? What am I thinking?" Jimmy said, "That you love me." I laughed, "You got me, Mr. J." He smiled again and popped back into his room.

5

TAKE FIVE

*J*immy and I passed a teenage boy on our way to the playground, a young man I'd never seen before. The kid smiled at Jimmy, gave him a high five, and kept walking. I looked at Jimmy, "Hey, who's your friend?" Jimmy looked away, still smiling. As a single person in her thirties, the anonymity of a big city had given me the freedom I needed to meet new people, move between groups of friends, and find myself—it was liberating. As a new parent to a nine-year-old boy, that same anonymity terrified me. No way was I going to be able to keep track of Jimmy's influences in the city. And with Ruby starting middle school next fall? *Holy crap.*

Soon after, Dan told me the Bureau called and offered him a transfer to a small office upstate forty miles from our lodge. "They've given us twenty-four hours to decide," he said, "what do you think?" I took it as a sign. "I'm in! Call and tell them we're going. This is no place to raise our family. Outside the city we would have more space, more resources, more time, less stress . . ." Dan interrupted me, "What about your career?" My heart stopped. I mumbled, "It'll be okay." It would have to be.

After we went to bed, I woke in the middle of the night thinking about our move and the sibling group still living in that foster home: The boys, Jason and Anthony, ages nine and five, had muscular dystrophy. Their sister Susie was seven. They'd been cleared for adoption for over two years.

"Dan? Dan? Can you please wake up?" He rolled over, "Are you okay?" My mind was spinning. "I don't know, I just keep thinking about, well, I mean, I know we are in over our heads here, but I can't stop thinking about those other three kids in the foster home." Dan was silent. I went on. "I mean, if our kids went through half of the stuff they've told us, then not only are the other three still in danger, they all survived that crap together! For six years! I think they should have each other, Ruby and Susie shared a bed, for Chrissake. Ruby talks about Anthony like he's her brother. I know it's crazy. I don't know what the hell I am thinking, I just keep coming back to it."

Again, silence. Then quietly, "I already made the call."

I bolted up into sitting. "You WHAT?"

"To inquire." He smiled.

"You called the agency to inquire about the other three kids? I can't believe you!"

"I inquired about their status."

"Oh my god, Dan! You inquired about their status?" The pitch of my voice was rising.

"And to offer our home as an adoptive resource."

"WHAT?" Louder.

"To feel out where the process was."

"AND?" Yelling.

"They're in a tough spot, Ann. The agency can't find a permanent home for them and they're being hit in the foster home."

"Oh my God." I flopped back down on the bed, breathless. "Oh my God."

The British songwriter Billy Bragg said, "The most important decisions in life are made between two people in bed." And there we were, in bed, in the middle of the night, Dan and I making an indefensible, emotional decision to adopt three additional troubled children we had not even met.

* * *

Siblings are as siblings do. These five were bonded siblings in every way but biologically. It was my dream that in our sympathetic home, these five could empathize about a past that Dan and I couldn't even imagine. As our children grew and began processing those years in foster care, they could witness for each, fact check, love and care for each other.

Once decided, I started to tell our loved ones about our decision. Our friends shook their heads, "It's too much." My brother laughed and said, "Well, if you're going to do it, overdo it!" Not the encouragement that we wanted, but we were committed.

We met with a social worker who actually cried when she learned we wanted all five, "It's been our dream, we never thought it could happen!" Placing siblings together is a challenge but placing five foster children from two different biological homes? "It's a miracle." When the kids were legally up for adoption, the foster parents declined their right of first refusal. Social workers asked Ms. Smith, the foster mom, why she didn't want to adopt them, and she said, "It's fine now, but what about when they are teenagers?" *Good point.*

We began our matching process, the kids' mini-reunion taking place on the sidewalk outside the agency. The five of them ran to each other, a mass of screams and hugs, then fast, loud talking, playful pushing and laughter. I heard Susie ask Ruby under her breath, "Do they have a TV we can watch?" Ruby rolled her eyes and said sarcastically, "Don't ask!" We took Susie, Anthony, and Jason for the spring break, then three weekends in a row, the matching process was condensed and so intensified our desire to adopt.

During these weekends, Dan and I were very active with all five: camping, traveling, playing, Ruby and Jimmy teaching the young ones how to swim and ride bikes. After each visit, I would walk the children back to the foster home and record in a marbled composition notebook a description of every scratch, bruise, and abrasion the children incurred on my watch and then sign at the bottom. It was a courtesy I had offered to Ms. Smith, with whom I had a cordial if superficial relationship. She had told me she was under investigation for child abuse through ACS stemming from allegations at Anthony's school. "Thank you, Ms. Ann. You have no idea what I am going through." Ms. Smith was busy. She was finishing school and had four bio kids of her own, three teenage boys and a four year-old girl. She complained of back pain. The husband worked. The foster kids were mostly supervised by the parents' teenage sons. Ms. Smith's sister lived in the basement apartment with her own children. These systems felt strange and unfamiliar to me.

Every time I entered the foster home, I would scan for information that might help me understand my children's experience, memories, and childhood: lighting, layout, floor coverings, smells, the little plastic table in the kitchen corner "where the foster kids ate," loud music, cockroaches. I would immediately shelve my observations without reflection and deliberately avoid forming opinions. I am a terrible liar. I wanted to be someone that Ms. Smith could talk to, confide in, even trust. I had to be able to look her in the eye.

After the matching period, we made a formal request to adopt the three children, have them placed permanently in our home, and move with us upstate. There was some turnover in the administration at the foster agency and we were suddenly met with resistance. Our social workers, whom we knew quite well, apologetically clammed up and were reassigned. We were told that the three younger children would not be able to leave New York City until the end of school in June. Our moving date was May 15. If we left the city without the younger three, we would not be able to advocate effectively for them.

Dan met with the new social workers a few times and was growing increasingly verbal in his frustration. I called a few times myself just to do damage control. I would say things like, "Yes, certainly, my husband does feel passionately about these children and I agree that he does have a way with words," and we'd all laugh a little.

Despite our efforts, it looked as if our plan was becoming another casualty of the system. The agency called, "The matching meetings with the children are being terminated. The current foster mother has requested the children be removed and we only have ten days to find a new home." I said, "They can move in with us." They hedged, "it has to be an approved foster home." *Dear Lord, give me strength to not go apeshit on these people.* "We *are* an approved foster home," I said, "currently fostering two wards of the state on behalf of your agency." There was a pause. "You are a foster home?" I felt contempt. "Yes," I said, "we are approved and would like to adopt all five children." Silence. "We'll call you back."

The agency called the next day, "We've found a temporary home for them and believe me, that's not easy to do for three kids on such short notice!" *Hmm. Wouldn't finding an adoptive home be even harder?* "Do you understand we are willing to adopt these children?" I asked, incredulous. "We'll consider it."

Furious, I called a lower level worker at the agency that I had become friendly with over the months. "I need to know where they are moving the three kids." My buddy laughed, "They're not moving! They convinced Ms. Smith to keep them for now." I was shocked, "They said Ms. Smith sent in her ten day notice." He said, "She sent the notice, but forgot to sign it. It has to be signed to be legal." Dan was listening on speakerphone, biting his tongue. We had two weeks to solve this before the movers came.

A moment of inspiration: "Wait!" I said to Dan, "watch this." I grabbed my phone, "Hello, Winnie? It's Ann Fox." I always called Ms. Smith by her first name, "How are you? How is your back?" I asked about her family, how's school coming along, then, "By the way we heard you are keeping the three younger kids. We know you are in a tight spot with the investigation and everything, and wanted to you to know we told the agency they could stay with us." There was a pause. Winnie was angry. "They told me they had nowhere else to go. Come and get them!"

I nodded encouragingly at Dan and said, "Okay, first you have to send a request for removal." Ms. Smith said in a low, controlled voice, "I already sent the request." I waited, holding my breath. "They told me you didn't sign it." There was silence and then an explosion, "I did sign it! They are lying! Come and get them. Get the children out of here!" I nodded again at Dan and said, "I will call the emergency supervisor at the agency. We can't do anything without permission." She yelled, "Call the supervisor and get them out. NOW!" We hung up and I called the supervisor explaining the situation. The supervisor confirmed, "We will have social workers there first thing in the morning."

Dan woke me up that night and whispered quietly, "Are we going to be able to do this?" I smiled. "Absolutely. I was made for this." *You what?* I could not believe I said that, it just came out. Dan kissed me and rolled back to sleep and my mind played it out. *Ann, you're a musician and historically self-absorbed. You've never even had a house plant! What makes you think you can do this?* Shh. I'm just latent, that's all. Those maternal instincts are going to kick in once those kids are here. *What if they don't? Five kids, Ann! What if you fail?* I have my family and I have Dan. They won't let me fail.

At ten the next morning, Dan and I became the proud parents of five beautiful children. It was the first of May, 2008. Mayday, mayday.

* * *

Our three new kids were in three different schools in three different neighborhoods. To get them there, Dan and I drove two hours each way through the Bronx and Long Island City with no parking and no margin for error; the schools locked their doors within fifteen minutes of each other. Dan would wait in our van while I ran in and signed each child out. We had sitters picking up Jimmy from school and meeting Ruby at her bus.

The first day I picked up Jason, numerous teachers, security guards, administrators, and aides came up to me, hugging me, thanking me, and crying openly. They handed me cards with their phone numbers, "This is my cell, call if you have any questions. I would have adopted him but we just couldn't, not with all his siblings." At Susie's school, her teacher pulled me aside, "Please keep in touch, call me anytime." Office staff stood up and called out, "God bless you," as I walked past holding the hand of my new daughter.

At Anthony's school, the physical therapist met me at the security desk and walked with me through the school halls, giving me instructions on how to care for him. Anthony's bus monitor interrupted us, hugged me, and started crying, "I would have adopted him if I could!" Then the nurse came over, "Thank God you are here, his teeth are rotting in his mouth, he has marks all over him, we call the police but nothing happens . . . " Anthony was waiting for me in the cafeteria, working on a yogurt with one of his aides. He recognized me and held out his arms. "Pick up!" I picked him up.

Five and a half years old, twenty-eight pounds and preverbal, Anthony had pale white skin with dark circles under his eyes. He wore metal hip to ankle braces over his pull-up diapers. As I carried him into the hallway, children and teachers started coming out of the classrooms. "Anthony! Yay Anthony! Hi Anthony! Is that your new Mom?" Anthony waved, as more students and teachers poured out into the hall, following us as we walked to the exit.

Teachers were crying and wiping their eyes. Anthony was smiling, waving to everyone. I kept walking, my eyes burning, fixed on the exit doors, feeling my part in this giant moment in a tiny life; little Anthony was free at last. They followed me out onto the steps, cheering and clapping while I buckled him into his brand new car seat. "Wow," said Dan, staring out the van window at the teeming, cheering crowd. I wiped my eyes, "You're not kidding." Dan turned to me from the driver's seat, tears in his eyes, "We're doing the right thing."

6

ROCK TUMBLER

The weekend came and with it, mayhem. Anthony was everywhere and then terrifyingly, nowhere. Susie was expressing her opinions on the furniture in permanent marker, tearing pages out of books and cutting holes in everyone's clothes with safety scissors. Jason was straddling Anthony's stomach while pressing his thumbs into his brother's eyes and a second later was pushing Ruby to the ground and sticking his knee in her back. Ruby was alternately taunting and grabbing toys away from Anthony, his high scream oscillating and cracking like a tortured, adolescent elf. Jimmy was a cameo, pushing and laughing, floating in and out of these scenes.

Time lost its purchase, warping us into an endless day with no rest, no rhythm, no light, no dark. Bedtime was the cue for Susie to scream and run out the door and down the stairs, tearing her clothes off as she went, crying, "Stop touching me, stop touching me," the stairwell amplifying her screams. Dan gave chase, brought her back up to the landing and held her while I put the other kids under various covers on makeshift beds with firm instructions to stay put. "You're hurting me, you're hurting me," Susie screamed. I opened the door, Dan whispered hurriedly, "I think it will look better if you hold her."

I sat at the top of the stairs with Susie, biting, scratching, and screaming on my lap. An hour later she cried herself to sleep and I carried her inside. Dan was lying on his back with Anthony on his stomach, the rhythm of his breathing putting Anthony to sleep. Dan put his finger to his lips. I nodded and quietly tucked sleeping Susie into a free corner of the guest bed. A few hours into our sleepless vigil, Dan whispered, "We need back up. Call Marie and get her out here on the next flight." We needed a professional. My older sister ran a pre-school, had homeschooled all five of her kids, and could travel with her youngest.

Thankfully, the weather gods pitied us: sunny and warm with a gentle breeze. We kept the kids outside in the park, hired sitters to help us push swings, shoot baskets, and chase after them when they ran away. Mistakenly, we sent two kids with one adult for a bathroom run. Taking the opportunity, Susie ran up the stairs past our floor to the roof and pushed the "alarm will sound" bar, triggering a call to the fire department. And while the adult was chasing Susie up the stairs, Jason was dialing 911, just for the hell of it, from our home phone.

Susie made another escape attempt in the wee hours. As I ran down the stairs after her, Dan called, "Take her to the van." We couldn't have her screaming infecting the rest of the kids. Susie stopped at the entrance doors to the apartment building, turned and faced me, teeth bared, her tiny, seven-year-old body bare except for her underwear. She screamed, "Stop touching me! Stop touching me!" I picked her up, a tiny mass of solid, lashing sinew. My brother heard the commotion and started racing down the stairs behind me, picking up her trail of clothes as he went. She was thrashing, scratching, biting, and spitting; I could barely hold her.

We struggled to get her in the van. Once inside, Susie stopped crying and started talking gibberish in weird voices, climbing up and over the seats and back again. John and I stared at Susie, then each other, then back at Susie. It was sobering. She was either hallucinating or pretending she was, neither option desirable. I whispered to John, "She might be out of her mind." My brother smiled, "Some might say the same about you." I said, "Do you think I'm nuts?" He said, "I think you're awesome. Going positive discipline on these kids with no television? That is what's crazy!"

We let Susie climb until she fell asleep. It was one in the morning. I put her clothes back on, and John picked her up and carried her home. Dan emerged from the bedroom and we whispered together in the kitchen. "We've got to get out of here. Did you call Marie?" I nodded, "She's on a flight out tomorrow."

The next day we threw a ninth birthday party for Jason in the park. The neighbors came, all our sitters were all there with Booker and our friends from the park. We kept scanning the street for signs of my sister. Finally, a cab pulled up to the gates of the park and my sister emerged with a carry-on bag in one hand and her four-year-old son in the other. Dan said, "The Susie Whisperer!" From twenty feet away, Dan caught her eye and pointed to the little lump on the park bench. Susie was hiding beneath a jacket, her body curled into the fetal position, face covered, limbs tight and tense. While we sang happy birthday and opened presents, Marie went to Susie, whom she'd never met, and knelt down beside her.

Glancing over from time to time, we could follow her progress: first an arm, then a leg. Marie was kneeling with her back to us, facing the bench. First the coat came off, then two light brown arms emerged, wrapping slowly around my sister's neck. A little head appeared on Marie's shoulder, then a smile. Dan looked at his watch and then over at me. He winked. Fifteen minutes start to finish. *Damn, she's good.* Susie was up and meeting her new cousin, my sister's Gabriel.

Dan called a meeting at the slide for Marie, John, and me. "We pack the van tonight after the kids are asleep. We load the children at 5 a.m., punch out, and drive straight to the lodge. Marie, you take Anthony and Gabe. Ann stays with Jimmy and Ruby, and John, you get Jason and Susie. Any questions?"

The breakdown was strategic. Dan figured I could use my relationship with Ruby and Jimmy as leverage and while Marie was the only one who could connect with Susie, she had Gabe and would not be able to give chase to anyone faster than Anthony. My brother was big and fast enough for Susie, and strong and Alpha enough for Jason. There were no questions. We dispersed. John followed after me for a few steps and whispered, "Wanna trade?" I laughed. "Hell no!"

* * *

Our fifteen-passenger van could barely hold the eleven of us, plus gear. And overwhelming the entire ride was the unsettling feeling that the kids might explode into violence at any second. Marie sat between two car seats on the first bench, Gabe left and Anthony right, reading, *Brown Bear, Brown Bear* in a calming, soft, sing-songy, voice; the stress reducing, beta inducing, sleep seducing voice of a seasoned mother.

I ruled the second row, Jimmy left and Ruby right, reading Rowling's *Harry Potter and the Sorcerer's Stone*, rendering a rolling counterpoint to the Brown Bear mantra. We rumbled down the parkway, the engine droning the tonic of the Taconic. Uncle John in the back, his deep voice a walking bass, walking through *Where the Sidewalk Ends*. Alternating his attention between Susie, then Jason, as needs arose, his free hand covering the seat belt release, while little fingers scratched at his wrists and digits. Dan was in the driver's seat, two eyes on the road, his third eye peering into the soul of every child chancing to glance at the rearview mirror. Charlie the dog was riding shotgun, sitting ramrod straight, ears up.

After a few hours, we stopped at a rest area and the engine killed. As if on cue, the children woke from their spell and exploded from the van, running and screaming like feral cats across the parking lot, scrambling through knee-high weeds towards a flowing culvert. "Hey! Stick around!" The four adults yelled, chasing them. Susie was running in the opposite direction, John caught her and cradled her snuggly in his arms. She spit in his face as Jason, appearing out of nowhere, approached slowly, staring coldly at his new uncle. John watched in disbelief as Jason picked up a rock and chucked it, hitting Susie, who was still cradled in John's arms. "Susie, I'm going to have to put you down. I think your brother needs me more than you do right now. Can you go get in the van?" She nodded.

John caught Jason in three long strides, picked him up, and started walking back to the van. "Not okay, Jason, not okay. Get in."

John sat between his charges, buckling them in, and sealing the latches beneath his hands. Susie clawed and bit him while Jason scratched at his uncle's hands, swearing. Meanwhile, I was corralling the other kids, Anthony screaming, Ruby taunting, and Jimmy laughing, disaffected. Dan yelled: "Get in the van!" We drove away.

It was another forty minutes before we got our groove back. We rebooted with a song, cheese sticks, and crackers. There was a temporary calm.

Brown Bear, Brown Bear, what do you see? I see some anger issues looking at me.

We rationed water in the interest of pee breaks, regulated blood sugar with apple slices. The next bathroom break we went in shifts, two at time. The rest waited in the van with the engine running. Finally, after seven hours, we got to the lodge.

* * *

That night, we put all the children in one room. Fail. So we pulled the troublemakers out and put them in a tent. Failure again. Then we set up another tent and divided the trouble-makers into two tents. Third time's a charm. By midnight, Marie had Anthony sleeping with her and Gabe, Jimmy was in the bunk room with Uncle John, Dan was in a sleeping bag between Ruby and Jason in the two tents, and I was crashed out in the van with Susie.

The next morning we left my brother at the lodge to cook for us and drove forty miles north to get the kids registered for school. We had prepped this little upstate district in advance so they knew we were coming; there were only six weeks left of the school year, four of our five kids had individualized educational plans, all were delayed, and all had behavior problems. The district responded like a small fire department that constantly drills in anticipation of that big fire, waiting for a chance to test their skills. We were that fire.

Dan filled out the paperwork, while Marie and I played with the kids at the playground. Almost immediately, Jason started throwing sand at the other kids, so I put him in timeout. Then, he started screaming, running away from me. I took him to a quiet, shady spot away from the other kids, and sat him down next to me. When that didn't work, I picked him up and carried him towards the van.

The principal of the school came out: "Do you need any help, Ms. Fox?"

"Thank you," I answered, "We've got it. We just need to finish a timeout but thank you."

The principal gave me a thumbs up: "Good work, Ms. Fox, let us know if we can help."

We finished the registration, loaded up the van, and dropped Dan to pick up another vehicle at the rental car place. Dan had to drive back to the city in two day to close up his office and he, like all of us, was showing signs of fatigue. We voted he should drive down to the lodge alone and in silence. Dan was keeping our family from spinning out into space, and needed some time to recharge.

Marie and I decided to stop at the Stewart's gas station on the way out of town and buy everyone ice cream. Let it be noted that refined sugar is a bad idea. Within minutes the kids were screaming and running around the parking lot, my shouts and warnings bouncing off defiant ears. Marie grabbed Gabe who was quickly being influenced by the manic energy, and took him inside the convenience store. I grabbed Jason and Susie by their shirt collars and said in my most excited voice, "Fox children! Come with me! Follow me behind the Stewart's!" Miraculously, they followed.

I had noticed a grassy knoll tucked back behind the store when we pulled in, covered in bright yellow dandelions. "Whomever picks the most dandelions for Aunt Marie and Gabe in the next ten minutes, gets to choose the movie tonight!" Our movie selection was limited to *The Sound of Music, Thomas and Friends*, and *Kiki's Delivery Service*, all of which we had seen several times before, but they went for it and started picking flowers.

Marie emerged with her son from the Stewart's to an eerie silence. She had watched me from the window and was wondering what I was doing in my stressed and sleep deprived state. She buckled Gabe into the van and fearing the worst, thought about calling the police as she walked slowly to the scene. Her doubts about my safety was an indication of how exhausted we both were and how little control we actually had over the children.

Gabe was delighted when Jimmy, the flower-picking winner, presented him with a gorgeous dandelion bouquet, and equally devastated when thirty seconds later, Jimmy demanded the dandelions back. Marie checked seat belts, I put Jason in the passenger seat next to me and started up the van. Within minutes it was clear we did not have enough adults to maintain safety. Jason unbuckled his seatbelt and ran to join the party that was ramping up in the back row. I grabbed him with my right hand and pulled the van over onto the shoulder. I put him back in his seat, fastened his belt, holding it closed with my right hand, while yelling at the other kids to keep it cool while we got back on the road. I could see Marie's face in profile in the rearview mirror, looking a hard left out the window over Gabe's head with her arm around her son in a protective posture.

I pulled into the next picnic area and stopped. "Marie? Have you ever driven a van this size?" Not waiting for an answer: "You are going to love it!" Marie jumped into the driver's seat. I barked, "Quiet!" loud enough for a momentary effect. Marie turned to Jason and said quietly, "If you do not stay seated with your seatbelt on, your mom will call the police and have them take you to the station. We will drive the other children safely home and come back and get you." She meant it and he knew it. He sat back in his seat and did not move.

While Marie was scaring Jason straight, the remaining four were silently receding. I had exactly one second to take control. Marie started driving. *GO!* I stood and started singing the ballad of Frankie and Johnny as loud as I could, "Frankie and Johnny were lovers, good Lawdy and how they could love . . ." I clapped in time, staring at each kid, crazy eyed, curled back lips, swinging my hips, knees bent and head down because I couldn't stand up straight in the moving van.

I walked down the rows of seats like a revivalist preacher, pointing, singing, moralizing, and pantomiming the ballad of the woman scorned. I had them sing the refrain while I yelled, "I can't hear you!" and hum along during the interludes. I taught them the traditional hand motions to the song which I was making up on the spot, "These are standard performance practice! Pay attention!" When the ballad ended, I did a forced modulation into "Boom-di-ada, boom-di-ada, I love the mountains, I love the rolling hills . . ." I had them clapping and swaying, louder, now softer, terraced dynamics, "Is that all you got? Your grandmother sings louder than that!" I had them sing rounds, timing the last selection, *diminuendo al niente, sotto voce* whisper and cadence as we pulled into the lodge driveway. The engine killed. I looked at Marie in terror. Dan was not there. The rental car was not there. The kids opened the sliding door and hurled out of the van like a tidal wave. I yelled to Marie, "Save yourself!"

Marie grabbed Gabe and ran inside. John came out and stood next to me as I watched in shocked silence as my children morphed into a ten-legged clump of screaming flesh and began careening around the yard, shouting and waving their arms. I should have stopped them, redirected them, made them safe but I just stood there, frozen in place. My hands went clammy and cold, my confidence folded like a paper napkin, and I felt fear for the first time since we got the kids. I needed someone to snap me out of it, slap me on the face with a bucket of ice cold smelling salts. Dan pulled up, got out of the rental car, and yelled, "Go inside!"

Everyone went in. Marie had set the table with the dinner John had made while we were away. I stood back, stumbling, staring, taking deep breaths. *Holy crap.* I needed a plan. Deep breath in and hold it, hold it, and exhale, come on. *You've got to get in there.* Give me a second. *This isn't church camp, girl. These kids aren't going home at the end of the week.*

I turned my mouth on and walked towards the table, "Ruby, help your Aunt Marie with those water pitchers, Jimmy sit yourself down right there across from your brother, everybody sit up straight, sing with me now, 'Oh the Lord is good to me, and so I thank the Lord, for giving me, the things I need, the sun and the rain and apple seed, the Lord is good to me.' Is that all you got? Your great-grandmother sings louder than that! Jason I want to hear you singing, don't make me come over there, we're doing this again and we're doing it right! 'Oh the Lord is good to me ...'"

*   *   *

Our lodge was in a beautiful country setting. But where most kids would run around, explore, and swim, our kids glommed together, tortured each other, fought and hit. I stood where Jake and I had sat and thrown rocks in the river, so long ago. "Here's an idea! Let's see who can throw a rock across the river!" Bad idea. Now they were throwing river rocks at one another. It occurred to me that they didn't know how to play.

We encouraged digging holes in the sand, building forts with the driftwood, looking for pretty rocks in the shallow parts of the river, taking nature walks. No takers. Instead, there was hitting, there were insults, there were strange, shifting alliances between the kids that broke down only when the children were allied against the adults.

Two days had passed, and Dan had to drive back to New York for a few days. John was going to hitch a ride down and get back to his life and work. In the afternoon before the men left, I sat alone on the beach with the kids, strategizing, while my brother slept on a towel down by the river. Marie and I had to hold down the fort and while she had seasoned-mom skills, for medical reasons she could not run or lift more than fifteen pounds.

Just then, Jason called Jimmy a freak, Jimmy picked up a river rock big enough to kill someone, and chucked it in Jason's direction. It got as far as four-year-old Gabe, grazed his arm, and landed thump. I yelled, "John! Jimmy's throwing rocks at the kids!" John bolted from his sleep, ran full speed at Jimmy who froze, his mouth open, as his uncle grabbed him, pulled him to the ground and started yelling one inch away from his face, "You will not throw rocks at other people! You will not hurt other people! It stops now!" Jimmy started crying. He had never seen his uncle like this, red-faced, heart racing from adrenaline. I also had never seen my brother like this. He was terrifying and effective.

Jimmy played quietly away from the others for the rest of the day. John returned to his towel by the river. I went and sat next to my brother. I could see his hands were shaking. Anthony was screaming; Susie had stolen his bucket and was calling him names. "John," I said, starting to cry, "you can't leave. You cannot leave Marie and me alone." He answered before I started begging, leaving me with a vestige of dignity, "I'll stay until Dan gets back."

Those three days without Dan were like a penance, an eternal purgatory for some heinous crime I had committed in a previous life. Screaming children, hitting and biting, dangers to themselves and others. But the weather held. We held. We sang, built fires, roasted hot dogs and marshmallows. I slept in the van with whichever child was the greatest threat. We went to the river every day: the holes got deeper, the sand castles taller, there was constant supervision, intervention, redirection and preemption. Jason and Susie were like kerosene and matches, barely stable apart and a guaranteed flamethrower in proximity to each other. Marie alternated keeping Ruby and Anthony with her and Gabe at the lodge.

One hot, sunny afternoon, Susie pushed Anthony into the deep part of the river. He started screaming and thrashing his way downstream. I ran for Anthony while John grabbed Susie, ignoring her spitting and swearing while his eyes scanned for motion among the other children. I returned Anthony to the river's edge, his soggy pull-up riding low, his little body trembling and shaking. Jason took the opportunity to make things worse, called him a cry baby and throwing sand at him. John handed wild-eyed Susie to me, took both of Jason's hands in his own, and led him to a timeout by the bridge. Jimmy came and sat by me. I was holding Susie, while trying to comfort the still sobbing Anthony. The hills were alive with the sound of Jason's one hit wonder, "You're hurting me, you're hurting me!" It occurred to me I didn't know how to parent.

I looked back at my brother in the timeout ditch with Jason; he smiled at me and pointed up into the sky. There was a bat circling over us. I whispered, "Look up, guys. There's a bat." Sudden silence ensued, eyes up, heads back, everyone motionless; the only thing moving was the bat. For five minutes we watched its awkward flight, out of place in the daylight; eyes fixed to its dipping down, jerking up, flapping for us, around and around. How strange at midday.

My brother stayed until Dan came back, but it was another six months before John could come visit us again; he said his heart would start racing just thinking about it. I wondered what the kids would remember from those early days.

Months later into our family life we returned to the lodge and on one sunny day, Jimmy sat down beside me at the river. He put his arm around me and pointed up into the trees. "Remember the bat, Mom? Remember the bat in the middle of the day?" I said, "I sure do, Jimmy. That was really something, wasn't it?"

7

NUCLEAR FAMILY

𝑀arie helped us move into our new house, a 4,300-square-foot brownstone on a former Air Force base overlooking Lake Champlain. It was enormous, with eight bedrooms and three floors that had sightlines across the parade field and the lake towards Vermont. It was so far from the Bronx; we might as well have flown to the moon. While I was frantically keeping my children from harming themselves and others, Marie bought school supplies, set up and stocked the kitchen, took measurements of everything and ordered mattresses. She cut the empty cardboard moving boxes to fit the windows in the children's rooms, so the summer light wouldn't wake them prematurely. She made us lasagnas and casseroles, then bought a freezer to put them in, and marked the height of every child against the kitchen door frame in pencil with their names and the date. She was doing everything that needed doing, everything I couldn't do while chasing after my children, using my big body to buffer and barricade as they acted out against this enormous disruption in their lives. Marie would have helped me in this process, but she couldn't, no one could, not if I wanted to be the mother of these five children. It had to be me, my body embracing them in this stressful, violent safekeeping.

One midnight, exhausted, I found Marie doing laundry in the basement. "Hi. I hate my life." Marie smiled, sorting and drying, "I know. Just remember, we can do anything as long as we can complain about it." I laughed. Then cried. "It's all so violent, all the screaming . . ."

Marie nodded, "Birthing is violent, screaming and bloody— you are birthing a family, Ann. It's sacred work. No shortcuts." I hung my head. Marie hugged me and sat me down on a chair. "You'll get through it. Rest when you can, and keep complaining. I'm here for you."

Before she left to go back home, Marie found us a live-in tutor who could start two weeks later. Until then, it was just Dan and me and the kids. Alone at last. Radiant, active, glowing, and unstable. Our nuclear family.

* * *

Dan had a vision for our family, a long view, and I trusted his judgment completely; he could see things I couldn't. I followed through on his hunches, implemented his policies. He was thoughtful, decisive, and he never missed. I told Marie, "This guy is kicking my parenting butt. He is off the charts." Marie responded, "You only need one good leader." Word.

Our division of labor fell clearly along our individual strengths, and we assumed our different roles without discussion. I was the boots on the ground parent, knee-deep in shit and minutiae. Dan's was an aerial view; he could see around corners, warn me of sneak attacks from the rear, and call the ambush before it happened. He had the forest, I had the trees. We were in constant phone contact. "Dan, I have a situation." In eight words or less he would make the call. "Isolate Jason, pull Ruby close, redirect Susie." Copy that.

The children equally feared him and loved him, waiting every day for him to come home and play with them. I would stand on the porch and watch Dan on the great lawn chasing them, grabbing their legs, dropping to the grass and rolling towards them, their laughing and screaming fusing into a single warbling shrill of excitement. I just stood there, watching him play, falling in love with this part of my husband I'd never met, this paternal man, the father of my children.

We took a family picnic to the lake on a beautiful afternoon, bright and sunny. Vermont's Green Mountains smiled at us from across the glistening expanse of water. We had the whole park to ourselves and our Frisbees, soccer balls, snacks, and sun hats. The day was going well. Dan was playing tag with the kids, everyone laughing. Then Dan's work phone rang. I froze.

We looked at each other. Dan picked up as I looked down at my watch. It was two o'clock on a Saturday. "I'm sorry. I have to go," he said and took off running up the hill. The children and I stood silently and watched as Dan disappeared around the corner. A huge hissing sound filled the air. I heard it, the kids heard it: the sickening, sucking sound of the power vacuum. The mood of the kids' play shifted immediately. I sprang into action, "Okay, guys! Time to pack up! Ruby, can you grab the charcoal bag? Let's see how quickly we can get home!" But Ruby was not interested. She had grabbed the Frisbee from Anthony and was holding it over his head, just out of reach, taunting him as he cried. Susie sprinted towards the woods and Jason took off after her, waving a stick and threatening her with violence. Jimmy stood at the picnic table watching and laughing while the paper plates blew into the lake.

I had tried to be like Dan, assert my dominance, command the kids with my words, but every time it fell flat. Dan kept telling me, "They have to respect you." But they didn't. Dan's booming voice spoke directly to them; his presence was primal, their obedience reflexive. He was the alpha male. I could use his exact same words but my voice, hollow and shrill, was ineffectual, or worse, comedic. "They don't believe me, Dan. They know I am not you. I have to say those things but I have to say them my way or they'll know I'm bluffing." Dan and I agreed this was not a gender issue; I know many women who rock the alpha vibe. I'm just not one of them. "Find your own way," Dan said, "but remember, they have to respect you."

I took off after Jason. I grabbed him by his shirtsleeve. He started punching. "COOL IT!" I said. He yelled back, "You're not the boss of me!" Ruby was laughing at Anthony, calling him a crybaby as he kept jumping for the Frisbee. "Ruby, STOP IT! It's time to go!" Jason started kicking my shins and grabbing at my arm, scratching at my hand that was gripping his shirtsleeve. I pulled him to the ground, but my focus was scattered and he knew it. "Ruby! PUT IT DOWN! We need to pack up! Jimmy! Help me out here!" Jimmy didn't even look at me; he and Susie were laughing at little Anthony, who was screaming profanities with such mastery and articulation that it stopped me dead in my tracks. Pre-verbal? Really? Jason landed a head butt to the left side of my jaw, chipping my front tooth. I needed containment and I needed it fast.

I lifted Jason by his shirt from the ground, my head still reeling from the blow, and took him to a picnic table away from the other kids. Jimmy and Susie were throwing charcoal at each other. Jason was yelling at me, "Leave me alone, bitch! Let me go! You're hurting me, you're hurting me! I'll kill you, you freak! Stop touching me!" Ruby was hitting Anthony with the Frisbee. "NOT OKAY!" I yelled. I had lost control. My heart was pounding.

I pulled one of Jason's thrashing arms back behind him, grabbed the back of his neck with my free hand and sat his skinny butt down on a picnic bench. "OW! OW! STOP!" he shouted. I played out possible scenarios in my mind, none of them good. I was not babysitting here. No one was going to come pick these kids up in an hour. These were my children. I had to figure this out. My hands were shaking, my heart rate soaring. I put my mouth one inch from Jason's ear and whispered, "If you so much as move, I will fucking kill you."

He froze. I left him sitting there. "Pack it up, first one home gets Oreo cookies. Let's go!" I was using a happy, excited voice as I grabbed Anthony and tried to collect our belongings. Jason was watching me, and I, him. The other kids rallied. "Jimmy, grab the backpack! Let's go! Come on guys! First one up the hill wins!" Anthony was twisting in my arms, trying to get down. I set him in the direction of the hill, "Go Anthony! Run, run!" I followed the kids halfway up the hill, then turned and walked back to Jason. Standing twenty feet from the picnic table where he sat stone still, I said in a soft, measured voice, "Follow at this distance. Do not speak." Jason, silent, shadowed us home.

We walked across the great lawn towards the house, my mind racing. What just happened? *You threatened to kill a nine-year-old child.* I didn't think I was capable of that. *Take it as a warning shot. You're tired. You're over-extended.* I'm scared. When I threatened him, my actions seemed completely appropriate. *Okay, it's okay. Let's start by preventing situations like this from happening again.* Right. I am not ready to be alone with all five, not yet. *You just have to get through the afternoon until Dan comes home.*

Back at the house, I took the kids on a bike ride, we kicked the soccer ball around, and went to the playground. The whole time, I was trying to keep it positive, keep it moving. Dan would help me tighten them back up when he got home. We watched *Kiki's Delivery Service* on our portable DVD player, and had cereal for dinner. Dan called at 6:30. Finally. *Thank God.* "Ann, I'm sorry. I have to be in Vermont for two days. I'll check in with you when I can." My heart stopped and my eyes teared, "Okay, thanks for calling. Safe travels!" I hung up. *Dear God*.

* * *

Time for bed. "Pajamas everyone!" I was helping Ruby put a clean sheet on her bed when I heard Anthony screaming. I dropped the sheet and ran. Anthony was on his back, lying on the floor while Jason was choking him with both hands. Susie was holding Anthony's arms down while Jimmy watched, laughing. There was a sickness at play, rabid and sadistic. I grabbed Anthony off the floor and ran back to Ruby's room, Anthony screaming in my arms. "Ruby, follow me!" She had not been infected by the other's attitude; I had to get her out of the house. We ran down the back staircase, through the living room, and out onto the porch. I sent Ruby to a friend's nearby, and I took Anthony to our next-door neighbor, Diane, whom I barely knew. She opened the door, "Hi!" I handed her a crying, naked Anthony in nothing but a pull-up. "I need you to watch him!" I said, running back to our house. "Anything I should know?" she yelled. I screamed back, "He likes baths." She'd figure it out.

Back at home, Jason and Susie were throwing things, their speech and gestures violent, while Jimmy sat on the floor, laughing. "Jimmy," I said, "Jimmy!" I pulled his arm. He looked up. "Stand up! I need your help! Jimmy! I need you to go in your room and shut the door." Non-responsive, listless, the Jimmy I knew was gone. He stared vacantly, grinning and laughing. I grabbed Susie under her arms, dragged her feet down the hall, and into her room. I shut the door and told her to stay there. She was laughing at me as I ran back to Jason's room. I pulled a "reverse timeout," on Jimmy, pushed him out of Jason's room and into the hall and closed the door behind me. I turned and faced Jason who was grabbing at his crotch, saying, "Suck it, bitch." I grappled him into my arms, knees to chin, arms tucked tightly in between, and slid to the floor, my back leaning against the closed door. I closed my eyes so I wouldn't cry while Jason, screaming and biting, clawed at me.

I hate this. I don't want this. I want someone else to do this. *There's no one else, Ann. This is your fight.* I don't know if I can do this. *Grow the fuck up. You're the adult. Love these children. It's hard love, harder love, but you need to do this because they need a mom.*

Jason interrupted my self-talk by screaming, "Bitch! You freak! Let go of me." His face was beet red as he told me what I could do to myself and where I could shove things. "QUIET!" I barked, in as deep a voice as I could. No effect. "QUIET!" I tightened my hold, squeezing him between my arms, my right hand pulling hard on my left wrist. He stopped. I relaxed. He started again. I tightened. I was not hurting him, but I was in control of him. When he stopped struggling, I relaxed. When he strained, I restrained him, back and forth for twenty minutes until finally he quieted down. I said firmly, "Get in bed," and let him go.

Susie was muttering to herself outside the door, pacing the hall as we struggled. I walked her to her room, "Go to bed," I said. I went downstairs. Jimmy was lying on the floor in the foyer, silent, soulless, with Charlie the dog lying quietly near. Jimmy had chosen a non-aggressive defense mechanism so I let him be. I called my neighbor, Lisa, to thank her and let her know Ruby could come home now. Anthony would have to wait. Lisa walked Ruby home carrying an apple-spice cake the two of them had made. Lisa hugged me. I didn't want to let her go, I wanted to cry and beg her not to leave me. I swallowed hard. "Thank you," I said. She smiled, "Anytime! We had fun, didn't we, Ruby?" I took Ruby upstairs to her room and told her to get her PJs on and get in bed.

There was poison in the air, meanness hung in the hallway

like a stench, putrid and sour. I had failed. The children had taken control of the house and I had allowed it to happen. Jimmy was still lying motionless at the base of the stairs. Susie, spooky and vacant, was picking at herself like a nervous animal chewing its paw. Jason was banging around in his room, talking to himself, his weird, ghostlike voices defining our family narrative.

I went into my bedroom and wrapped my shaking hands around the thin, wooden neck of my guitar. I tuned as I walked, sussing my acoustic options, looking for an advantage. I sat on the floor in the hallway outside my door, *strum, strum,* tipped my head back and aimed my voice at the sweet spot at the top of the stairwell. My voice ricocheted like a hot shower in a tiled bathroom. I sang and sang: music as crowd control, music as medicine. Jimmy came upstairs and put his head on my shoulder. "How many roads must a man walk down . . ." The girls called out, "Can we come sing?" Of course. They sat beside me. Jason stayed in his room. The other three calmed down, resting their heads on my legs, close and warm, music as mortar, music the mother I was trying to be.

"Goodnight, Mr. J," I said, kissing Jimmy's head. I hugged the girls, "love you, Sweeties." They smiled, snuggly, "love you too, Mom." It was 10:30 p.m. when I picked up Anthony, he had been in the bath at the neighbors the entire time. He smelled of lotion. I put him to bed in the T-shirt Diane had provided. I went downstairs, ate half of Lisa's apple-spice cake, and fell asleep in my clothes.

The next morning, I played Bach on the piano for my children while they slept. Bach is the voice of peace in the extreme and order in the universe, written by and for all things well-tempered. And from that day forward, I woke them each morning playing Bach on piano and I sang to them nightly with the guitar. No matter how violent or vulgar the day, no matter how base or ungodly the bedlam, coming and going, prelude and postlude, music would bless us, atone and forgive us.

* * *

Dan and I needed to make a safe, predictable home for our children; a home filled with kindness, respect, clear expectations, and consistent follow through. We asked the school district for a copy of each child's discipline program to help streamline the transition between home and classroom. The school used an emotionally detached system of consequences called, "123 Magic." In it, the child is given three opportunities to stop bad behavior. If the behavior continues, she gets put in timeout for the number of minutes she is in years. If she won't do the timeout, she is taken to her room, and the timeout does not begin until she chooses to sit quietly. Following the timeout, there is no discussion or moralizing about the behavior and the child moves on. It was simple and easy to understand.

While the school's version seemed simple, in our house, this method was generally accompanied with kicking, hitting, scratching, and biting as I made them do their timeouts. I soon found that taking them to their rooms for timeouts was proving unsafe for a number of reasons, broken glass and second floor windows not the least of them. We converted an empty, windowless storage room on the third floor into the dedicated timeout room. The door opened in and we put foldable wrestling mats on the floor with vinyl covers for easy cleanup of emotional discharge: mucus, saliva, blood, and rarely, but disturbingly, urine. There was no lock. The door had to be held closed from the outside by an adult.

Jason's timeouts lasted on average ninety minutes. Susie could go two-and-a-half hours, no problem. Both of them would kick the door from the inside, tell me they had to use the bathroom, tell me they were ready to be done, then scream and talk to themselves in bizarre, scary voices. As soon as there was a moment of silence, I would start the timer. But just the sound of setting the timer or the sound of the timer ringing to announce they were done would set them off. "Mom, mom, mom, I'm ready, I am calm now, MOM! FUCK YOU. I AM READY! OPEN THE DOOR!!! Mom, mom, mom, mom . . . OPEN THE DOOR, YOU CRACK WHORE!" *Wow. Crack whore? Really?* The goal of the children was to engage me. Any attention, even negative attention, would be seen as a reward, so I tried to stick with our 123 program: keep the responsibility on them and make it their choice to do the timeout or not.

Bathroom breaks were the worst. "Mom! I have to pee! I'm going to pee myself, I'm not kidding! MOM! Open the door!" Most times I would hold Jason by his shirt while he peed, if he actually had to pee. Usually he'd just stand at the toilet, then turn and smile at me, wag his tongue and say, "Fool!" I'd walk him back to the room, kicking and screaming, scratching and writhing. I hated it.

Most timeouts ended with the child becoming exhausted and sleeping it off. Then two months in, Susie figured out that if she just did the seven minutes and skipped the fight, she would be back outside and at the playground in no time. The first time she had a timeout in the chair, she was shocked. She kept telling her siblings, "Just do the timeout, it's SO SHORT! Seven minutes is like nothing!"

But Jason would not give it up. One afternoon I was trying to get him back in the room after a bathroom break. He was grabbing at my clothes, kicking and screaming, "Don't leave me in here, don't leave, I hate you, I hate you!" I was as gentle as I could be while putting him into a non-escalating restraint, "And I love you, Jason. I love you too much to let you behave like this." He screamed, his face turning red, "No! You don't! You hate me! You've always hated me!" I said, "You're my son, I love you and nothing will ever change that. You're a good boy, you just made a bad choice and now you've got nine minutes. Just get it done."

Jason suddenly went limp in my arms and started sobbing. "No!" he yelled through his sobs, "I'm a bad boy! I'm a hateful boy!" I held him. All my instincts told me to kiss him, tell him no, you are a good boy, you had a rough start, we'll get past this. But when a child with an attachment disorder says he's bad, it is counterproductive to deny it or try and talk him out of it; it's his reality. He will think you are saying he's good because you don't know the truth, and then he will set about trying to prove to you that he is bad, bad enough to reject, bad enough to send away. I towed the line. "I'm sorry you feel that way, Jason. That must be really hard." He was sobbing, his limp little body shaking in our now defunct restraint, strands of my hair sticking to his sweaty fingers, his snot and tears making an ever widening stain on my pant leg. "I don't know who told you that, buddy, but I like you. I think you're a great kid . . ." He was asleep.

I sat there quietly for a few minutes. I had to make sure he was really sleeping. I tested him, ran my fingers quietly through his sweaty hair, "Jason?" He was definitely out. I started crying. I stroked his head and held him to me, kissing him. I whispered, "You are a good boy, Jason, you had a rough start." I wiped my tears on my T-shirt, "We'll get past this, Jason. It's not your fault. You are a good boy." I laid him tenderly onto the mat and stood up. My body shook spontaneously. I took some deep breaths and ran downstairs.

8

SUSIE

*W*hen we adopted her, Susie was seven years old and losing her mind. We had no medical records for any of the kids, and were particularly concerned she might have some serious mental issues. Every night around eleven she would emerge from her room, a ghostlike waif with hollow eyes, and float through our massive house, whispering to herself, gasping and starting at the visions in her head. Dan and I would follow her, watch her as she traced the walls with her fingertips, "Do you think she's psychotic?" I asked Dan, quietly. If she was truly ill, she might need a level of care that we couldn't provide.

I called in our situation to the local children's mental health clinic, which was conveniently within walking distance to the house. I filled out the applications for all of the kids and returned them to the office the same day. They said they would call back, but didn't. The next day I sat vigil in the office until someone would see me. We'd been put on a waiting list for the intake sessions and told there was an even longer waiting list for the therapists. "But you never know," a receptionist told me, "something might open up."

Meanwhile, Susie was stealing, lying, violent, and defiant. I was at the school every day and in touch with the teachers throughout the day. They were incredibly helpful, sharing information with me, completely accepting of both her and our situation. One day she would not come out from under her desk, the next she wouldn't get off the top of her desk. She was caught kissing the other children, going through the other children's backpacks and desks, stealing toys and books from the classrooms and library. Away from school, she was trying to jump from moving vehicles, and climbing out of her second floor window.

We needed help. I called the mental health services again. "Hi. This is Ann Fox. You can either agree to see us within twenty-four hours, or I will call 911 and you will have to see us within twenty-four hours. This is not a threat." Well, when I put it that way, it seemed they had a new hire who might have room for one or two of the children. We scheduled an intake the following Monday. "Super. Thank you so much. Can you tell me the name of the new therapist?" "Darcy Mason." I wrote it down. "Thank you again, we will see you on Monday." I hung up the phone, hit redial, and disguised my voice. I asked to speak with Darcy Mason in a high-pitched, upstate accent. "Just a moment please, I will put you through."

"This is Darcy." I used my normal voice. "Hi Darcy, my name is Ann Fox. I have a recently placed, pre-adoptive foster child who is in crisis. I have promised her we would get her a feeling doctor as soon as possible to help her with her feelings. She is seven and asking every day to see the feeling doctor. I am calling as her pre-adoptive mother of five weeks to see if you can help us." Darcy was moved. She said, "The poor little thing." I pressed her, "We need help, Darcy." She saw us that afternoon.

At the session, Darcy asked Susie how things were going at home. Susie said it was really different from the foster home in the Bronx: "Our new family is not fair." *Here we go.* "In what way is your new family not fair?" Susie thought for a moment. "Here the kids hit the parents but the parents don't hit back." *Thanks, Susie, back me up.* After that, Darcy saw us twice a week to help Susie.

Soon I had therapists for every child, and I went with them to every session. As the new mother, I was a complicated person for our children. I was hard to love, accept, or trust. All five children all believed at a fundamental level that their biological mother had rejected them for whatever reason, and going to the "feeling doctor" together provided a platform for us to talk about these difficult mother issues, along with the laundry list of issues for any abused and neglected child.

The pediatrician visits soon followed. We told the doctor about Susie's trouble sleeping, and he suggested we give her one antihistamine before bed for a week to help get her sleep cycle back on track. It was the most wonderful week ever, I didn't want it to end. Neither did Susie. The first night without a Benadryl, she cried and cried, tossed and turned. I told her she didn't have to sleep, she only had to rest, to pretend to sleep. "Close your eyes, breathe slowly, feel your stomach going up and down . . ." I took her on guided visualizations, gave her a bath, rubbed lavender-scented baby oil on her back. Nothing worked. Finally she asked if she could have the sleeping pills. "Oh, Susie," I said, "I can't make that decision. I would need to talk to Dr. Beguine." She pleaded for me to call him. "Okay, but I need you to rest until I come back." I went down to the kitchen and tore a tiny corner off a slice of sandwich bread.

I rolled the tiny piece of bread between my fingers until it was round and smooth. I got a cup of water, climbed the stairs back to her room, and with great ceremony stood in her doorway. I waited for Susie to open her eyes, then walked over and sat by her bed. "I spoke with the doctor and he said we could try this new sleeping pill but you must know it is VERY strong.

You need to swallow it whole, with water, and then as soon as you take it you must lie down and close your eyes." She took it soberly, respectfully. I took the cup from her hand and she lay back down. It knocked her out. She woke the next morning rested, saying it was the best sleep she ever had. The bread pills were so effective that after a month of taking them she didn't need medication of any kind.

* * *

Six months into her new school, Susie dialed 911 from a school conference room and told the dispatcher that a man was beating her and then hung up. Susie's one-on-one aide had left the room for twenty seconds, and was shocked when the police arrived. The police and the principal confronted Susie with what she had done. She denied it and then completely shut down. They put her in the "blue room," a padded, carpeted timeout room, until I was able to come pick her up.

The next morning Susie would not dress or eat, and refused to go to school. In the short time we'd known Susie, we'd learned that she made better choices when we made them for her. "If you do not get dressed, I will carry you to school in your pajamas. You will dress in the principal's office and go to your class." Dan and I had done it more than once. I would call ahead and give the principal a heads up and she would meet us in the parking lot and begin talking Susie down, as Dan or I carried her inside.

A series of forced extractions from Susie's classroom followed the 911 incident. I met with Susie's teacher, the principal, and the school psychologist, and we agreed on a plan for me to come get Susie before she had a full-blown episode. I told them about Susie's "tells," her physical attributes that preceded a meltdown. I imitated her for the teachers, pursing my lips, staring blankly and pulling at my fingertips. They recognized her immediately, "Wow, you're good. That looks just like her!" *Thank you, I'm here all week.* They were to call me as soon as she started pulling on her fingers and I would come immediately.

A few days later, I was one block away picking up night splints for Anthony when I got the call that an ambulance was on the way to take Susie to the hospital for a psychiatric evaluation. I was furious. This was not the plan. I pulled up just in time to watch three EMTs subduing Susie. She was screaming like a wounded animal as they held her down, wrapping her in a thick rubber blanket and strapping her onto a gurney. This is not what we wanted. I rode in the ambulance and Dan met us at the emergency room. He told her jokes while we waited, got her laughing and giggling. Susie was already scheduled for a psychiatric evaluation the next day, so they let us leave the emergency room with no interview and only a few hours of waiting.

The psychiatrist interviewed Susie, and then met with Darcy, Dan, and me. The question came down to whether Susie's behavior was a choice or the result of a condition beyond her control. She was diagnosed with oppositional defiant disorder and might possibly respond to medication for ADHD. We had only known her for six months at this point, and felt medication was premature. We wanted to find out who she was first.

I worried about Susie more than the others. She was the only one of the five who, in addition to lashing out, would also self-harm. She had figured out that if she scratched the inside of her nose until it bled freely, she could get out of most situations. I had mentioned the prolific nose bleeds to our pediatrician and upon examination, he said she had broken through the lining of her right nostril and into the vein so many times that if she did it even a few more times, it would not heal. They would have to cauterize it, which would create other problems down the road.

A week after the ambulance incident, I decided to go for a

walk. All the kids were at school and the sun was making a rare appearance, so I forwarded the home phone to my cell phone and got about ten minutes from the house when the school called: Susie was in distress. I called our tutor, John, and he met me with his car and drove me to the school. I ran inside to find Susie tucked tightly into the far corner of the blue room, head down, motionless, the blue carpeting splattered red from her free-flowing nosebleed. I went to her, gently stroked her back and whispered, "We're going home, Sweetie." Legally, no one could help me remove her and I was not asking, but the entire staff stood instinctively close, offering support as I lifted Susie, struggling, up off the floor. I moved as quickly as possible through the office and into the parking lot.

The principal, school psychologist, child advocate, and two others followed me out. Susie pulled an arm free from my restraint and started hitting and scratching. She struggled and one of her legs broke free. I started to run. There were two adults running along beside me to catch us if we fell. Another adult had run ahead and was holding the car door open. I dove, Susie first, into the back seat where I struggled to regain my hold of her. She was thrashing and screaming. The principal shut the door and John started driving.

I held her tightly with her head tipped slightly back, trying to stop the flow of blood from her nose. As we drove, the screaming turned to sobbing, and the writhing slowed to short outbursts every fifteen seconds. There was blood everywhere, down her shirt, running up her face and pooling near her eyes. I looked at the tutor in the rearview mirror. His eyes were fixed on the road.

I had felt many times in the past months like an imposter, a fake, someone who was "mothering" but not a "mother." I was waiting for the moment when I'd mothered enough, put in enough false labor to make it real. I figured I would know it when it happened. I sat quietly, looking out the window as we drove through the downtown, the shadows from the buildings blinking for us, the gentle trees with gentler leaves, and little Susie twitching in my arms. *You did it. You're a mom.*

Just then, Susie sneezed. Blood sprayed from her nose onto the ceiling of the car, the side window, the rear window, and the upholstery. My face was spotted and dripping. Susie shuddered in her post-sobbing calm and I looked up at the tutor in the mirror. He was not taking his eyes of the road for love or money. A minute passed before I said, "Hey, remember that guy in *Pulp Fiction*? The guy that cleaned up the car after John Travolta shot the guy in the head? What was his name?" The tutor finally looked up at me in the rearview mirror and then quickly looked back to the road. "Wolf. His name was Wolf." I laughed. "Man, do I need his number!" We pulled into the driveway. John wasn't laughing. "Sorry about your car," I said, "I'll clean it up."

* * *

I gently pinched Susie's nose at the bridge as I led her to the bathroom. I started the shower for her and helped her undress. "Get cleaned up, Honey, I'll be right back." I went into Dan's and my bathroom and washed my face. I changed my clothes and ran through a few scenarios depending on Susie's next move. At some point she would have to complete the original timeout she was given in school for whatever bad choice she had made. I was hoping she was exhausted, that I could let her sleep it off and then have her sit in the chair for her seven minutes.

I walked her to her bedroom and helped her into some clean clothes. Her nose had stopped bleeding but she was wide awake, defiant as ever. "Let's go, Sweetie. Let's do that timeout and then get on with the day." No response. Her eyes were glassed over. "That's one, Susie. At three we are going to the timeout room." Nothing. She was digging in. "That's two . . . . That's three." I took her by the arm and she pulled away, hitting and screaming. I carried her upstairs, and put her face down in the far corner of the timeout room with her arms behind her back, legs together, and then ran for the door. She was two steps behind me, scratching and screaming at the door. Eerie silence, then *BAM* kicking as hard as she could with the bottom of her foot at one second intervals. For ten minutes she kicked, and I held the door closed and leaned against the frame, trying to relax. *Deep breath, Ahhh*. As long as she was kicking I knew what she was doing.

The kicking stopped. I threw the door open and ran at her yelling, "You keep that finger out of your nose or I'll keep it out for you!" I pulled her tunneling fingers away from her face. I held her down again. She did not resist. I let her up and her hand shot back up to her nose. I grabbed it away and held it to her side. "You want to play with me, Susie? Game on! Nobody hurts my kids, not even my kids! If you can't control your body, I will control it for you."

She started struggling. Half-walking, half-carrying her, I got her back down the stairs, her tiny close-trimmed nails clawing at my wrists and arms. On the way out the back door, I grabbed my heavy nylon jacket and got Susie into the back seat of the van. I held her face down with her hands behind her back while she screamed and kicked. "As soon as you stop struggling I will let you up." For fifteen minutes she screamed at me, scratched at me as I held her hands together behind her back.

Finally she stopped. I released her and she sat up. I put her arms to her side and velcroed her into my thick, conveniently blood-red-colored jacket. The collar, when zipped all the way up was like one of those white plastic cones vets put around dogs' heads to keep them from chewing themselves. "Sit up straight, keep your eyes forward and keep your hands outside the bottom of the jacket where I can see them." I closed the van door and stepped back just behind her sight line. She waited a moment, then turned to look for me. I opened the van door, pushed her back onto the seat, face down and held her there for a minute. She was crying but not struggling. I let her up. "Sit up straight, eyes forward, hands where I can see them." I closed the door and stepped away. I circled the van slowly. I let her see me watching her, then I'd pull away, into her blind spot. Three minutes passed before I saw a little finger wriggling up from the inside of the coat collar. I jump into the van, yelling, "I said hands down!" pushing her onto the seat again. She cried, but did not struggle. "You sit up straight, eyes forward, hands in your lap where I can see them." I closed the door and stepped away.

Three more minutes pass. Susie looked straight ahead with her signature glare, both vacant and defiant. I made my rounds and saw her hands clawing at each other in her lap. I yelled as I opened the door, "You're going to scratch yourself? I don't think so! These are MY fingers now, Susie. I own these fingers!" I put her gently face down on the seat. "I'm not going to let this happen to you!"

She does not cry, she does not struggle. *Dammit.* It feels six kinds of wrong to hold a child down who is not resisting. When a child continually crosses the line, I have to redraw the line further away from the dangerous behavior I sit her back up, wipe the snot of her face, and tell her to sit up straight, "look forward and keep your hands on the seat." I place her hands flat on the seat, but she pulls them away. I shove them back onto the seat, fingers under her legs. She starts to cry but leaves them there. I close the door and start walking around the van.

Susie sits straight, eyes forward, hands on top of her legs, pinky fingers stretching down so their tips brush the vinyl seat. She's making a point. I give it to her. I open the door. She doesn't move, doesn't look at me. I say gently, "How are you doing, Susie? Are you okay? Do you need to use the bathroom?"

She whispers, "I'm okay." I ask if she's ready to do her timeout and she nods, "Yes, Mom." I exhale. "That's my girl. I'll go get the timer."

Throughout her episode, Susie had managed to rack up two hours and forty minutes of timeout time. I set the timer for an hour and set it on the dashboard so she could see it. I gave her a cup of water and told her I would check on her. With her eyes looking straight ahead she asked quietly, "Mom, how long is two hours and forty minutes?" I said, "Susie, it's longer than the longest movie you have ever seen. Show me some good behavior out here and maybe I will let you do some of it inside."

I step out of the van and close the door quietly. The other kids are home from school. The tutor is giving them a snack in the kitchen. I look at Susie through the window. She looks relaxed and calm. After twenty minutes, I unzip her from the coat and carry her inside. She rests her head on my shoulder and drapes her arms around me. I lay her gently in her bed and pull the blanket over her, stroking her hair. "You can finish the timeout in your bed," I whisper. "Thanks, Mom." I kiss her head. "I love you, Susie."

"I love you, too, Mom."

9

A NEW NORMAL

I had five back-to-back meetings with the Special Ed Office to discuss the children's individualized educational plans. I arrived with five color-coded folders, white athletic tape tight around my sprained wrist, a sty in my right eye, a bruise on the corner of my mouth from a head butt, and two slightly chipped teeth. The committee greeted me warmly, everyone smiling nicely and mock-shaking my sprained hand, "What nice folders! So organized."

Various teachers, aides, advocates, school psychologists, and principals sat around the table and discussed each child in turn. I took copious notes. My kids had been in school for thirty days and in this time, these people knew as much or more about my children than either Dan or I did. They had done comprehensive testing and the reports were devastating. I was writing down numbers like seventh percentile, twelfth percentile, and fourth percentile in my color-coded notebooks; words like "borderline," "egregious," and "global delays." One of the children had scored in the fortieth percentile in one category and I let out a "Yes!"

After the second session, I started to feel a little defensive.

It was ungrounded, of course. No one was suggesting these test results were a reflection on my parenting. Jason had been diagnosed as "borderline mentally retarded." He tested so low, they were not sure if the diagnosis was correct; his vocabulary was so small that the testing might not accurately reflect his abilities. "He has about a 400-word vocabulary," one of the teachers said. I laughed, "Really? Because he's taught *me* a few new words!" Some of the teachers laughed with me. One said seriously, "We're not talking about those kinds of words, Ms. Fox." I apologized, "I know, I'm sorry. I was kidding." I was near tears.

Anthony was up next. As they went around the table with their numbers and results, I had to take deliberate breaths to keep from crying. The tragedy of Jason, the nine-year-old who could not tie his own shoes was paling before the fate of the little brother who never would. Anthony was testing poorly in an ungraded, skills-based class. He couldn't hold a pencil, needed toilet training, and had trouble eating. Ninth percentile, fifteenth percentile, third percentile . . .

I interrupted, "Right! How about that smile, huh? I'm looking at ninety-seventh percentile right there!" Everyone chimed in, "absolutely, what a great smile." I went on. "Good. Hugs, ninety-fifth percentile, cute laugh ninety-eighth . . ." Everyone was nodding in agreement. The head of special education said, "These are wonderful children, Ms. Fox. I think we should take a break." I went outside and sat in the car.

I'd met with a psychiatrist earlier that week who was doing the intake sessions for our kids. She asked me if Dan and I were trying to save these children. I said no, "We just want to make it better." She looked surprised and sat quietly, waiting to see if I had anything to add. I didn't. The psychiatrist said my expectations were realistic: "Some of your children could still end up addicts, homeless, or in prison, even after being adopted into a loving home. We just don't have enough information yet about the long term effects of trauma on a developing brain."

All of the diagnoses were overwhelming. *Shit!* I banged my hands on the steering wheel. *The long term effects of trauma . . . okay, I'm just guessing here but I am going to say . . . not good.* What the hell happened to my children? *The question is what happens next.* I don't have any training. *You have a healthy brain. Use it.* I put my head on the steering wheel and started crying. *Why are you crying? They don't need your pity.* I'm not crying for them. *Feeling sorry for yourself? Not productive!* I am crying because it isn't fair. *Make it fairer!*

* * *

I was born in Berkeley in the nineteen-sixties, then moved with my family to Palo Alto when I was four. My dad had a PhD in neurophysiology and my mother, a master's in child development. I thought everyone lived like me, precious and loved, never hit, never hungry. I grew up happy, healthy, strong, and confident. I had never heard of foster care, not even on television. We didn't have a television. I was taught as a child that I was on this earth to experience joy and fulfill the nature of my design. These were my expectations for life. I knew who I was and where I came from. I never doubted that I was worthy or deserving and I was given an education to help me to achieve my potential.

I regret I was not there for my children's formative, critical stages of neurogenesis. But the past was behind us, I had to look forward and do my best to compensate for their fearful, love-starved, stimulus-poor start.

The next night after dinner, I called the kids together. "Fox children, piano lessons will begin this week. You will practice thirty minutes each day. The practice schedule is here on the whiteboard with your name and time for your practice unit. No one will be made to practice. If you do not practice, you will sit facing the wall for the duration of your practice time. When you have done your practicing, you will receive fifty cents. If you put your fifty cents into your savings account, your Dad and I will double it and it will become a dollar. Practice five days a week, and you will have five dollars in your savings account. Are there any questions?"

Ruby raised her hand, "Do we have to?" I nodded. "Yes. Fox children play the piano. They practice thirty minutes every day. This is what Fox children do." Jason asked, "What if we don't want to?" I smiled, "You will sit and face the wall for thirty minutes while your siblings are making bank."

I was bluffing. I had no idea if the Fox children would practice, and had no way to enforce a thirty-minute consequence if they didn't. Hell, I couldn't get a Fox child to sit for a nine-minute timeout. I'd found a piano teacher who was a retired second grade teacher, lived within walking distance, and could take all five. I put a wooden music cabinet next to the piano and made labels with each child's name by their own shelf. I began playing for the kids throughout the day, stopping at the piano as I passed by. I used the piano as one might use a cup of tea, a moment for oneself to savor and enjoy, modeling for my children the pleasure one gets from making music.

I never interfered with their practicing. I would answer questions, but never teach. Passing as they played, I'd say, "You sound incredible! I love it. Play that one again, you sound so good." In a free minute I would sit with them and make up a left-hand accompaniment. I wanted them to love the piano. "Jason, did you know that your grandfather learned how to play on this very piano when he was just a boy?" Jason looked confused. "I have a grandfather?" *Right.*

The kids started popping the ivory off the piano keys, one by one, and leaving them all over the house. *Dammit.* I collected them, quietly, one by one, and put them in the back of a dresser drawer. Our technician said it would be too expensive to put them back on, but I saved them anyway. I never confronted the children, never said a word. There was only one way to stop this vandalism and I knew exactly what to do. We needed a grand piano. A big one, a real looker, and we needed to put it right in the middle of the living room, in front of the French doors and close enough to the window for the light to pour onto my artists. We needed to put an enormous mirror at the end of the piano, angled for a view of the audience and their own gorgeous selves as they came and went.

I knew it would work. A grand piano is a presence in the house, a piece of art, commanding respect and inspiring in itself. Massive weight on temple legs, Samson strength with brutal grace; handsome, kinetic, and yes, a little dangerous. It's compound curves like the back of a horse, the open lid a lion's mouth. It is complicated, beautiful, and the height of romance.

All children crave attention, mine as much, or more, than the next. For those thirty minutes of fame each day, each kid was center stage, blazing, amazing, singing at the top of their lungs. Studies show that instrumental practice is most productive when a parent sits and listens. With a grand piano, sitting or not, the kid knows you are listening. Everyone is listening. It's a seven-foot long, eight-hundred pound talking stick. They loved it: "Mom, it's my turn to practice next!" They loved performing for our guests, for the neighbors, for me.

No one argues about the benefits of teaching children music: the positive effects on the brain, coordination, critical thinking, and discipline, not to mention self-expression. But there is also a hidden benefit for parents: when my children were practicing, I knew exactly where they were and what they were doing.

* * *

After music came food. In the foster home, our children ate at a small plastic table, away from the biological kids, and were beaten if they didn't eat. In the Fox home, no one had to eat anything they didn't want to. I took requests and spared no expense. Processed foods were avoided, fresh fruit and vegetables strongly recommended, but only if you wanted to eat anything else. Menus were designed to engage a youthful palate, provide the vitamins and minerals their bodies needed to grow healthy and strong, and educate young eaters about other cultures through world cuisine. Our family sat for three meals a day, singing together before we ate, elbows off the table and manners politely enforced.

New dishes were met with a healthy skepticism. Jimmy, nicknamed "Food Hero," was fearless in taking the first bite of a new dish: tikka masala, injera, fajita—the kid tried everything. His siblings, watched with rapt attention while he tested the unknown.

I branched out. Cheese wasn't just orange anymore: meet feta, fontina, and homemade ricotta. Spaghetti had a skinny little sister called capellini, and cousins called fettucine and farfalle. We served racquette pasta with green peas during the US Open. We had lox for bagel night, latkes for breakfast. Anthony called me "Edemama" on soybean night; I had to cut him off when his pile of husks was bigger than his head. Dan would tell us the story of Stroganoff, the Russian chef who would carry an onion under his armpit for two days before using it in his famous sauce.

The kitchen was my classroom. We learned to follow directions, work as a team, and respect the clock. Cooking math was built in as every recipe had to be doubled, tripled, or quadrupled. And with cooking came lessons in hygiene, chemistry, and nutrition. We learned the secrets of yeast, the virtues of the single rise versus double rise bread, quick breads. And lessons too in geography: Where did our food come from? It backfired once while I was teaching Anthony to name the states on a blank map of the US. I pointed to Wisconsin on a blank map, quizzing Anthony on the fifty states. He said, "mozzarella." I gave him partial credit.

One night Susie asked, "Did you put pecorino romano in

the risotto?" *Impressive!* Ruby and I had experimented by mixing a quarter cup in with the pound of fresh parmesan. "How did you guess?" Susie said proudly, "At first I thought it was the fresh asparagus instead of our usual artichoke hearts." *What kid talks about food like this?* "But then I realized it was the salt from the sheep's milk romano that was giving it that extra layer." My kids, apparently! We had a house full of foodies.

The kitchen was also my sniper's perch. I could see Anthony in the sandbox from the window; I had a sight line to the living room two steps back from the sink; I could see the tutor desk in a strategically placed mirror and was gathering critical information about the activity on the second floor from the footfall over my head. Aware of the entire house, I could be present but not hovering, available and productive.

On occasion a child would threaten me with a hunger strike. Good luck with that. Once Jason made it all the way to dinner in protest of what he called an "unfair grounding." I stuck my head into his room just before dinnertime. "Hi, honey. I just wanted to check and see if you would like some cabbage soup with hot oatmeal bread." He hesitated. "Uh, uh, no." I opened his door so the smell of the fresh baked bread could waft into his room. "Really? Not even a little bit?" He stumbled. "Uh, uh. Okay, but just a little bit." Three servings later, we had him where we wanted him: full and happy, laughing and joking. Appetite's victory, honor's defeat.

* * *

And while I sang for our suppers to make our house home, Dan fought to forge our family in the air, on land and sea. He took us camping, no frills and often. Oatmeal for breakfast, ramen for lunch, hot dogs for dinner, marshmallows for dessert. Condiments as follows: ketchup, mustard, bug spray. We hiked and sang, threw sticks for Charlie, and got mosquito bites all over. We played tag in the clearings, hide-and-seek in the woods, discovered nature's most scenic timeout spots—there's no better way to do your time than staring at the Green Mountains of Vermont, the High Peaks of the Adirondacks, or both, depending on the elevation of your bad choice.

Next came canoeing. We packed our gear in dry bags, kitchen gear in a duffel, and the guitar in a plastic garbage bag. We'd push off for one of the many islands dotting Lake Champlain; our regatta included, but was not limited to, a flat-bottom twelve-foot boat with a tiny outboard for the dog, the French horn, and other precious non-paddling cargo, plus two seventeen-foot aluminum canoes. From our base camp island, we would swim together to neighboring islands, our voices conversing across the conductive water, Charlie's barks the backbeats to Anthony's shrill at the thrill of such beauty so close.

And to help put things in perspective, Dan would rotate taking the kids up in his four-place Cherokee light airplane. I headed the ground crew, waiting and waiting, we could hear the plane before we could see it. We spelled out messages on the big lawn with rolls of paper towels and would start jumping and waving as the plane flew overhead. Dan would fly the kids to a regional town, land on a grass field, and buy them lunch at the airport diner. The flyers' voices were as high and fast as the plane itself, squealing with delight: "We saw the island where we camped, Mom, and Dad let me steer! I got to fly the plane, Mom!" I could feel their excitement, the thrill of a small plane. These were moments of happiness.

And when the weather got too cold for camping . . . movie night. Movie night with Dad was the reason for living, the reason to behave during the week. Dan would arrange the furniture around a large flat screen monitor and set out blankets on the couches and chairs. After dinner on Friday, the children would ask to be excused from the table. Dan would nod and say, "Pajamas. Stay in your room." He would grant amnesty to those grounded. Viewing was only denied to those who had committed an act of violence that same day and even then he may still let them watch.

Walking to the base of the stairs, he would say their names one by one. He'd wait, build the suspense and then say, "Movie." A brief stampede down the stairs and into assigned seats. No talking. If there was an argument at any time during the movie, the movie would be stopped and everyone sent to his or her room. Dan would start the movie, then ceremoniously sit himself right in the middle of them, sometimes on them, sometimes between them and when the screaming subsided, he would sit there with them, watching with them, everybody together. And if everything went well, he might show another movie on Saturday.

He did not take requests. His programming was thoughtful and deliberate. He would show a popular animation film, a documentary on origami or topiary, *Fiddler on the Roof*, maybe an action film or a foreign film with subtitles. "Anybody have a problem with that? No one has to watch, you are always free to go to your room for the duration of the movie." Everyone watched. There was no screen time outside of movie night.

From what we could tell, television and gaming had been the go-to in the foster home. Our children's developing brains had been bathed in unsupervised television and video games. *World Wrestling Entertainment* was their model for behavior, and *Grand Theft Auto* their moral compass. Not on our watch. We introduced our kids to nature TV: the river, the stars, the woods. The programming was slow-paced, quiet and calming. Even city kids would watch. All we had to do was remove cell phones, computers, internet, DVD players, radios, televisions, handheld devices, make hot chocolate, and sit with them.

We did recognize that our children would also have to be computer literate in order to function in the world, so we gave them twenty minutes of free time on the computer each day. I say "free" but they had to earn it. First they had to complete twenty minutes of a typing tutorial, twenty minutes of online math exercises, and then answer a research question in the marble composition notebook:

> *Where did Langston Hughes go for college?*
> *What is the equivalent in cup measures of thirty-eight*
>   *tablespoons?*
> *How many tragedies did Shakespeare write? How many*
>   *comedies?*
> *What does the acronym NAACP stand for?*
> *What is the life expectancy of the common housefly?*

Then, and only then, could a child go to pre-selected, age-appropriate, educational, and vetted websites. There was one approved two-dimensional gaming website where they were free to play any and all games, so long as it did not involve shooting, hitting, or the pistol-whipping of any representation of life forms. Also off limits were games involving people dressed inappropriately or exhibiting inappropriate behavior. Games like soccer, moto-cross, or biplane dogfight? Enjoy! Not exactly the latest technology but deprivation makes one grateful for what one gets.

10

HAUNTED HOUSE

We were still living in a haunted house, the past whispering at us from the corners, hiding in darkness, voices, and shadows. Our days were filled with gasps and twitches, reflexive jumping at sudden moves, loud noises, or a light reflecting off a shiny surface. I warned the kids when a hug was coming, or else my touch, trying to calm, could spook them. Our kids didn't cry over spilled milk; they screamed, wide-eyed and frozen. Night was full of fitful sleeps, quiet tears, and crazy terrors. We left the lights on while they stirred in their sleep, blankets pulled over their heads.

I called my friend Brena from the West Coast. She was a trauma therapist who worked with returning veterans. All our kids were diagnosed with PTSD. Brena flew out to work with us for a week doing bilateral exercises, tossing balls back and forth while talking to them. The goal, as I understood it, was to have them remember the trauma and while talking about it, stimulate the left and right side of their bodies in some way, tapping on their knees or shoulders, listening to white noise recordings that shifted the sound from one ear to another, all the while reminding them that they were safe now.

"How are you feeling now? Are you comfortable? Is anyone hurting you?" Brena sat in on some of the therapy sessions; the children sat on my lap, and I would alternately tap their left and right knees while they talked.

Brena was also an amateur horn player, and we were trading therapy for horn lessons. After a late night of music making, she asked me how I was doing. "Ha, me?" I was fine, stressed, but holding up. She was concerned about Dan and me, our marriage and stress levels. I said, "Darcy, the kids' therapist, thinks I have PTSD." Brena started chuckling, "There is nothing 'post' about your stress. You're in the middle of it, it's traumatic and they're right to be concerned. Pay attention, watch for burnout. You're doing great."

Did Brena's therapy work? We were carpet bombing these kids, so it was hard to pinpoint which therapy was taking out which disorder. But I could tie Anthony's thunder issues to the trauma therapy. Rainstorms were a trigger for all the kids, but Anthony was particularly affected by the noise. The day before Brena left, we were all in the kitchen when a thunder clapped, loud and close. Anthony started screaming. I looked at Brena. She said, "You do it." I knelt behind Anthony, his little body rigid with terror, lungs gasping between shrieks. I put my hands on his shoulders and I started tapping, left, right, seven times total, then break. "This storm must be really scary for you, Anthony. But you are safe now." Tap, tap, tap, "Everyone loves you here, Anthony. That thunder isn't hurting you." Tap, tap, tap. Anthony stopped screaming. He turned and stared at me. I smiled and hugged him. "Do you want to see it, Anthony?" He nodded. We went out onto the porch and watched the storm, the water sheeting off the roof, over-banking the gutters. I held him and we watched together, quietly.

The next thunderstorm came a few weeks later. Anthony froze and then looked at me, shocked. Together we waited for his scream, but it never came. He stared, "Not afraid." Small victories.

At the end of our first summer, we played a game of evening softball, our eyes squinting after the ball, fading into our twilight play. We came inside, glowing from exercise, smiling and exhausted. We ate ice cream sundaes, while Dan was working late. The kids were relaxed and chatty as the conversation turned slowly from home runs and short stops to stories from the foster home. They were laughing about it, sharing: "Remember when . . ."

Ms. Smith had stepped on an arm and broke it. Mr. Smith threw the car keys at a head and missed, hitting and cutting the throat, blood running down their clothes. They were shamed, called names, ridiculed, and beaten, and made to watch each other get beaten. These stories, new to me, were horrible and graphic. I let them talk; I wanted to know. They showed me the kitchen utensils of choice the foster family used, first to taunt then to beat them, quick and hard, "like this," said Ruby as she drove the metal spoon down on top of a small, imaginary head. They showed me scars on their bodies I hadn't seen before, explained some I'd seen, but not mentioned. Then something shifted. Their voices dropped and the air went thick, their narrative slipped from past tense into present, "She calls me stupid. She hits Anthony on the stomach with a stick." *Shut it down!*

I stood up from my chair and leaned over the table. "Those adults made bad choices. None of these things should have happened. You have parents now, parents who love you. I promise no one will ever hit you again. I'm your mother now, and this is my watch."

My children stopped and stared expectantly at me. I rested my fists on the table, leaned towards them and raised my voice, "If you think anyone's going to hurt my kids, you better think again." Susie asked, "You're not afraid of her?" I gave an angry look, "Of Ms. Smith? Let me tell you about Ms. Smith, Susie.

If Ms. Smith comes near my kids, she'd better be afraid of me!" I gesticulated, "Nobody hurts my kids, not on my watch!" The kids started laughing, looking at one another.

It started to feel a little like a rally, so I went for it. "I'm your Mama Bear! Mess with my cubs? Then you mess with me!" I dropped my voice. "Did you ever see a Mama Bear when someone messes with her cubs?" They stared, shook their heads. I paused and then suddenly, throat shreddingly loud, "ROARRR!" Anthony screamed. I threw my head back, "ROARRR!" They laughed, excited. "Again! Again Mama!" "ROARRR!" Anthony was clapping, "You my Mama Bear! You Mama Bear!" I raised my arms, "Who hurts my kids?" They shouted back, "Nobody hurts your kids!" I paced. "That's right! Ms. Smith better watch out. You mess with my cubs, you mess with Mama Bear." Anthony yelled, "Mama Bear! Again! Again!" I cued them and all the children roared on my down-beat. Then I cut them off, conducting them, put finger to my lips, and whispered, "Nobody hurts my kids."

With everyone happy, "Teeth brushed, in your beds!" They scrambled for the stairs, "Will you sing to us?" I winked, "You bet!" They all went to their rooms, PJs on, waiting for me to call them out for singing.

I sat for a minute in the kitchen and cried. Sobbed, actually. *Get your shit together.* I went upstairs and tuned the guitar. The kids took their seats beside me in the hallway and we went around the circle picking songs. They loved the simple songs: "You are my Sunshine," "Edelweiss," "Edelweiss," "Edelweiss," "Again? But we just sang it three times! Okay, okay." They loved repetition, calmed by the familiarity. I'd start them soft, then loud, then call out, "instrumental," and have them whistle a verse. They were adorable; I loved them so much. I heard Dan come in through the open kitchen door. "Goodnight, lovies."

I ran downstairs, closed the kitchen door for privacy, and told Dan about the kids' disclosures, trying not to cry. The details were horrific. He asked me if I thought they were feeding on each other, exaggerating, trying to shock me. "I can't be sure. I was careful not to show any reaction. I cut them off when it got heavy and then showed anger at the perpetrators." Dan called them down one by one from their rooms and interviewed them, sitting with them on the couch in the living room. Questions only, listening thoughtfully, careful, respectfully, asking for details, then off to bed. We met again in the kitchen. They were telling the truth.

The nature of the abuse was consistent with the initial given report; the extent, severity, and frequency was much greater than we originally thought, but Dan and I both agreed it did not warrant filing a new report. Dan suggested I encourage the kids to talk about it in therapy. "Let the therapists report it to the agency and from those reports, let the agency close the foster home." We were trying to move the kids forward.

I asked the social workers in New York if the home had been closed. "No, but we have not put any new kids in there." I would ask them every time we spoke. "You're reading the therapist's reports, right? Do you read those reports?" They weren't putting new kids in, but they weren't closing it either. I stopped asking. I didn't want to know.

*   *   *

"So what do we do now?" I asked Dan. He said, "Starting tomorrow, we keep them laughing." Copy that.

11

YOU CAN'T BE SERIOUS

"Endless stairs." The kids loved it. I loved it. Whenever Dan did "endless stairs," it was endless laughter, guaranteed. The kids were in bed by eight, teeth brushed and in pajamas. After singing, they could read until 8:30, then kisses and lights out. The stragglers would grab a last minute bathroom run or glass of water, followed by that slightly charged, artificial silence before a big family falls asleep. Dan would take Charlie outside for a short walk, then come back in and climb the stairs.

Creak. Creak. Creak. Creak. Half way up, he'd take three steps back down, then up four stairs, same cadence, same creak. Down five, up three, never faster, never slower, until Ruby would call out, "Dad!" Then Susie, "Dad!" *Creak. Creak. Creak. Creak.* Jimmy and Anthony, sharing a room, yelling in unison, "Dad!" *Creak. Creak.* Jason finally, "Dad!" *Creak. Creak.* "Dad! Dad!"

Then silence. Dan was motionless on the stairs, everyone breathless, waiting, baiting. Suddenly, 200 pounds of adoptive Dad would crash up the remaining stairs and run down the hallway into a dark, but random, room. Everyone was shrieking, terrified it would be them, disappointed if it wasn't. Dan would wrestle them, tickle them, stuff their pillows under their nightshirts and move on to the next room. Dan would wish them goodnight, then sneak one last pillow throw. Dan would come into our bedroom, his hair all messed up, smiling, while the kids would sort out their bedding, giggling, "*Hee hee hee.* Dad. *Hee hee.*"

The biggest laughs came when Dan would get Jimmy going at the dinner table. Dan and Jimmy sat at opposite ends of the table, silent bookends, eating quietly, watching the dinner drama playing out. There was constant conversing, giggles, at times arguing, with me directing. "Pass those rolls, Susie, and watch those elbows. Keep eating Anthony; easy on the butter there, Miss R." Without warning, Jimmy would erupt in uncontrollable laughter, dropping his fork and grabbing a napkin, foodstuffs escaping his mouth and nose. Dan had caught Jimmy's eye, and then raised his eyebrows and stared at him. That's all it took to get Jimmy laughing, swaying back and forth, struggling to stay on his chair while the whole table was laughing at him laughing. Finally, finally it would taper off and everyone would compose themselves and get back to eating. Ruby would sigh, "That was some good times." Dan would wait for the first full silence then say, "Whew!" and the whole thing would start up again, Jimmy swaying in his chair, head back, doubled over, grabbing his stomach.

After dinner, we would retire to the living room for the Dan and Anthony show. The stars would enter with a slow, but breakneck, Charlie Chaplin chase around the couch, both of them up on their toes, laughing, with Anthony screaming, "I'm going to get you, Dad!" Sure enough, Anthony would catch him, the both of them landing on the couch, Dan pretending to struggle beneath Anthony's twenty-eight pounds. Then he'd fold Anthony in half, upside down and Anthony would scream, laughing, "Mom! Help! Help!" I'd say, "It can't be helped, Anthony," and all the kids would shout, "It can't be helped,

Anthony!" Dan would let him go and the climbing would start all over again.

* * *

Humor is very important, and should be taken very seriously. I weighed heavily which of my comedic devices would be most effective in fulfilling the new "keep them laughing" mandate. Roughhousing was out. I couldn't engage the children physically in the way Dan could; I wasn't strong enough, and I was already being attacked daily. Scatological humor, arguably the highest form of humor, had always been my go to; loaded with universal appeal and sound effects, the bathroom is a veritable dumping ground of timeless classics. I decided to pass on that approach, fearing the children were too young to navigate the fine line between sophistication and vulgarity. Besides, Anthony was already working the angle with his nightly bathroom reports to the dinner table: "Big! Big!" always a winner, as was my personal favorite: "Raisins!"

I decided to go with "crazy mom." I started flipping their pancakes and French toast at them from eight feet away. "No, Mom! No!" Already airborne, "Oops, too late!" I told them I was training their reflexes. Grabbing plates, lunging, screaming, and scrambling, they always managed to catch them. And if they didn't, Charlie had a great breakfast.

As the children came into the kitchen for a snack, they would find me, back turned to them, talking on a banana as if it were a phone. I would wink, "Mm hm . . . mm hm . . . why yes, she just walked in! Hold on a second," then hand the banana to them, "Honey, it's for you." First they rolled their eyes, but soon started playing along. "Hello? Yes, this is Susie . . . Yes, I agree she is completely crazy." I put M&Ms on the broccoli-and-sausage pizza. "Mom! You don't put candy on pizza!" I looked concerned, "What? What are you talking about?"

Pointing, "Mom! The M&MS!" I pretended not to see any. "What are you talking about?"

I would play popular music in the car and start nodding my head in time with the music, working a slow shimmy while driving safely. "Mom! Please stop, you're embarrassing us!" Perfect. Next, I would start gently pumping the breaks in time to the music as we approached a stop, the laws of physics making movers of them all. "Jimmy's dancing, what's the problem?" Jimmy, sitting in the back seat, stone faced and looking out the window would try not to smile as his head and torso pulsed forward and back. "He's feelin' it!"

Laundry was a limitless source of material. "Mom, have you seen my pink hoodie?" I would come upstairs either wearing the item, way too tight, and hand them a pair of Anthony's underwear, "Here you go!" or if the request was underwear-related, I would put said underwear on my head and shrug, "'Can't find it!" I would throw soft things at them: Anthony's stuffed panda, socks, a loaf of bread. After checking on them in their rooms at night, I would kiss them goodnight and leave the room through their closet door. I'd wink at them before closing the door behind me, cup of tea in hand, and then shut the door. I'd wait for about a minute and then come back out, looking embarrassed, and try to sneak away.

The only thing better than getting a kid laughing is having them make you laugh. To positively affect an adult is hugely empowering for a kid. I encouraged my kids to make me laugh, tell me knock-knock jokes, make animal sounds, setting them up for one-liners. If their joke didn't work, I would moan and start laughing anyway, "Oh man! That was the WORST!" They could tell I was enjoying them because, well, I *was*. I left props out and laughed at the jokes they didn't know they were making. "Sweetie, you just made a joke! You said these hard-boiled eggs were hard to beat. Get it? Hard to beat?" *Wait for it. . . .* "Oh, yeah! Wow, I was funny!"

Still, the house remained incredibly strict. Rules were consistently enforced and a baseline of behavior was maintained or the child would be put in timeout. Humor made the good times better and the bad times shorter. After a violent outbreak, a joke was better than a hug.

* * *

We don't have any baby pictures of our kids, no baby blankets or tiny shoes. Or memories, for that matter. So birthdays are a big deal for our family, as we celebrate and compensate for the mysteries surrounding their births. The birthday kid gets to picks the menu, the games, the guests, and the gifts. Piñatas, cartoon themes, pin the tail, treasure hunt, Twister—whatever they wanted. I had one request for "chess" under games. *Really? All right then.* I borrowed the regulation sets and timers from the library chess club, and we set up tournament style tables on the porch. I was unsure it would work but the guests, including our incredibly supportive adult neighbors, played chess all afternoon; playing, watching, coaching. Chess as a party game. Who knew?

We are a birthday machine. Birthday cakes are made from Rice Krispies treats. The child chooses the shape. We vary the recipe to match the engineering demands; you need structural integrity for a free standing air foil on a formula race car or the sharp dorsal fin on a shark. Dan and I make these cakes together: he shapes the cakes and I frost them. Over the years we've made musical instruments—a grand piano, a violin, and a horn of course—topographically correct mountain ranges, a chess set with board and pieces, sports gear, trains, planes, automobiles, and an array of historical landmarks.

Jimmy's birthday is in early November, just as we are coming down off our Halloween sugar high. For this first birthday upstate, the birthday boy wanted sushi, root beer, pasta carbonara, and General Tso's chicken for dinner. And for a game, he wanted to bob for apples. The temperature was dropping throughout the day and as the hour of bobbing approached, I cornered Dan, "It's too cold to bob for apples. We need to regroup." Dan nodded, "I'll take care of it." He slipped away while Jimmy opened presents and the kids had cake and root beer floats, which Anthony called, "root beer floaters!" Ew! Gross!

We went outside with our bags of Granny Smiths to find a canoe filled with warm water. Dan had run a hot water hose from the laundry room. I was moved by this, by this canoe full of warm water on this cold birthday. This solution defines my husband: practical in his impracticalness, a romantic answer to a technical problem. I looked at him across the noisy green lawn, past the children floating apples in the steam. He was standing back, arms folded, watching the kids. He looked up and saw me, raised his eyebrows, smiling. I smiled back.

The kids were waiting for me, kneeling, leaning against the canoe with their heads up, hands behind their backs. I looked down at my watch and shouted, "Ready? Go!" They had three minutes to bite into as many apples as they could and pull them out. I laughed at their laughter, their joy, their splashing. I laughed at myself, my marriage, my love.

12

ANTHONY

*a*nthony would not shut up. He had gone from pre-verbal to never-ceasing verbal within a few months of living with us. He liked to perseverate, repeating the same stories again, and again, and again. His favorite one went like this: "Melissa take a wagon outside and fix it." It's a little story about his teacher Melissa and her wagon. One day her wagon broke and well, the rest is history. Twenty, thirty times a day we heard about the wagon. The kids weren't allowed to tease him about it, but sometimes we would smile at one another while he was looping, the same smile we shared when Dad was snoring loudly on the couch.

Growing up in a dangerous environment, Anthony survived by being cute and making people feel special. He is what is called an "indiscriminate attacher," making everyone feel that they, and only they, can save him. He plays the baby, asking complete strangers to pick him up, and then gazes into their eyes like an infant Casanova. He'll remember your name and everything about you, flattering you until you start to believe you, and only you, are on this earth to love and protect him. I have to tell adults repeatedly, "Please do not to pick him up and cuddle him. He's six years old." They can't help themselves. Even educators will say, "I know I shouldn't pick him up, but he's so cute!" as Anthony wraps his arms around their necks and put his head on their shoulder. I had to remove him from an after-school program when one of the younger counselors became obsessed with him. It was kind of intense. I met with her on several occasions, explaining our situation and asking for her support in helping Anthony behave like a six year old and attach to his adoptive parents. "Please, do not to pick him up, do not to carry him around, and do not to cuddle him." She wouldn't hear it. "You don't understand," she told me. "He needs me." A blessing and a curse: his baby charm kept Anthony alive in an abusive world, and now safe, it kept him infantilized.

Behind this loving, innocent demeanor, however, was an angry little human who could express his rage with adult sophistication. His behavior was cruel and devious. He called his classmates names, swore at them, and grabbed the little ones by their necks when no one was looking. He was aggressive to animals and babies. Once my sister, Michelle, saw him bullying Jimmy and Ruby, his high-pitched voice knifing at his older siblings, "Your parents are dead! They didn't love you! You have no one!" Jimmy, hurt, begged him to stop, "Anthony, don't say that!" Anthony, sadistic, "They are dead! You don't have parents!" Ruby was crying, "Anthony, stop! It's not true!" Michelle was disturbed. She came back and told me what she'd seen. "I would never have believed he could be so hateful if I hadn't seen it for myself. It was chilling."

Anthony broke every toy we gave him, broke the zippers off his coats, and dug holes in the plaster walls of his room with his fingers. He was systematically destroying the bathroom: yanking on the spigots, cranking on the faucets like they were handbrakes for a runaway train, and unscrewing the bolts on the bottom of the toilet so that water soaked into the basement through the floorboards.

And I get it. He's in a small body he was neglected, malnourished, and mistreated, but no different from anyone else in wanting to leave his mark on the world. One night Anthony snuck out of his room, took our video camera, and made fifteen short films of his hands screwing around with the computers in the dark. Throughout the films is a whispering voice over, "I am Anthony Fox, I am Anthony Fox, I am Anthony Fox . . ." It was profound and pathetic. I didn't know if I should laugh or cry. When we confronted him the next day about the broken computers, his denial was like an exclamation mark. He wanted us to know he did it. He wanted us to know that he is Anthony Fox, and with the limited tools he was given, he was leaving his tag. "I am Anthony Fox! Anthony Fox was here!"

* * *

A year into our parenting, we were getting a lot of pressure from both the school and child psychiatrist to put Anthony on Ritalin. No one was telling us explicitly to do it, but the suggestion was always there. Our pediatrician made a good case for a trial, saying if Anthony's problems stemmed from ADHD, the medication would help him; if it was not ADHD, then the Ritalin would have no effect and we would take him off of it. "The medication will keep him from feeling frustrated with his learning in school." Anthony frustrated? I am pretty sure the teachers were frustrated with Anthony. I was definitely frustrated with Anthony.

We gave it a shot. A few days into the trial, Anthony's behavior got worse. He was getting out of his room at night, climbing on the kitchen counters, playing with the stove, putting pans in the oven, and scribbling all over the walls and computer screens. It wasn't working. Or maybe it was working and we just had so many other variables in play that we could not tease out what was causing this flare in behavior. We took him off the Ritalin and pulled him out of summer school.

* * *

A problem with disciplining Anthony was trying to figure out what his mental capacity was at the time of his infraction. Was it the impaired, impulsive toddler acting his delayed age? Or was it the advanced manipulator, pleading incompetence to get a lesser sentence? We were not always sure. As noted, our standard length of a timeout is the child's age in minutes. "Okay, Anthony, take a timeout. You have six minutes." He'd act as if I'd baked him a cake. "Six minutes? Thanks, Mom! Woo hoo." Hmm. "Actually, let's make that twenty minutes." Again, excited, "Twenty? Alright, thanks, Mom!" I upped it to forty and he looked sad. But could even he sit still for forty minutes? Did he even know what forty minutes was? I would set the timer for ten minutes and then watch him. Just before he would start to wiggle in the timeout chair, I would turn the timer off and let it ring. I wanted to help him. I wanted him to succeed.

I focused on Anthony the toddler. He was not safe unattended. We had two carpets on the first floor, one by the kitchen door and one at the main entrance, which we named "the magic carpets." They were industrial looking, red and black with rubber trim. I would put him on whichever carpet was closest to me while I worked. He was allowed to sit or kneel, but not stand. He could play with his toys as long as he kept them and himself on the carpet. Anthony loved his magic carpets. He would play for hours and hours, watching me, basking in benign attention. He would talk to himself and roll back and forth like a two year old. I would give him an empty cereal box and a paper bag and he would tear the box into tiny pieces and put the pieces in the bag, laughing.

But he wasn't a toddler. He was perceptive, sometimes freakishly so. He could tell I was looking for the measuring spoons. "You put them in the squeaky drawer." The squeaky drawer? He pointed to a drawer. It squeaked when I opened it to find the spoons. I hadn't noticed the drawer squeaked. "Do any of the other drawers squeak?" He shook his head. I checked. He was right.

When I sprained my ankle on a family camping trip, I wore a white, elastic ankle support over my white sock, in my sneaker and under long pants. Barely visible, I wore it every day for a month without a mention. The first day I came into the kitchen without it, Anthony asked, "Is your ankle better, Mama?" Dan bought two identical jackets for work. I hadn't noticed and if I had, would not have been able to tell them apart. "Hey, Dad, you changed your jacket. It looks good." It was uncanny

Watching an animated film during movie night, Anthony accidently read out loud a sign over a cartoon gas station, "Dino Pump!" We looked at him, surprised. He turned bright red. He had told us this entire time he didn't know how to read. His hyper-vigilance was impressive, his listening skills bionic. I was talking to a friend in the kitchen while Anthony was engaged, playing with his trains in the next room on his magic carpet. She asked me a question about Jason and I told her we could speak later, when Anthony wasn't listening. She said, "Oh, he's not listening!" I winked at her. Quietly and breathily, "Anthony, which sibling are we talking about?" He answered instantly, "Jason!"

And yet, Anthony couldn't do simple tasks, like set the table. I would give him a stack of plates and have him count them, one for each member of the family. "Good, now set them out where each person sits." He would put two plates together, almost touching, and then one at the end of the table and three on the other end. I coached him, reminding him who sat where. He couldn't do it. Or wouldn't. I don't know. Was he just screwing around? Playing dumb was a defense mechanism for Anthony but also a control mechanism, a way of screwing with his authority figures.

But how could I help my little guy? He needed to succeed at something, I needed to give him some directions he could execute, rules he could follow. When I was a kid, my Mom would pass me a plate of warm cookies and say, "Be sure and take the biggest one!" She wasn't being sarcastic, she was showing me she knew what it was like to be me, giving me permission to be my selfish little self and hover forever over the cookies with my greedy little fingers tingling with anticipation: calculating, comparing, you touch it you take it! She'd smile at me, "Did you get the biggest one?" *Oh yes, I did.* "Nice work, honey."

On St. Patrick's Day, Anthony and I snuck into all the bathrooms in the house while no one was looking. I told him to put five drops of green food coloring into each toilet bowl. His eyes got big. "Shh! It's a secret!" He was ecstatic.

"Now Anthony, when people see this, they are going to ask, 'who did it?' and you have to pretend it wasn't you. We want them to think a leprechaun used the toilet. Leprechauns have green pee." Anthony said, "But I did it." I knelt down and looked him in the eyes, "This is a practical joke, Anthony. We are pretending something happened that didn't. I am giving you special dispensation to lie. Let's practice. 'Gee! I wonder who peed in the toilet! The water is green!' Now, Anthony, you say what?" He said, "A leprechaun?"

I prepped one of the tutors before we sat down at the table for lunch. The tutor said, "If you'll excuse me, I need to use the restroom." She went into the bathroom and exclaimed, "Gee! I wonder who peed in the toilet! The water is green!" Anthony burst out, "I did it! I did it! I put the green in the toilet!" Oh, well.

About six months into our relationship, I was sitting with Anthony in the kitchen, waiting for him to finish his dinner. I was exhausted, but couldn't leave him alone at the table or he would give his food to the dog. It was dark outside and rain was falling. I should have been doing dishes, writing checks, opening the mail, but my brain had shut down. I just sat there, staring at nothing. *Anthony, eat dammit.* It was 7:05. It felt like midnight. I still had to help Jimmy with his homework.

Anthony had not gained one ounce in six months. We put butter on his peanut butter sandwiches, gave him half and half instead of milk. Nothing worked. We tried everything to get him to eat: coaxing, pleading, threatening, bribing. Nothing worked. I was trying out the "it takes as long as it takes" method for his eating. Guess what? It takes too damn long! I thought about the wet laundry sitting in the washer since yesterday, folded my arms and put my head down on the table.

"Mama?" Anthony said, his voice uncharacteristically calm. "Mama? This my table?" I lifted my head slowly and smiled. "Yes, Anthony. This is your table." He pointed out the kitchen window to the neighbors' house. "My neighbors?" I nodded. "This my house, Mama?" I told him yes, this was his house. "My Mama?" I said, "I'm your Mama, Anthony." Anthony slowly looked around the room and then at me. "Is perfect," he said. "My Mama. My table. Perfect." And then he took a bite.

13

GRAFTING A FAMILY TREE

*a*ttachment is the gold standard in adoption. It is the single most important goal in securing the emotional health of your children, their future lives and relationships. Attachment is a biological and emotional event between a child and parent, an enduring, affectionate bond connecting the child to a safe, secure, and comforting adult. Its importance cannot be stressed enough.

In the first three years of life, the human brain grows to 90 percent of its adult size, and forms the bulk of the neural pathways for our emotional, behavioral, social, and intellectual responses. If during those early years a child's bonding cycle is interrupted for any reason—from ambivalent parenting to abuse to neglect—the brain can scar significantly, and alter the growth and development of the child. When children are unable to attach, they can be diagnosed with reactive attachment disorder, depending on the severity of their behavior and inability to form loving relationships. With the Fox kids, it was pretty much five for five. Jimmy's on the cusp.

A lot has been written about ways to cultivate and promote attachment in adoption, almost all of it describing activities for an infant—not exactly applicable to our situation. "Hold the infant to your chest without clothing on for maximum skin-on-skin exposure." *Skip*. "Minimize stress and chaos in the house." *Good luck with that*. But it was imperative these kids attach to me. I was trying everything I could think of and failing. *Keep trying*.

I thought back to my own childhood, before medication, and remembered my mother rocking me on her lap in the rocking chair. I took Susie with me to the thrift store, and we bought a rocking chair for the living room. "Children," I announced over lunch that day, "this is a rocking chair. This is how we did it in the olden days. This summer we are kicking it up old school! For those of you about to rock, I salute you!"

I started with Anthony, rocking him every day for thirty to forty minutes. I'd take his little head in my hand and press it gently to my shoulder. "Shh." I'd hold him to me, not too tight, and breathe deeply, "Shh," slowly, contagiously. He was quiet, but resisting, tense. "Shh," rock, rock, and then suddenly, like someone flipping a switch, his tiny body would relax, his energy level would drop and he would go into some kind of beta zone, awake but very calm. He spoke softly, without affect, his arms loose, but affectionate. I rocked all the kids. Jimmy and Ruby were in a different weight class, with their arms hanging every-where and long legs draping down; I had to keep shifting them from side to side every five minutes or so but it they loved it. Everyone loved it, especially Susie. Even Jason, nervous at first, came around. He liked to sit with his back to me, his arms rest-ing on my arms as they rested on the arm rests, his head rolled way back on my left shoulder. We rocked all summer, the best bonding and attachment therapy I could think of. But it wasn't enough.

I complained to one of our feeling doctors at a collateral ses-sion, "Why don't they love me? It's been a year. I would totally love me by now!" She smiled knowingly, "Their trauma was so profound, they can't trust anyone. They are still fearing for their lives. It's going to take a long time for them to trust enough to feel love, if ever." *Shit. That was hard to hear.*

My voice fell into a pre-cry rasp, "But, there are moments when I feel like I've reached them, like we've connected." I paused, discouraged, "Then the next minute they come at me in a rage, hitting and kicking, biting . . ."

"That's the PTSD disrupting the attachment. Whatever gains you make attaching disappear as soon as the PTSD gets triggered. And when that happens, everything, every emotion feels like a fight to your children. Because of the early trauma, it's the only coping mechanism their brains have." She tried to explain their reality. "Children of abuse have no floor in their house. They may live in a beautiful, loving home but for them, everything feels tenuous, like they are floating on a cloud and the slightest breeze will blow it all away." That was even harder to hear.

I told Dan about my talk with the therapist. He nodded. "With no floor, there is no self." I shuddered. "They may never heal. It's like an incurable disease. Incurable but wholly preventable." Dan took a deep breath. "It is what it is."

I lay awake that night, staring at the ceiling, despairing. With no self, there is no self-esteem, no self-knowledge or self-help. With no self, there is no self-love. My children may never feel my love for them. *True. Your kids may never feel your love, but their kids might. Do it for them.*

* * *

Jimmy and I got a foothold on his attachment during our time in Manhattan. Like a wink or a secret handshake, we could talk without speaking and be close when far apart. This was a very good thing; I was so busy with his siblings, that days would go by without a meaningful word between us. Jimmy was still wetting the bed and waking him up to take him to the bathroom in the middle of the night was counting as our one-on-one time. I had to spot him as he staggered down the hall, half asleep. I'd leave the bathroom door open and face away from him for privacy while checking on him constantly over my shoulder.

I'm not saying Jimmy and I didn't have issues, but they paled in comparison to his siblings. I engaged him one day by accident. It shouldn't have happened. I was stressed from a Jason encounter when I burst into Jimmy's room, "What's this about failing your science test? Are you kidding me? What part of the stem and leaf plot do you not understand?!" Jimmy stared at me for a minute then started to cry. "Do you know how hard it is to be good?" He was angry and hurt. *Shit.* "I'm sorry, Jimmy, I'm sorry." I sat beside him on the bed and hugged him. He stopped crying, I patted his shoulder and said, "Put your shoes on, we're going out." I texted the tutor to watch the others. Jimmy and I went to a Mexican place, ordered tacos, and played with the fart machine app on my smartphone. We went to the comic book store and argued Manga versus Marvel. Which would you rather be? Magneto or Wolverine? Shape shifter? "Sure, they are great for plot but what do they do really?" Good point.

After that, Jimmy and I promised to go on a date every month. If we couldn't find a free day, I'd wake him late to use the bathroom and then take him for a midnight movie, sneaking out in the dark of night, popcorn, soda, and pinky swear, "We shall never speak of this to anyone."

* * *

Susie's depressions were hard to describe, like a complex, fine, but most un-subtle wine. *A spicy mix of full-bodied defiance and hints of abhorrence, this nuanced little mood is impertinent without being pert, violent and surly with a cat pee finish.*

So after many unsuccessful attempts, I tried to change it up one afternoon. "Now, Susie, this is going to feel weird but

I want you to lie down next to me and put your head right here." I steer her stiff head over my heart, her angry ear tucked between shoulder and clavicle, her arms folded tightly. "You're doing great, Susie. I know this is the last thing you feel like doing." In tense silence I wrap my arm around her shoulder and gently stroke her hair. I match the rate of my breathing with hers, drape her left arm across my stomach as it rises and falls with my breaths.

Susie was finally starting to relax. "Okay, Susie, are you ready? I call this one 'the secret weapon.' Think you can handle it?" She smiled. I turned her arm over gently, exposing the soft inside of her forearm and gently ran my index finger from her wrist to the bend in her elbow. We lie there quietly, my finger tracing softly back and forth, "Shh, shh, everything is going to be okay." Susie raised her head and smiled at me. I smiled back. I tickled her and we start to wrestle, laughing and laughing. "Mom! Mom!"

* * *

Anthony was born into foster care, and left alone in a crib at the very moment his brain was supposed to be learning how to trust. When he reached out for care and affection, no one reached back. When he cried out, no one answered. Maybe his brain deduced he wasn't worth it, that if he wanted affection he'd have to work for it. His hugging, eye-gazing, "I love you so much, Mommy," were not necessarily indications that he was attaching to me. He hugged and loved and gazed everyone so much. He was like a solicitous lap cat: snuggly, patronizing, and free. The need for control is another symptom of attachment disorders. Our relationship changed forever the day I had to restrain him.

Anthony was all but begging for me to hold him down: swearing, lying, breaking things, talking smack, and refusing to stay in timeout. We were at a family picnic and I warned him that if I counted to three, I was going to hold him down. He crossed the line so I lay him down on the grass, away from everyone else, and with my right index finger held his tiny wrists together behind his back. He started writhing and flexing, twenty-eight pounds of pure defiance, "Let me know when you are ready to get up," I said routinely. He'd seen me do this to Jason a thousand times. "Stop! Stop! You're hurting me!" said the mini-me, mimicking Jason to a tee. Twenty-five minutes later, the sweaty and snot-covered Anthony was ready to get up. I released him. He hurriedly crawled into my lap and started crying.

He hugged me, tighter than ever before, "I love you, Mama," he cried. "I love you, Anthony." He sobbed, "I promise I will show you good behavior, Mama." I comforted him, "You're a good boy, Anthony, and you will always be my son, even if you make poor choices." Still crying, he asked me to hug him tighter.

That night, Anthony and I snuggled, same as every night before bed. I would sing him a little song about the two of us, my impromptu lyrics describing the details of the day we just spent together. I ended with the refrain, "I love you, Anthony, my precious, precious boy. My sweet sugar lump." He loved it. As soon as he was able to put the words together, he outed me in front of the family at the dinner table by screaming, "You're my precious, precious Mama!" I dropped my jaw, "Anthony! That is my line! You can't steal my line!" He kept going, "Sweet sugar lump!" I pretended to be mad, the laughter from the other kids fueling his squealing, "Sugar lump!" I threw up my hands, "I've got writers working overtime to come up with this stuff, and he thinks he can come and steal my best material!" Anthony was manic, "I steal your lines, precious, precious Mama!"

* * *

Jason was the hardest to reach. I tried everything I could think of, reading to him, working together with him on projects, gently rubbing his back until he fell asleep. It felt impossible and I was already spending more time with my squeaky wheel than any other kid.

One day after a particularly difficult encounter with Jason, I was so frustrated, I told Dan over lunch that I'd had it. Dan said, "I know you're exhausted but there is a little boy in there, we have to keep trying." I raised my voice. "At what cost? We have four other kids! Jason is sixty percent of our time, resources, and energy!" Dan said, "He needs it." I was angry. "What about the other kids? It's not fair to them." Dan said, "The other kids are watching. They are learning who we are by watching us work with Jason." Dan offered to take the afternoon off so I could go for a run. I shook my head, "Thanks, I'm good." Dan left. I sat in the kitchen, disgusted with myself, with Jason, with everything.

Charlie came over and put his head on my knee. "Really, Charlie? What do you want?" I said. He lay down at my feet and didn't move. Charlie didn't want anything. He could tell I was suffering and had come over to be with me, just like he did for the kids when they were stressed. Charlie would lie at their feet or by their beds. He didn't try to solve anything or offer advice. He could sense when a member of his pack was hurting and went to them with no judgment, just awareness.

I scratched Charlie behind his ears and climbed up to the third floor. I told Jason to go to his room and finish his homework. I sat on the floor outside his door, leaned my head against the wall, and closed my eyes. "You okay, Mom?" Jason asked. "I'm fine, Jason, thanks. I'm just going to sit here for a little bit."

* * *

Ruby took a karate class every Wednesday night. She seemed to be enjoying it. She loved wearing her red karate jacket and crossing the park to get there all by herself. She was hard to miss; a bright red triangle walking over a solid green of the grass, independent, finding her way. It was summer and the sun was still up and everyone was outside playing soccer. Ruby would turn and wave as she walked to karate, "Bye, Mom!" I'd wave back.

One night I got a call from the karate teacher, "Ms. Fox, I just wanted to let you know that one of our parents saw Ruby in the gym basement in her uniform." And? I didn't know where this was going. "I see. Was she late for class? Is everything okay?" There was a pause. "Ms. Fox, Ruby has not been to class for two months." I flushed with anger. "I see. Thank you." *Dammit!* I ran to the gym, no sign of her. I had the tutor cover the other kids and I ran to the car to start looking. I called Dan and he said, "I'm on my way." I called the mothers of Ruby's friends, no luck.

Then Dan called; he'd found her at the playground. "I can't believe it," I said, "I checked the playground first thing. I didn't see any red karate uniform." I swear I could hear him smiling on the phone. "She took it off." Of course she did. I said, "I guess that's why you're a special agent and I make buzzing sounds with my lips into a brass tube. I'll meet you at home." I was pissed. I told Dan, "I'm ready! You and me, bad cop, bad cop! Let's drop the hammer, let's roll!" Dan smiled and shook his head, "No, Ann. This is our chance. She's scared. This is our chance to bring her to us." *No way.* "What? Really? Now? No consequences?" I was speechless.

The three of us sat in the kitchen while the two of them talked. How did he know what to say? I watched him reach out to her and connect. "I know you don't always feel like you belong here, honey, but this is your home. We know you didn't choose us, your Mom and I chose you, but this is your home. We will always love you, no matter what. Nothing is going to change that." With the tone of his voice and his choice of words, he drew her in. "You've been through a lot, honey. I know it's hard.

I'm not you, I don't know exactly how you feel but I care about you. I am proud of you, Ruby. You're my daughter. We're going to stand by you and we're going to help you. You are not alone." She looked at him and started crying. He gave me a nod, and I put my arm around her. We sat with her while she cried and cried, her head down, sobbing. When she stopped, she lifted her head and smiled at us. Her entire demeanor had changed: her face was relaxed, her shoulders low and soft. Her eyes and her mouth moved organically, like a person with a twitch who suddenly stops twitching. She was present and at peace. Ruby had attached, or so it seemed. Or until the PTSD kicked in and disrupted it. For that minute, anyway, she was our daughter.

Well, Dan's daughter, really; mine by extension. I'm okay with that. Mothers are complicated. They are complicated even in healthy biological relationships. I try and imagine what it's like to deal with an adoptive mother while your bio mom is absent but still alive. I conjure the angst of my worst break-up ever, multiply it by a thousand and then imagine that the state has just married me off to a stranger. Ruby may never attach to me. Who am I kidding? If I can just keep these kids alive for no other reason than to give me shit, then I'm good. It means they're alive. And if they have me to hate, then at least they have someone: someone with feelings, someone to rail against, bitch about, argue with and blame. And when they get older they can call each other and complain about me, "Can you believe her? She is so mean!" My gift to them. Bitching about your mother is one of the great joys of siblinghood and this family is about giving something to someone else. If the takeaway is a mother to hate, I'm good.

14

USE YOUR WORDS

*T*he modifiers just kept coming. We had a bank of
impoverished words to further describe the children
we were raising: oppositional, delayed, high risk, conduct disorder, self-harming, at risk, dysthymic . . . We needed
a Punnett square to help parse the behaviors and motivations;
is this a dominant emotion or a double recessive? The list was
endless.

Our kids are missing some basic emotions. Most children
with early trauma don't experience guilt. They skip remorse and
go directly to shame; they haven't done something bad—they
are bad. I am always careful to distinguish, "You're a family girl
now, you don't need to steal anymore. You're a great kid, you
made a poor choice and now you need to take responsibility
for that choice." We wrote letters to the victims of our frequent thefts, "Dear Store, I am a bad girl . . ." *Whoa! Let's try
that again.* Language is important, especially when one poorly
chosen word can derail a kid into self-loathing.

Some of our kids don't experience empathy. It's not their
fault. My parent impulse is to ask, "How would it make you
feel if someone took your stuff? Would you like it if someone

hit you and called you names?" The very question is an insult to their reality. I should be asking, "How would it make you feel to be loved and respected? Would you like it if someone cared about you and told you how precious you are?" It's a daily exercise.

We work on social cues. "When people are talking, you must wait your turn." The kids want to know, "How long do I wait? How do I know when it's my turn?" These are real questions, ones that are easier to practice than answer. I tell them families are where we practice appropriate behavior and making good choices.

We practice hugging, listening to our bodies, telling us when it's time to let go. "Mom! It's just like in music, when it starts to slow down, we know it's almost over!" I say, "Hanging out like this, talking about stuff? This is what parents do who love their children." I tell the kids when I am loving them, I make a point of pointing it out. Because they don't feel or recognize love. Yet. Maybe never. *Keep trying.*

Our kids don't know trust. I explain it, give examples, at times saying, "Just try it! Pretend you trust me and see what happens!" Dan says they have to learn to trust, and if they can't trust us, we must give them an environment they can trust, a home for them that is predictable and consistent with clear expectations and clear consequences. I hang two whiteboards in the kitchen, one for our daily schedule, in fifteen-minute intervals, one for the weekly schedule, and a large paper calendar for our month, color coded by child. Planning is key.

If a child is acting out, I first ask myself, *Have I done my job? Did they get enough sleep? Is their blood sugar high enough? Have they exercised today? Have they practiced piano? Have I hugged them and told them I loved them?* If not, I will redirect, shape their day, take them swimming, feed them PB and J. If I've done all I can to prepare them for success, I will count them to three and I will put them in timeout. If they cannot control their bodies,

I will control it for them. I follow through. Consistently. Every single time for every single kid.

* * *

Our children have difficulty taking responsibility for their actions. I heard a thump and a crashing sound and ran upstairs to find Susie standing barefoot in a room full of broken glass. I told her not to move and ran to get a broom. When I got back, she insisted that her light fixture just broke all of a sudden and that, "I ain't done nothing!" I said, "Susie, your soccer ball is right there in the middle of the floor. I heard it hit the light and then hit the floor." She said, "I tol'you I ain't kicking no soccer ball!"

I like to take these opportunities to explain the double negative to my children. This is less about grammar and more about disrupting their habitual denials, deflecting the focus away from a guaranteed confrontation and making them think for a second about what they were actually saying.

After months of admitting, "I'm not doing nothing!" I finally got Jimmy to deny a travesty with, "I'm not doing anything!" Everyone knew Jimmy had thrown the board game on the ground but instead of a consequence for his behavior, I rewarded him for his grammar. "Jimmy! You're a genius! Did everyone hear that? He didn't use a double negative!" I hugged him, laughing, "Finally!"

Our children lie. It's not their fault. They were trained to lie, taught to lie, told to lie or else be beaten. Lying can make them feel powerful and in control, if only for a minute. Some of our kids are better liars than others; some are excellent. Ruby was terrible. She had a thousand tells: frowning, looking away, stuttering, pretending she didn't hear or understand the question. It was tricky. Confronting Ruby about her lying reinforced her negative self-view, so she'd lie even more because that's what liars do.

"Time for bed, sweetie, did you brush your teeth?"

"What?"

"Have you brushed your teeth?"

"Huh?"

"Ruby, look at me, honey. Have you brushed your teeth?"

"T-t-t-tonight?"

"Yes, tonight."

"Uh . . . yeah." I take her with me to the bathroom where together we discover that her toothbrush is completely dry.

"W-w-w-well, I didn't use that one."

"Which one did you use?"

"Huh?"

"Which toothbrush did you use?"

"The one in my backpack."

"You have a toothbrush in your backpack? I did not know that, but let's go take a look."

"Well, it's not in there now. I left it at school."

"You left the toothbrush you just used at school? You're not a liar, babe. Tell me the truth. If you didn't brush your teeth, just say so. You can brush them now and we can move on."

"But I'm not lying! I did brush my teeth! I just, I don't know!"

"Ruby. Brush your teeth and go to bed."

"But I swear it! I'm telling the truth! I brushed them! Why don't you believe me? You hate me!"

It was so hard to break through to these kids. I can remember on one hand the times my father raised his voice at me, each with a memorable effect. My kids, on the other hand, had been desensitized, inured to criticism. Yelling was futile and they'd already figured out I wasn't going to hit them. I asked Ruby's therapist about the lying to see if she had any ideas. "Do you have any suggestions?" I asked. She shook her head, "No. Not really." Great.

I needed to find help. Lynyrd Skynyrd was not my usual

go-to for parenting tips but in this instance, I could not deny the simple logic in their double on double negative, "Don't ask me no questions and I won't tell you no lies."

"Ruby," I said, "I can't make you tell me the truth, but I can give you a break from lying. For two weeks I'm not going to ask you any questions. You won't be able to lie because I will already know everything. For two weeks we will either be together or you will be in your room." She ran errands with me, went shopping, helped me with meals, paying bills, and doing laundry. I went with her to lap swim, to the feeling doctor, to the library, and talked with her in the present tense over meals, just the two of us. She stayed home from school. I would check on her in her room and say, "Hi," but never ask how she was doing. It worked. Two weeks, no questions, no lies. When it was over, Dan asked her, "How does it feel?" Ruby smiled. "It feels weird, but I like it. In the Bronx, I lied to keep from getting in trouble. Here, I get in trouble for lying." Good call.

* * *

Our kids are defensive. They act tough and pretend they know everything. When we first took Jimmy and Ruby to the pool, they assured us they knew how to swim. *Super!* Proud and excited, they walked all the way up Columbus Avenue to the West Side YMCA wearing their new goggles and swim caps. When we got to the pool, they refused to get in. "But, I thought you said you knew how to swim." They'd never seen a pool. Hell, they'd never seen a pond or a natural body of water. The first time Jimmy saw the Hudson River he thought it was the ocean. "Wow! Look at all that water!" The first time Jimmy saw the ocean, he thought it was heaven.

The problem with insisting you know everything is that you lose face if you ask a question and, without asking questions, it's really hard to learn. I started talking over their heads in order to clue them into how much there really is to learn, maybe force a question or two and if nothing else, increase their vocabulary. It gave me no end of pleasure to hear Ruby ask, "Mom, can I get special dispensation to taste the cookie dough? Tasting is a chef's prerogative, correct?"

We hung six ceramic camping cups on the wall in the kitchen, one for each Fox child, plus a spare. The kids asked about the extra and I told them, "That cup is for Elijah." The children stared at me, but didn't ask; to ask would have been admitting they didn't know. The cup was actually for guests but I loved the symbolism of Elijah, our Old Testament prophet, turning the hearts of the children to their parents. That's how I read it, anyway. Visitors asked about the cup and the children always answered, "It's for Elijah!" One guest asked, "Do you think he'd mind if I borrowed it?" Ruby said, "He? Elijah is a man?"

*   *   *

Susie was suffering. I remembered my grandmother telling me that to know a poem by heart is to have a friend for life. "You will never be alone and your mind will have a place to rest." Well, Susie needed a friend and her mind was also low on fuel and flying over the strangest seas. She needed a landing zone ASAP. We sat in the rocking chair and I helped her memorize Emily Dickinson's "'Hope' is the thing with feathers." It worked. Incredible. I gathered the other kids and told them, "This summer we are going to memorize poetry. Memorizing poetry is what Fox children do."

I printed off some short poems in large, non-threatening fonts, and wrote a dollar amount in the upper right hand corner, their reward for learning it word for word. When they were ready, I would film them reciting it. Jason did William Carlos Williams's "This is just to say"; Ruby did "Peaches" by

Sandra Cisneros; and Jimmy recited "Quiet Girl" by Langston Hughes. To Anthony I gave the opening line to Hamlet's soliloquy, "To be or not to be, that is the question." I was shocked and delighted when he recited it verbatim; by the end of day, all the kids had memorized their poems.

I handed out the next assignments. By the end of the summer, I was out several hundred dollars and happily so. The kids had memorized a body of work: Shakespeare's sonnets, the Gettysburg Address, Edward Lear, Ogden Nash, Robert Frost, Maya Angelou, Henry Wadsworth Longfellow. We held our first poetry slam and invited our neighbors over for readings, recitations, and refreshments. Loud and proud, the kids stood up and recited their pieces. They were incredible. Everyone applauded, duly impressed. Ruby's "Invictus" brought tears, Jimmy's moving recitation of Dr. King's "I Have a Dream" speech was unparalleled, but Anthony, our dark horse, pulled out of nowhere and stole the show.

I had started him on Hamlet's soliloquy as a joke, more or less. Jimmy and I were reading *Hamlet* together that summer, and while the opening line of the soliloquy is short, it is compelling. Anthony wouldn't let it go. He wanted to learn the rest of it. I printed it out for him, section by section, and by the end of the summer slams, he had memorized the first third of it. He was last on the program and when he got to "The proud man's contumely, the pangs of despised love," his little voice crescendoed with each line until it cracked with excitement on his big closer, "and THE LAW'S DELAY!" The crowd, small as it was, went wild. And Anthony, small as he was, felt his accomplishment.

Subsequent slams brought more and more lines. Anthony was like a dog with a bone. "Mom? What does Fardels mean? What is a bare bodkin?" He learned other poems as well, taking solo lines in the group recitations of "Custard the Dragon," "The Owl and the Pussycat," and "The Midnight Ride of Paul

Revere." He picked up poems from listening to the other kids practice theirs. But the soliloquy was his trademark conversation stopper. He recited it to his feeling doctor during one of his sessions. The therapist stared at him, then at me. "I'm going to have to rewrite his treatment plan."

Memorizing poems was more than just making friends, it was more than a confidence boost in public speaking, it was actually changing their speech patterns. Our friends with kids were openly envious of our poetry slams, "I wish I could get junior to memorize poetry." I'd remind them that junior had been read to as an infant and raised listening to vocabulary rich discourse. Our kids were just beginning to learn the power of language.

15

LAWFUL

*M*y goal was to help our children grow up happy, healthy, strong, and confident. To that end, I promised I would get them the best help available in our home, in the courts, at the doctors', and in the schools. I promised to help them make good, safe choices. I monitored our inner circle, vetted our play-dates, and always called for references. Happy, healthy, strong, and confident. It was my mantra. I ended agreements, broke contracts, and quit programs and people that were not advancing our cause. Neutral didn't cut it. It was not enough to do no harm. We were behind and needed motion, efficient intervention, fast and effective love. I felt an urgency about my parenting; the tide of adolescence was coming in and there was no standing still.

Therapists were a particular challenge for me. At times I felt they were reading to us from a playbook, wherein the parent was a big part of the problem. Sitting in the waiting room, I could see where this bias came from: we watched parents teasing their kids until they cried, belittling, shaming, and cursing; nothing our kids had not seen or experienced before. I would take my kid *du jour* into the vestibule with me, away from the waiting room, kneel down, and look them in the eye. "Did you see how that adult is treating that little boy? It is disrespectful. That adult is making a bad choice. Adults need to show children how to behave but not all adults have good behavior. These are not bad people, but they are making bad choices."

In the therapy sessions, I was a follower. I would answer background questions, fill in holes if the child didn't want to answer. "Would it be okay if your Mom told me what happened?" The child would nod and I would say, "Sure thing, but you correct me if I miss something." If the sessions weren't progressing, I would call a collateral meeting with the therapists and share my concerns, discuss strategy, maybe offer more background information that might help steer the talking towards a more productive end. The next session, I would sit in respectful silence, waiting for improvement. The children always knew when I lost confidence. In the very moment I lost faith in a situation, the child would turn and look at me.

I had one therapist who insisted that one of the kids would simply grow out of particularly egregious behaviors "over time." She thought I was overreacting. We ended our planning meeting with her saying, "Look, just because a child lights matches does not mean they have been sexually abused." *Lighting matches?* I'd not heard that one before. I went home to find that the child in question had been lighting matches while I was with the therapist.

After several months, I finally found an adoption specialist, a therapist trained in attachment and adoption issues. During the intake session, she told me that often, after an adoption becomes legal, some children will completely freak out. "Some parents do not tell the child the adoption is legal, just in case. I just wanted to mention it as an option." I considered it, Dan did not. Dan said the strength of our parenting was our honesty. We told the kids the adoption was coming and I braced myself.

* * *

Our adoption took place in Westchester, New York, eighteen months after the children were placed with us. Our lawyer had hooked it up, and while it was a five-hour drive, it was the soonest date we could get. We were going to be part of a national adoption day in which several families would be adopted on the same afternoon. I was so ready for this to happen, for the kids to be inextricably ours and for social services to be out of my life forever.

Scooby-Doo was at the courthouse to meet us, and a life-sized Elmo picked Anthony up and carried him around. Anthony went with it, introducing Elmo to everyone. "Elmo, this is my Dad. Dad, this is Elmo. Elmo, this is my brother Jimmy. Jimmy, Elmo." He went through the whole family, plus our two tutors, Uncle John, and our friends who came up from the city. The kids looked gorgeous: new suits and dresses, hair newly cut, combed or braided.

The proceedings began. We sat at a table with reams of paper waiting for signatures. We were asked to read aloud the kids' names and then spell the names into a microphone. When the judge asked Dan to read Susie's full name aloud and then spell it, he struggled with the letters, choking on emotion. He looked over at Susie and winked. She was glowing with pride. The children were nervous because they couldn't fully understand what this adoption meant for their future. Dan and I were nervous because we fully understood what it meant for ours.

After the legalities, we piled into the van and started for home. We stopped at a diner in Albany for our celebration dinner. Ten minutes into the meal, Jason insisted Jimmy's fried shrimp was his, he started yelling, stood up, and threatened to kill his Dad. Jason was tired. We were all tired. It had been a long, emotional day. I counted Jason to three and took him out to the van, steering him past the staring customers by the collar of his jacket.

It was dark outside, the blacktop wet from a drizzling rain, and reflections from the diner lights glowed in the shallow slick. Twenty feet from the restaurant, Jason started thrashing and screaming: "Let go of me! Let go of me!" I crouched down behind him, wrapped my arms around his wiry torso and tightened slowly, half hug, half boa constrictor. "I hate you!" Tighter. I held him. He stopped writhing. I whispered in his ear, "Be quiet." We stayed a minute longer and then I let him go. He walked with me to the van.

I had him sit in the front seat, "eyes forward, not a sound." I sat behind him on the second bench. Ten minutes later Dan came out with Ruby. Not a word was spoken. She climbed in the van, I pointed her to the seat behind me; "eyes forward, not one sound." The rain on the windows picked up the reflection of the diner lights, dripping and streaking. The three of us sat in complete silence while the others finished celebrating our first dinner together as a lawfully legal family.

* * *

My first act as an adoptive parent was to put an eye-hook lock on the timeout room. As foster parents, Dan and I were given a contract stating we would never hit our foster children, berate their biological parents or ethnicity, force the children to crawl over uncooked rice or beans (*what the . . . ?),* have them kneel in a corner with their hands behind their heads, withhold food as a means of punishment, or bind their hands or feet. We also agreed not to lock them in a room. These policies, born of abuse, painted a picture of the worst side of humanity. We signed it, wishing the world were a better place.

Jason in particular had abused the lock-free clause to take control of the house. So long as I was holding him down, or standing outside the timeout room holding the door closed, I had my back turned to the four other children. I could see how he had won their loyalty in the Bronx. They themselves had told us stories of Jason drawing the heat, pulling focus, taking the abuse while the rest of them were made to watch. He had an incredible will. Even in the moment that he was turning our house upside down, I admired him and hoped that someday his incredible will would serve him. I had spent the worst part of our first eighteen months together holding that timeout door closed, ignoring his siren cries, manipulations, and threats.

With the lock in place, the power shift was immediate and complete. The first time Jason heard me walk down the hall away from his tirade, he went berserk. "Where are you going? Get back here! You can't leave me here, get back here you fucking bitch!" Then, crying and pleading, "Don't leave me! Come back! Please, please come back!" I shut the door to the third floor behind me. *Click.* He started kicking and screaming. I walked slowly down the stairs, breathing deeply. I went into the kitchen and set the timer for ten minutes. I poured myself some tea. I could still hear him but only faintly, like the sound of a distant radio.

When we first started this consequence, Dan had explained to me the psychology of locking someone in a room. It was way beyond a safety issue. We were not giving them a consequence. We were not giving them anything. We were taking something away. We were taking their freedom away, and we would be responsible for everything that went on behind that door. Any child in a locked room would be checked on a minimum of every ten minutes. They would not be left if we felt they were at any risk of hurting themselves in our empty, windowless timeout room. That first ten minutes, I did nothing but sip my tea.

After ten minutes, I headed back upstairs. Jason heard my footsteps on the third floor and flew into a rage as I approached the door, "How's it going, Jason? You okay?" He screamed, "Fuck you, bitch!" I opened the door to make sure he was alright. I closed the door and dropped the metal hook into the eye. "The timeout starts when the fit stops, buddy. Your choice, you've got ten minutes." In a soft, childish voice, "Mom? Mom? Don't leave me, please, I'm scared. I have to use the bathroom, you can't leave me." He had used the bathroom just before I had carried him up those stairs ten minutes before; I was pretty sure he'd make it.

He was going nuts. I took no pleasure in this. The goal was to rehabilitate this child, reclaim him, make an omelet from all the eggs he was throwing at me. I felt like throwing up as I walked away. I went downstairs, set the timer for ten minutes, and read with Anthony. "I do not like green eggs and ham, I do not like them, Sam I am." We could hear Jason's distant screaming, hear him kicking the door and banging on the floor. "It's his choice, Anthony. As soon as he does his ten minutes he can be free. Nobody's hurting him." Anthony said, "I know, Mom." Eventually, Jason completed his ten minutes.

* * *

My second act as an adoptive parent was to make contact with the kids' biological mothers. Our lawyer advised me to take a post office box in a different state, near a friend or relative who could receive and forward mail for me. I thought about these women a lot. Without knowing them or their circumstances, I knew they'd had their children taken from them, I knew they wondered about them, missed them and worried. I wanted to send photos of their beautiful, healthy children with poems written by their brilliant athlete/musician/elementary-school scholar/artist/comedic/chess masters. I put myself in these women's shoes. These envelopes from a post box would help me on a down day, remind me to hope, that life was carrying on.

My children think of these women constantly, a thousand times a day, longing, wishing, wondering, *Does she miss me? Does she love me? Why did she give me away? Was it me?* The therapeutic community has a label for this devastating longing, this all-consuming ache. It's called "lack of closure." Seriously? Such toothless, passive words are an insult, diminish our experience. "Lactose intolerance" sounds more passionate than "lack of closure." And while we're at it, how about "failure to thrive"? It sounds like an orchid is wilting when in fact a child is dying, strapped in a high chair in a darkened room, alone. I have no words.

The agency wouldn't give me the addresses. "Once the adoption goes through, the case is closed." Can I mail the photos to you and have you forward to the mothers? "I'm sorry, we cannot discuss this." I called social services, shelters; the numbers I had were cold. No one would help me. After dozens of calls ending with, "I'm sorry, we can't help you," I started to lose it. "Then help them! I'm not the one who needs help! Help THEM, goddammit! I have their children! Can you take my contact information? Can you get a message to them from me?" Silence. "I'm sorry, ma'am. We can't help you."

"I miss my real Mom," they'd say, crying. I comfort them, "I know you do. I would, too." How confusing for a little heart, needing to attach to someone, unable to love in the present tense, worried that feeling close to me is betraying their real mom. The older kids can remember their moms. Kind of. Susie and Anthony have no memory at all. What is it they long for? Is it love? The idea of love? Maybe I have it all wrong. Maybe their longing is love.

Loving these children is easy for me, no mystery there; we love the things we care for. Is my love the same love the bio moms feel? The same love that my mother feels for me? I don't know. Does it matter? Love can be a lot of different things, or many things at once. It can spring up organically, uncontrolled and wild. It can be a decision, a seed we plant and water. These children want to be with their birth mothers. Of course they do. It wasn't my choice to remove them, and it certainly wasn't theirs. But here we are and love is love, it has its own life. It is working inside of us, having its way. We are learning to say, "I love you."

16

JASON

The first impression I have of Jason is from a story told over dinner by Jimmy and Ruby while we were a family of four in Manhattan. The foster parents couldn't get Jason to eat faster, "So they took the metal spoon and beat him on the head, but he just kept eating slow and he was smiling at us the whole time. They kept hitting and hitting and there was blood running down his face, but he just kept smiling at us and eating slow." The kids admired him. Hell, I admired him. It was hard not to. Jason was central to every story I heard about the foster home. There was abuse at the hands of the adults, abuse by the older biological children in the home, and a shocking lack of supervision. Jason was in charge of the foster kids. He was the ring leader, the child king. He filled a void.

"Remember when they hung Anthony by his shirt on the hook on the door and then beat his stomach with a stick?" Another kid jumped in, "Remember when Marilyn beat Ruby for washing her feet in the sink?" I wanted details. "Who was Marilyn?" I asked. "She was Ms. Smith's sister, she lived in the apartment downstairs. She watched us during the summers." Apparently the Smiths would go to Jamaica during the summer. I asked if Marilyn would come and live upstairs. "No, she had two of her own kids. She stayed in the basement. She would come up and check on us sometimes. And beat us." I asked the kids what they would do all summer. "Whatever we wanted." And who was in charge? Jason. He was the feared and malevolent Lord of the Flies.

The picture was becoming ever clearer. The reason Jason hated us so much was because we had taken his power away. He was competing with Dan and me for the hearts and minds of his siblings. He would whisper to them outside their bedroom doors, the bathroom doors, "They hate us! They want to hurt us! Don't do what they tell you, they're trying to control us!" The longer we were together as a family, the less influence he had over the others, and the more desperate he was to get it back.

The day after our adoption, Jason had another in a series of psychiatric evaluations. There was talk of using an off-label drug for ADHD to treat his oppositional defiant disorder, just one of Jason's many diagnoses. His teachers, therapist, and pediatrician were suggesting that if Jason's defiance was impulsive, there was a chance his brain was not releasing the stop chemical which prompts a person to pause, assess, and choose an appropriate response to a given situation. This was the first time meeting with this psychiatrist, and Jason was in rare form, prowling around the room, agitated, speaking in different voices, and curling his lips back in a weird smirk. I let the line out for about ten minutes, so the doctor could get the whole picture and then I reeled him back in. Consistency was my sharpest parental weapon and I did not want Jason to think that his bad behavior would be tolerated anywhere, ever.

"Okay, Jason, it's time to put the cars back," I said, as he was smashing them together, trying to provoke a response from me. "But I'm not finished playing with them," he said, in a baby voice. "It's time, Bud. Let's pack it up."

Jason did not respond and kept crashing the cars together, ignoring me. "That's one." He yelled angrily, "You can't count me! I said I'm not finished!" I counted two.

"But it's not fair! You can't tell me what to do!" He jumped up, kicked the cars with his foot then grabbed a car with his hand and held it behind his head, threatening to throw it at me. "That's three."

I stood up and took his hand with the car in it. Jason screamed and began kicking me. I took the car, then picked him up and cradled him tightly. His face was red: "Stop! Stop, you're hurting me!"

I said firmly, "As soon as you stop squirming, buddy, I'll let you do your timeout." The psychiatrist was taking it all in. Jason writhed for another five minutes and then stopped. I let him go. "Have a seat in the chair, buddy. Ten minutes." The doctor excused himself while Jason sat. After ten minutes, Jason and I went to the waiting room. I let him play quietly while I talked with the doctor.

The psychiatrist was thoughtful. "Let's assume Jason doesn't have access to the chemical stop mechanism in his brain. If we were to medicate him, give him that extra second before acting to consider his choices and potential consequences . . . well, I think Jason would make the same choice. All we have left are anti-psychotics." I said, "Thank you. We'll just keep working with him behaviorally. He had a rough start. We're hoping he comes around."

* * *

He wasn't coming around. We were trying to stay positive, and keep him moving forward, but nothing was working. He'd been kicked out of karate for desecrating the dojo and talking back to the sensai. Chess club didn't like cheaters, especially those who threw pieces when they were called out. Jason was expelled from summer school for sticking his finger in a student's eye while his teacher and the parent of the child were sitting next to them. Soapstone-carving class ended when Jason chased a fifteen year old around the room with a saw. ("I was kidding! It was just a joke!")

We had meeting after meeting on Jason's behalf: the principal, the school psychologist, teachers, therapists, Dan, myself, and our live-in tutor. We would sit in a conference room, all of us trying, all of us frustrated. Someone said, "What if we sent him to Four Winds downstate, checked him in for a month, and let them figure out what the hell his diagnosis is? We're throwing labels around like conduct disorder, oppositional defiant disorder, post-traumatic stress disorder, reactive attachment disorder. Which is it?" His therapist and I looked at each other. "He has all of them," I said. Dan jumped in. "Whatever his diagnosis is, none of these disorders can be treated medically. We have to treat him behaviorally, which we are doing. Sending him away for any amount of time is not the message we want to send to this child." Jason's therapist added, "His new home is the best place this child can be. He is with his siblings, and he has two loving parents who are treating him consistently."

The teachers were afraid to keep testing him. He needed the behavioral support mandated in his Individualized Educational Plan, but his IEP was based on his learning issues. Academically, he was reading above grade level and his solid math scores would disqualify him from the closely supervised classroom needed to control his behavior. However, all of his teachers agreed strongly that he should not be mainstreamed; he lacked empathy. And yet, everyone who did not know him well adored him. The neighbors, the receptionists, the librarians, essentially everyone who didn't actually have to deal with him on a regular basis, would tell me what a soft spot they had for him. "What a smile! That is one special kid." They wouldn't believe his behavior at home could be that bad. They thought I was too strict with him. "Remember, there's a hurt boy in there. You just need to love him." Of course I love him. Jason was easy to love, just really hard to live with.

When she came to visit, my own mother took his side: "He's just a boy, honey. You're too hard on him." I smiled. "You're right, Mom. Say, why don't the two of you go for a swim at the YMCA?" I watched the car drive away, stop abruptly at the end of the drive, and turn around. My mother screeched back and stormed into the kitchen. "I have never been spoken to like that by anyone, let alone a ten year old! You need to teach that child a lesson! I want him out of my sight!" Jason was yelling at her from the sidewalk, "Liar! You liar! You're just trying to get me in trouble! Grandma's a liar!" My mom looked at me, eyes wide, pupils dilating. "I'll handle it, Mom, just ignore him." *That's one . . .*

He was wearing me down. Jason's therapist told me he was testing me, "Just keep doing what you are doing. He's in a tough spot. He trusts no one." I dug deep and found my pride. If all this was just a test of my mettle by a ten year old, then I was bloody hell going to pass or get my head slammed in a door trying.

* * *

Jason slammed my head in a door. It was not an accident. As I was leaving his room, he called to me, "Mom?" I stopped, leaned my head back into his room to see what he wanted, and *BAM!* The door met my temple, driving my head into the door frame. He had set me up. The pressure was intense. I groaned and grabbed my head, easing myself down to the floor while Jason stood laughing at me. I grabbed his arm as I slid down, pulling him to the floor with me. I rolled him over onto his stomach, put his hands behind his back and yelled, "NOT OKAY!" He started screaming, "Stop it! You're hurting me! Stop! Stop!" I picked Jason up and took him outside to the van, away from his audience. It took him two hours to stop screaming.

Dan and I gave Jason two weeks of lockdown for my head injury. The longest grounding up until then had been two days. He ate alone on a ten-minute timer, had no piano, no swim, no outside play, no access to the other kids. The effect of his absence on the other children was profound, a game changer. Meals became more relaxed; we conversed, there was laughter and lightness. We played games together after dinner, read aloud together, passing the book from reader to reader. I got to spend time with my four other children, all of them funny and smart and markedly more open and calm away from Jason's influence. It was a huge piece of information.

After his grounding, Jason was welcomed back for two days before we had to ground him again. Infractions during that two-day period included but were not limited to: throwing rocks at passing cars, holding smaller children under water in the swimming pool, carving his name into the veneer on the piano, using the vacuum cleaner to torture the dog, and punching Jimmy repeatedly in the groin.

What to do with our angry, ousted dictator? Exile. If it was good enough for Napoleon, it was good enough for Jason. We packed up his bedroom on the second floor, moved him to a room on the third floor, and grounded him for a month. He was the only child on the floor. There was a tutor living in the room next to him with whom he shared the third-floor bathroom. He used the back staircase to get up and down and was not allowed on the second floor. He was livid. For days his cheeks burned with rage. "It's not fair! You hate me!" He plotted his revenge. He showed me his secret journal, in which he chronicled the crimes of adults against children. "Just because adults are bigger they boss us around. Children can take care of themselves. There is no difference between adults and children. We should be left to manage ourselves."

Jason showed me picture after picture of himself as a stick figure, shooting, stabbing, blood spurting from adult-sized stick figures, rockets flying at spherical heads with no ears. On his couch was a cloth doll, a gift from Aunt Marie, marked up with sharpies, cut with scissors, clothes gone, hair shorn, and every orifice violated. "Vengeancy is the only thing on my mind," he said, growling at me. I said, "You mean 'vengeance,' Honey. 'Vengeancy' isn't a word, but I love that you are working on your vocabulary." Time to redirect that energy.

Dan bought him a simple, sturdy, handmade dollhouse at a garage sale. It cost ten dollars unfurnished, but had good light and lots of potential. I carried it upstairs and talked Jason through the basics of real estate. "It's a fixer-upper, Jason. We got in low. If you put some sweat equity into this beauty, we can flip it, and walk away with some serious bank. I bet you could double our investment." He was listening. "My suggestion? Put your money into the bathrooms and kitchens. That's where you're going to get the biggest return on your investment in the resale." I handed him a new set of markers for the common rooms, "Don't fear color!" I said. He was interested, "What about the bedrooms, Mom?" He was looking for suggestions. "Feng Shui. Look it up." Jason grabbed a pencil and paper, "Can you spell that for me?"

We discussed window treatments and lighting fixtures. "If you upgrade the electric, the value added would be significant." We had an electronics lesson. We bought wiring, a breadboard, tiny buzzers, and lights, and a miniature fan that could run off an AA battery. "What about outside lights? You know, for the yard." I nodded. "Well, then I guess you're going to have make a yard." Dan bought him some magazines on landscaping in miniature, borrowing from the model railroad tradition.

We gave Jason reams of plain white paper, six rolls of scotch tape, and set up project tables for him. He covered the tables with paper and made cities with streets and buildings, parking garages for his Hot Wheels cars. We brought out the Lego trust, four file boxes full of Legos that his Aunt Marie loaned us. He swam at the YMCA every day. I supervised him at chess club on Fridays, drove him to and from school, walked him to piano lessons, and therapy sessions. He rode his bike, ate his meals with just me. And Jason read. He read aloud to me, he read alone to himself, and he read along to books on tapes. Monday afternoons I let him use the kitchen to bake bread, which he would sell to the neighbors, still warm, for $2.50 a loaf. Friday night was movie night; the only time he could see his siblings. Dan and I sat on the couch between him and the other kids.

He was for all purposes an only child. He hated it, and complained bitterly. Once he was down on the first floor, he did not want to go back up to his room. Every time I asked him to go upstairs, he experienced an abbreviated version of the five stages of loss: denial, bargaining, anger; and instead of grief and acceptance, Jason would substitute profanity and violence. After one of his more dramatic episodes, Jason accused me of being an abusive parent. I asked my jailbird to sit down for a minute and list for me his activities from the two previous days. He wrote it all down on a piece of cardstock. The list was extensive, full of fun and varied activities.

I put the list up on the refrigerator with a magnet. He looked sheepishly at me, grinned and tried to backpedal, "Okay, okay, so maybe I exaggerated a little."

17

ANN FOX

"My, but you've gotten bigger!" said Debbie, a friend from Albany who was up visiting. Debbie was talking to the undersized, but slowly growing, Anthony. Standing at the sink with my back to the dinner table, I said, "Thanks for saying that. I think a lot of people notice, but they never say anything." Dan laughed audibly into his napkin as I turned around, smiling at our guest. Debbie was mortified, blushing. I rushed to apologize, "Oh, Debbie, I'm sorry. I was teasing! I knew you were talking to Anthony." Dan was still laughing. *Not helping!*

I struggled to recover, "Let's just say everyone is growing around here and it's not just the kids! I've put on twenty pounds! More salad anyone? Anthony, would you like some more half and half?"

Jimmy said, "Mom weighs 148 pounds." I winked at him. "Thanks, Jimmy!" Dan would not stop laughing. Jimmy and I had weighed ourselves the day before, and clicked in at exactly the same weight, a coincidence Jimmy loved sharing with any and all. "Guess what? Mom and I both weigh 148 pounds!"

It was the most I had weighed in my life. I was super fit

when I joined this family and had been resting on my laurels ever since. My big fat laurels. My laurels were so big, they no longer fit in my clothes. We were trying to put some pounds on our little ones, so we stocked our kitchen with nutritious, but calorie-rich, food. I found myself eating when I wasn't hungry, eating just to eat. My sister told me it's called "stress eating," that I was compensating for zero downtime, and lack of self-care. And it was working for me. Eating delicious food was a way of being nice to myself, of loving myself, while everyone else was hatin' on me. "I hate you! I hate you! You're mean!" Really? Because this avocado and feta salad with basil-infused olive oil says I'm awesome.

*   *   *

"Five kids! I don't know how you do it!" I get that a lot. It's a figure of speech, a way for people to acknowledge that I am doing something difficult, without actually having to do it themselves. But they do know. People know how I do it, they just do not want to imagine it. Like the Donner party surviving for three months in the Sierras with no provisions, or giving birth in a cab, or winning a hot dog-eating contest. We all kind of know what's involved—it's just not pleasant to think about. For someone living one of these scenarios, however, survival is in the details. "Five kids! How do you do it?" Me? Seriously? I have a badass partner, sensible footwear, abundant health, and for the first forty-three years of my life, I did pretty much everything I wanted to do. I also go to New York City one day a week to teach and play music. That one day is my reason for living, the light at the end of the tunnel. I call it, "Every Child Left Behind."

I wake at 3 a.m., alert and excited. I dress in a skirt, a jacket, and shoes without laces. Dan goes over the checklist of things I need to take with me: French horn, mouthpiece, music, mutes, phone, charger, wallet, keys. "Love you," I say. "Be safe," he says. We kiss and I leave, elated, skipping my way to the car. As the Vermont ferry pulls away from the dock, I step out of the car. My defenses power down, the cold wind quieting as I breathe in deep, thirsty breaths. I am alone. Me. Alone. I board the plane in Burlington, land at JFK, and catch the train into the city. It's light now, and I look out the window, my reflexive eyes flicking left and right as they track the passing trees, the rapid eye movement defragging my brain, rebooting. By the time I get to NYU, I am a different person. I brush my teeth in the bathroom, wash my face, and put lipstick on. I wear my hair down because I can; no one's going to grab it or pull it. I unlock my studio and do something I'm good at: teaching.

I love my students. Most of them are at the graduate level: smart, self-starting, and sophisticated. My job is to listen to them, polish and mentor them from advanced student to promising professional. I am doing for them what my teachers did for me: alchemy, changing sound into meaning, craft into art. I teach them techniques to make the playing more comfortable, the player more confident, how to manage exposure, and take musical risks. I am happy when they improve. I don't want our lessons to end.

An instrumentalist is only as good as they are able to play on any given day. That goes for everybody. When I'm at home with the kids, I leave my horns all over the house and play them constantly, multi-tasking my scales, flexibility exercises, and physical maintenance, while keeping the kids in line, cooking, baking. I wake up at midnight to take my bedwetters to the bathroom, then go down to the basement and do my focused practicing from midnight until 1:30 or 2 in the morning. If a student starts a lesson with, "I didn't have time to practice this week," all I have to do is look at them, and say, "Really?"

If my phone rings while I'm teaching, it is Dan, and he only calls in an emergency. I pick up, give him the location of the insurance cards and the address for the hospital, then hang up and let it go. I am six hours away, there is nothing I can do about it. Dan called one night during a 10 p.m. lesson. Susie had run away, "Any friends close by? Any house she might go to? We've got two feet of snow on the ground and her footprints end at the street." I gave two addresses and went back to teaching. I had forgotten to unforward our landline upstate to my cell phone, and as the police arrived and neighbors came out in force, no one realized I wasn't at home and I found myself organizing the search party. "I apologize for this," I said to my student. "Not at all," he said. We stayed focused between interruptions, on task and productive.

But as time went on, the news was getting worse, the calls more frequent. My student said, "Professor Ellsworth, if you'd rather, we can reschedule. I'm sure this is very upsetting for you." I took a moment. "Thank you, but if you can tolerate the disruptions, I'd like to continue. We can solve your issues in the next twenty minutes, fix the few things that need correcting, and be done. This," I held up the phone. "This I cannot solve. This cannot be fixed. They'll find her and she'll run again. But if I can help you mark these phrases, so the breathing becomes a part of the line, I will have fixed something. I really need to fix something." He nodded, "Of course. I'll begin at the recapitulation." I love my students.

Many of them have come to visit the house upstate, stayed with us, rehearsed in the living room. We did a two-day horn immersion conference at the local SUNY where I was adjunct. My students gave lectures, master classes, new music recitals, and horn ensemble concerts. Donna played cards with Anthony; Harley taught Jimmy how to make omelets. The Fox kids wanted to play their piano pieces for them, sing and play their secondary instruments. My students listened, coaching them, making comments, encouraging.

* * *

It's hard on the kids when I leave. I know it's not ideal. But like the workers at Chernobyl tasked with sealing the radioactive core of the damaged reactor, there are limits to how much radiation a body can take. You either respect the turnaround time, or risk over-exposure. I know my limits. I have measured my performance, tried and tested it over those brutal, soul crushing, no-school stretches of summer and winter "break." At the start, I am brilliant, nimble, and clear. But after ten days or so, things drop off precipitously. I lose my patience, my sense of humor, and my hair starts falling out by the handful. My sister says, "Maybe it's because you haven't showered for two weeks." *Ha ha, not funny*. I feel gripped and grabby, manually overriding the speed of my breathing, to slow the release of adrenaline into my bloodstream. Can I put a child in timeout for staring at me? At fifteen days, I throw our porcelain tea cups off of the back porch, smashing them onto the driveway, overhand pitches smacking and popping on the black top.

I think maybe if I run really, really fast, my demons won't catch me. But they do. After twenty days without a break, I drop the kids at summer school, swimming lessons, and piano. I park at the marina and run onto the docks, dive fully dressed into Lake Champlain, and swim down, down, down, shockingly cold, away from the boats. It's dark and quiet, the water pressure pressing on me, uniform pounds per inches cubed, reverse fever cooling my melt down. Acid stress leaching and seeping out of me into nature's forgiving neutral. It's so cold. I love you, Lake. One of the tutors has to pull me out. I lie on the deck, my jeans sticking to my legs like wet cement.

* * *

Before we got the kids, I was living my dream. I was playing well and had the work that I wanted. I was touring a lot, staying in spa hotels, playing incredible music in the world's great concert halls with amazing musicians. Back in town, I would swim and play squash every day and eat expensive, delicious, high octane food. When I wasn't working, I was climbing mountains in the Adirondacks. I was in amazing shape.

I remember being at an elementary school on the East Side of New York City, demonstrating the horn to children sitting in concentric circles at my feet. I unscrewed my detachable bell ("the amplifier of the brass instrument") and showed them how the horn sounded softer without it. Still talking, I held the horn up to screw the bell back on, feeling for the click in my right hand, that little click telling me the threads were seated and I could spin it back on. It's second nature, something I do several times every day. Someone in the band cracked a joke, I was laughing and distracted, and thinking the bell was seated, gave the thick three-inch ring a sharp twist to the right. The bell flew off the horn, out of my hand, and began a spinning tumble through the air.

I watched it falling, thinking how unfortunate it was that I had just sold my other bell to a colleague the day before, how I hoped the bell would not hit the children in the front circle near my feet, then acknowledged that if it did hit the children, it would no doubt survive unscathed, and then chastised myself for putting the potential mitigation of damage to my instrument above the health of a child. Suddenly, everything stopped and the auditorium went into a shocked silence. I had caught the bell with my foot, the flare up, and the ring sitting snug on the tip of my boot. The audience froze and then broke into applause. I reached down and took my bell and bowing deeply, had an epiphany.

I had way more resources than I was using, way more energy, time, and money than I needed and I felt ready do something more with my life. I was too comfortable. If I wanted to keep growing as a musician, I need more depth as a human. I needed to shake it up. Transformation doesn't happen in the comfort zone.

I wasn't alone. A lot of my peers were in the same place, trying to figure out what comes next. My friends were biking across exotic third-world countries, running marathons, scuba diving, enjoying their excess health and wealth in increasingly exotic and challenging environments. I was always invited and I always considered, closing my eyes and imagining myself at Machu Picchu, breathing hard on the crest of a polar mountain, the crunch of the ice pack beneath my crampons. But that was the problem: I could imagine it. The one adventure I could *not* imagine was parenting.

After spending Thanksgiving with our new family, my sister Michelle called it, "extreme parenting." She flew back to Colorado and hanging out with her climbing friends, listening to them talk about their base jumping and free climbs, "It was so extreme! Super rad!" Michelle sat silently for a while and then said, "You think that's extreme? My sister and her partner adopted five special-needs kids through foster care. Y'all got nothin."

18

SILENT SPRING

a month after moving Jason to the third floor, something went very wrong. Ruby started having screaming outbursts at the table. Jimmy was avoiding eye contact and walking away from me while I was speaking to him. Susie was spending an unhealthy amount of time hiding under the desk in her room, and Anthony's abuse of the first-floor bathroom was reaching artistic levels. I tried reaching out and spent quality time with each of the kids, "Is there anything you want to talk about? Any worries? This behavior doesn't seem like you." Nothing.

Something was not right. Ruby, Jimmy, and Susie all had discipline referrals from school, while Jason was upbeat and cocky. I dropped him off and called Dan. "What the hell is going on?" Dan called it: "Jason has access. Shut him down. We need to find out what he's been doing."

We moved the children into individual rooms on the second floor, no more shared spaces. We put everyone but Anthony in lock-down: no piano, basketball, soccer, or swim. The children ate one at a time with just me and a timer at the table; there were no snacks after school or desserts after dinner.

We questioned Jimmy first; he had the most to lose and rolled like a bowling ball. "Jason came into my room and told me to throw my toys over the banister." I stared at him, my arms folded, "Why'd ya do it, Jimmy?" He bowed his head. "Jason said it wasn't fair that you took Anthony's toys away and he told Susie to come into my room, I don't know why. And Jason was standing outside the bathroom door a lot, whispering to Susie and stuff." Jimmy was released. Ruby's turn. "Jason said it wasn't fair that the kids had to stay in their rooms. He said kids should be able to go where they want to and that you guys hate us and are trying to control us." Ruby was released.

Susie would not give it up. I had to find an angle. I stopped by her room for a routine check. The air was heavy with perfume, a controlled substance in our house. Susie loved all things smelly—lotions, hair products, perfume, and deodorants—but could not moderate her usage. Left alone with a bottle of anything, she would rub it into her hair and clothes, squeeze the contents into a desk drawer, and then smear it onto her walls and bedclothes. Single doses of lotion were squeezed into her hand by an adult. Susie had broken a rule while grounded. This was my ticket in.

"Susie, what's this dripping from your hair, honey?" She shrugged, "I don't know what you are talking about." I smiled, "I can smell it, Babe. Where did you get it?" Lying straight to my face she said, "I don't have it. I didn't do anything." These kids had a very high tolerance for discipline and once they figured I wasn't going to hurt them, I had very few options. "Sweetie, I am going to go through your room until I find what I'm looking for. I'm going to put everything that is not a book into this bag and keep it. As soon as you tell me what it is and where you put it, I will return it. It's up to you." I picked up her Yellow Teletubby. Her eyes went wide. Into the bag. I picked up her Polly Pocket, gave her a second to consider, and then tossed it in the bag. I tossed Polly's fold-out home, Polly's clothes and shoes, jewelry box, colored pencils, clock radio. She was riveted, but silent. "I'm going to find it, Susie. Or you can just tell me where it is and I will stop. I don't want to take your stuff."

I moved to her dresser where a tiny ceramic tea set sat arranged, waiting elegantly for some miniature guest to arrive. Susie bolted up. She loved this tea set. I moved slowly, building the tension. I picked up a saucer and threw it in the bag. I picked up a cup. Susie yelled, "It was in your bathroom closet! I found it in your bathroom!" She had gone into our bathroom, found a bottle, put the contents in her hair, and then put the bottle back. I asked her what was in the bottle. "I don't know, I couldn't read it." I softened. "My job is to keep you safe, Susie. I can't keep you safe if you lie to me. Take a minute, I'll be back." I left the room.

I had worked Jason over earlier that day "They told me everything, Pal. Jimmy, Ruby, Susie . . . I know what happened. I just need to hear it from you." Jason was indignant. "They are just making stuff up to get me in trouble!" I asked him why his siblings would do that. "Because that's what I do to them!"

After threatening to take away his Legos, he cried out, "I told Susie to climb down the stairs while you and Dad were watching a movie and find out what it was! You can see the movie by looking in the glass on the painting over the stairs!" I put the box down and turned and faced him. "What else?" I folded my arms. "I told her to go into Jimmy's room and take his Hot Wheels and bring them to me." I nodded. "Did she do it?" He nodded yes. "That's good," I said, "That's all for now."

I came into her room, sat down beside her, rubbed her back, and suggested she take some deep breaths. "Sweetie, Jason has already told us everything. We know what happened but it's important that you say it. You need to tell me the truth."

She started crying. I used my soothing voice, "I know you love Jason. I love him, too. No one is going to get in trouble. Just tell me in your own words." Susie lied, "I don't know, I don't know anything . . . nothing happened, I don't know what you are talking about." She was crying harder now.

"Susie. He told you to go into Jimmy's room and steal his Hot Wheel cars. He told you to sneak down the stairs and look at the reflection in the picture frame to find out what movie your Dad and I were watching." She turned suddenly, eyes wide with betrayal. "He told you that?" I nodded. "He told us everything, Sweetie. Everything." Her face went white. *Look at her! She looks terrified. He threatened her.* "What did he say would happen if you told?" She sobbed, "He said he would call the Smiths and tell them where I was."

I pressed her. I asked her yes and no questions to which she nodded or shook her head. The news was not good, it was horrible and wrong and not my news to share. *Oh, God.* I held her close to me and she began sobbing. "Susie, none of this is your fault. Children need supervision, this is not on you." I felt sick. *This is not about you. She's loyal to Jason, but you need to get her on your side.* "No one is going to get in trouble, I love Jason as much as you. It's not his fault either." *Show anger and stop breathing like that.* "Those adults were not keeping you safe. I am angry at them." *You need to normalize it for her.* I can't—I got nothing. I am out of my depth! *Then change the subject. Move on.*

"Susie, I want you to think of a food that would not be improved by adding either bacon or chocolate." It's an impossible question, like finding a word that rhymes with "orange," but it got her thinking.

Not all bonds between humans are healthy. They say the strength of the fear based trauma bond is more destructive and powerful than any other bond, stronger than every healthy bond we were trying so hard to build. It explained the "kids versus parents" vibe that we were currently living in. While studies on trauma bonds are painful and disturbing to take in, they explain certain human behaviors that cannot otherwise be understood.

Our children did what they had to do to survive. They allied themselves and stayed together, innocent and unhealthy. They stayed alive, kicking and screaming and scratching, fighters all, strong as nature, strong as life. Their brains are young and, yes, messed and messy. To break the trauma bond between them will require a forceps, delirium tremens. We said healthy, strong, and confident and our word is *our* bond. This is not a stock home. And love is a powerful methadone.

I cried when I told Dan about Susie's disclosures. He was sad, but not surprised. We weren't there in the Bronx, and we may never know what really happened. "But if a quarter of what she said is true," Dan said, "we have a situation in our home. Zero access. No exceptions." Copy that.

* * *

Before any of the children were placed with us, we requested copies of their medical records from the agency. When those were not forthcoming, we petitioned the court for them multiple times over the next several months. Nothing. We made access to their medical files a condition of the adoption. Still no files. We adopted them anyway, and filed a court order forcing the agency to give us copies. Months later the records came in the mail, a heavy cardboard box eight inches deep— eight inches of scratchy photocopies of diagnoses, second opinions, recommendations, and handwritten notes scrawled in the margins of psych evaluations. I started going through the files at night after the kids were asleep. I wanted to know why Jason and Anthony weren't growing. Lord knows they were eating. I would read for an hour, then cry myself to sleep. After a few nights, I stopped reading. These files showed me the horrible things that were done to them, but could never show me why.

It took us eighteen months, but we figured out on our own

most of what was in those files: If we'd had those records before the adoption, we would have made better decisions, informed decisions, smarter and faster-acting decisions. In our abbreviated family life, everything is a race against time. That was eighteen months we'll never get back. Eighteen months of blindly parenting the best we could. We had been operating without a complete picture in any way. Hell, we learned that one of the children was allergic to penicillin. That child could have died. Who benefits from withholding that information from a child's guardians and doctors?

We shall not overcome. We can't, it's too much. Instead, we shall overwhelm, make a life for our children so full and so delicious, there will be no room for need, no room left for pain, only light and love. Stuffed with family bonds, extended, farm-fresh cousin bonds, hydroponic parent bonds, and organic child-dog bonds. Their trauma bond was like a rat in a siege; we eat it to sustain life, to survive. But now the siege was over and that rat has no place at the table of joy. Each day I looked at them, silently pleading, *choose love, my loves, come closer, come closer, welcome yourselves to the land of enough, the land of excess, at least for the moment, at least for today.*

*   *   *

It's April 2010 and Easter breaks our long, cold, lonely winter. Baskets include, but are not limited to: giant one-pound chocolate bunnies, jelly beans, malted eggs, sunglasses, toys, swimsuits and towels, and a rainbow coalition of marshmallow Peeps sticking and tangling in the green plastic grass.

We hold our third Easter sunrise service for ourselves and our neighbors overlooking the lake. It's not really a sunrise service anymore. Previous years, we would get up at 5:30, build a fire on the beach, and I'd play the alphorn as the sun came up, but the number of neighbors turning out for the service definitely increased when we moved it to 10. There is still a small group of diehards, trekking through the dark as we cross to the lake to watch the sun come up, its rays spiking like a sugar high in the small of group of Fox children first thing in the morning. "Of course we're going! It's a tradition! We do this every year!"

As we walk across the field for the second service, the sun is high in the sky. The kids point to the colored patches of grass where we'd dyed our eggs outside: blue, orange, purple, yellow, and red. Jimmy carries the warm cinnamon rolls we made at six that morning, while Susie carries the guitar. Ruby has the programs, while I carry the pot of hot chocolate and Anthony carries the cups. The neighbors arrive with deviled eggs, coffee, and a token green vegetable.

We stand in a big circle while Susie hands out the programs, "The words for the songs are on the back." The kids have written poems about Easter, nature, and rebirth. We have special musical numbers, recorder duets, and original songs. Jimmy steps into the circle to say his poem, "Our Sun is a Spring Bling!/Wakes you up in the morning, Ting!" A neighbor leads us in a sun salutation, and then we eat. Dan stays home during the service and hides six dozen hard-boiled eggs. If you want a real Easter egg hunt, get a man who finds things for a living to hide them. It's intense. I could tell you more but I'd have to kill you.

Our special today is honey-baked ham with seeded mustard, scalloped potatoes baked in heavy cream, homemade crescent rolls, asparagus, and a mixed green salad with goat cheese, apples, walnuts, and dried cranberries and a balsamic vinaigrette. For dessert, the children have made a cherry cream pie and a white bunny cake with furry coconut frosting and weird sprinkles in its eyes, giving it a distinctive, very creepy, look. My dad always said tradition is about doing the wrong things for the right reasons. So be it. It's a weapons exchange: trauma for tradition, bonds for bonbons, baskets and rebirth, at least for this moment, if just for today.

19

DO THE MATH

*H*ome school. I never thought it could happen to me. I didn't fit the profile. I loved the teachers, staff, and administration that made up our school district. I had no illusions that I could do a better job teaching than a professional educator, and I sure as hell didn't think God wanted me to homeschool. We were our third year with the kids when we made the decision to take our children out of public school. I made it clear that they were home to learn appropriate behavior and get back in school as soon as possible.

Ruby, already held back once for fifth grade, had managed to get three discipline referrals in two weeks for hitting and physical altercations. During that same period, she also bit another child at the YMCA. When confronted, she said it was an accident. A biting accident. *Wow*. While Dan and I discussed options, I began appearing at Ruby's school during recess. She loved tetherball; I could hear her screaming at her classmates from the parking lot. There she was, my gorgeous girl; a head taller than everyone else and twice as loud. A little fifth grader approached me, "Are you Ruby's mom?" I said, "I am." My arms were folded in a displeased stance and my eyes fixed on Ruby through my dark glasses. "Everyone's afraid of her! She's mean!" I took a deep breath. "I'm on it."

Ruby was not intrinsically mean. She was a sweet girl who had been treated badly. She would act out to get attention, get too over-excited so that the adrenaline would rush her brain to its default setting: violence. Ruby needed to be socialized, but 400 middle school students were not the calming influence I was looking for. Socialization is the big argument against homeschooling and I agree, children need to learn how to get along with other kids. If they are only exposed to adults, their social development will skew. And, in the case of my kids, if they are never exposed to adults to teach them that strangling, hitting, and biting are not appropriate, they are definitely skewed. Good luck making friends and maintaining relationships. Ruby needed a break from other kids, including her siblings. She needed adults to help her mature, to love and respect her, to model good behavior, and to teach her how to love and respect herself.

Homeschooling for Ruby was a perfect fit. She thrived on the one-on-one instruction and attention, she applied herself and aimed to please. While at home, Ruby wrote a memoir, she learned oil painting, had a voice teacher, a sewing tutor, and learned to cook. We listened to her read aloud, listened to her practice piano and sing. And we talked with her and listened to what she had to say. She played sports, took swimming lessons, did research projects at the library, and worked on her computer skills. She had a dance tutor, and learned to control her body to a creative and expressive end. Ruby was thriving.

* * *

Within a month of bringing Ruby home, we pulled Jason out of school for abusing one his classmates. The school had an effective discipline plan for Jason but as good as they were, we were better. The school could follow through until 4 p.m. We could follow through round-the-clock. I was in charge of behavior and discipline, while I let the tutors take care of the academics. He was impossible. Trust me when I say I spent more time wrangling Jason than the tutors spent teaching. Our science tutor, a PhD candidate in entomology, was taking a year off from her program to help us out. Ten minutes into her science unit, I heard Jason screaming, "You can't teach science! You don't know anything! You're a woman! And besides, you're Chinese!" I started running up the stairs and rounded the corner just in time to see the whiteboard, covered in the most beautiful, colorful, hand drawn cicada being thrown across the room towards the tutor. "Lesson's over," I'd say, grabbing him by the back of his shirt and steering him towards the timeout chair.

The tutors were burning out on him. I gave them a break and taught him math for a semester. Our lessons were always a battle.

"Okay, buddy, you left this problem blank on your worksheet, how come?"

"I don't know what shape a merry-go-round is. How can I find the circumference if I don't know what shape it is?" *He knows what shape it is.*

"Because it gives you the radius. Only one shape has a radius, what is that shape?"

"I don't know." *He's playing dumb. He wants a confrontation. Don't give it to him.*

"A circle. That's what this chapter is about, Jason, finding the area and circumference of a circle. I'll make up some practice sheets for you."

"No, no, I don't need any practice! I know how to do it!"

I started walking away. "See you soon, Pal."

"No! No!"

I closed the door to his room behind me, returning twenty

minutes later with ten custom-made radius and circumference problems. At the top were the formulas and a gentle reminder, "If a shape has a radius, it is a circle. All the shapes below are circles." Jason looked at the problems and using a whiny, half crying baby voice said, "I don't need these, I know how to do it." I smiled, "Good, then it shouldn't take long to finish. Knock it out, Buddy." He started screaming, "That's not how they teach in real school! In real school they would help me! You don't know how to teach! Get me a teacher!"

I turned and walked away, "Get it done, Jason, I'll be back in twenty minutes." He ran at me and jumped on my back, knocking me off balance.

This is not how I'd pictured mothering.

*   *   *

When a special meeting is called for your special-needs child by the director of special education, you just know it is going to be, well, *special*. We met to discuss getting an additional one-on-one aide to work with Anthony in the classroom. His class currently had eight kids with one teacher and three aides, but the teacher was petitioning for another aide just for Anthony. "It's like he has eight arms!" the teacher said. "You can't turn your back on this child. He needs constant supervision." Another teacher added, "He also learns better when it's one-on-one. Of course, all children do, but Anthony especially."

Anthony was in a skills-based class that focused on things like eating, brushing teeth, dressing yourself, and using the bathroom. His classmates were severely autistic, had Down syndrome, or were delayed. Anthony's behavior was manipulative, hiding in the corner, would lure his classmates to him, *psst, psst*, tell them to take something, break something, go pee on something, or worse, someone, and then watch them get in trouble. And without a one-on-one aide, he was getting away with it.

Anthony would marinate all day in a classroom loud with screaming and restraining, then come home, wired from the stimulation, and continue acting out. I'd count him, put him in timeout, then send him back the next morning to soak for another day in the very behavior I kept insisting was unacceptable. Anthony was showing me he needed for an intervention in every destructive way he could. It was his turn for homeschool. But Anthony was my homeschool nightmare, the giant mosquito I could not swat, the noisy, angry, starving mosquito with attachment issues. *Dear Lord.* Dan said, "Homeschool is the only chance he has of getting out of his classification." He was right, of course, and we decided to bring him home. I had just become the one-on-one aide.

* * *

Dan and I had been given a continuing subsidy from the state for our five special-needs kids. We had planned to save it for the college fund but quickly realized there would be no college if we didn't invest now in bringing them up to speed. We had managed so far with one live-in tutor and a few day tutors to help us after school with homework and projects. But with more kids at home than in school, we went from one live-in tutor to three. I upgraded my title to Behavior Czar, while the tutors taught. The district let us use textbooks and syllabi for the classes I desperately wished the kids were attending. Much of our success at homeschooling depended on the tutors. Some tutors could not work with Jason, some were afraid of Ruby. At one point I had a tutor leave midyear. I begged her to stay, offered to double her salary, "I feel bad," she said, "but it's just too hard." She had a point. We needed to streamline. Dan and I discussed with the district the option of putting Ruby and Jason back in school part time, or as we called it, "The Outpatient Program."

Jason returned to Maple Street Elementary with no recess and no lunch period; I took him to lap swim during the lunch break and fed him in the car on the drive back. The school district offered to bus Jason to school and we gratefully accepted. After his third day on the bus, the monitor walked Jason to our front door, and with trembling hands and a shaky voice told me of Jason's abuse of the other children, safety issues, and flagrant disrespect for authority. Jason was no longer welcome on the bus.

Two weeks in, Jason was no longer welcome in gym class either. Another week passed and he was pulled out of structured reading and library time as well. I spent more time driving him to and from school than he spent in the classroom and still, I cherished the moments he was out of the house. Another week passed, and he was home for good. The principal called. "I have never known a more deceptive, manipulative child than Jason. Get him out of here." This was coming from someone who had worked with a lot of deceptive, manipulative children. It was terrible news yet strangely validating.

Ruby returned to middle school for core classes only. She was not allowed to have a locker and had no unsupervised access to other students. In the three minutes between bells, she had to check in with her guidance counselor and she came home every day for lunch. We were very clear with Ruby, "Engage another child physically and we will pull you back out of school." A month into her modified program, Ruby punched two of her classmates in the face during math class. I met her in the principal's office. Even her telling of her side of the story was damning and calculated.

After these failed attempts, I was forced to accept homeschooling as my new calling and took up the mantle of educator. It fit me like a hair shirt, and the fact that homeschooling was so successful just made it itchier.

20

WHITE MOM

On his first visit to our apartment, Jimmy said, "There are a lot of white people in Manhattan." It was true, but in New York City, if Jimmy and Ruby didn't look like us, at least they looked like our friends and neighbors. I wanted to prepare Jimmy and Ruby for our move upstate: "Just so you know, there's not a lot of diversity going on up there." One of our neighbors took me aside as soon as we moved in, "When the base was still open, people would see a black kid and assume his dad was the Air Force. Now they assume the kid is here because his dad is in the prison." Race was going to be an issue in a multiracial family like ours. How we dealt with racial identity, culture, and heritage would affect the health and future of our children. A lot of my African American friends from the city had weighed in on our adoption of Jimmy and Ruby. The majority of them were for it, "mix it up!" but others were not comfortable with it: "The experience is too different. You will never understand." It was complicated, but we talked about it, acknowledged and argued the hugeness and complexity of race relations in our country.

Jimmy and Ruby came with Dan and me to Middle

Collegiate Church in the East Village. There was a black pastor there who was in a mixed marriage, and had a PhD in race relations. She had the vocabulary to talk it, the experience to walk it, and the compassion to bless and include. Our first service there, the congregation welcomed us as one of their own: diverse. We were all the same in being different. Jimmy and Ruby sang in the youth choir, standing up there in front of the altar with the other children like a box of Crayolas: jeans, dresses, freckles, dreads, gingers, cornrows, beads, high heels, high tops. It was beautiful. Dan leaned over and whispered, "It takes a city."

Standing in the registration line for a soccer camp in Lake Placid, surrounded by a sea of blond, blue-eyed children bobbing around their blond, blue-eyed parents, Ruby said, "Good thing you got me these socks, Mom." She loved her new red checkered soccer socks. "This way you'll be able to tell which one is me out on the soccer field!" I smiled, "You think so, Honey?" I saw an Indian family with two kids join the end of the line. I had to stop myself from waving at them, "Yoo hoo! Over here!"

When Susie ran in from our local soccer practice to tell me that some man called her a racial slur, I felt my whole body flood with anger and told her to point him out to me. The soccer field was crowded, she was pointing to the far side of the lawn. I told her to follow me and started running, my head pounding, wondering what the hell I was going to do if and when I caught this asshole. The harder I ran, the more I realized my body was preparing itself for a confrontation which might not be the best role modeling for my Susie. "Mom! Mom!" she was screaming, "He's gone!" I slowed to a stop, relieved. That would not have gone well.

Ruby described our family once as, "Dark chocolate, chocolate, milk chocolate, and vanilla." I said, "Yummy!" Then Ruby said, "Wait, you can be white chocolate instead of vanilla. I know how much you like chocolate." Our neighbors called us the "Rainbow Coalition."

But it wasn't all easy. A kid called Jimmy the "N" word and the kid's mother told me about it at Ruby's basketball game, "I wanted to tell you before you heard it from someone else. Junior didn't mean it, I don't think he even knows what that word means." Her face was beet red, "We're all just live and let live up here. I raised my kids to be color blind." My face went red. *Easy, girl.* Color blind? So it was by chance that her son called my son—one of three black kids in a three mile radius, the other two also living in my house—the "N" word? *Give her a break, Ann. Her kid might have just been trying it on. Ignorant doesn't always mean racist.* I replied, tensely, "Thanks for telling me. If you'd like, I'd be happy talk with your son about it. Jimmy's black, it's a part of who he is. To pretend we don't see that is to pretend he's someone else." The mother said guardedly, "It's okay, I talked to Junior. He won't do it again." I had made her defensive. *Shit.*

After this encounter, I called a city friend who studied race relations. "I need a summit, like a round-table discussion where we invite the neighbors and the neighbor's kids, and we talk about race and deal with it! I want you to come up here and do like a mini race-sensitivity conference."

My friend laughed and said, "Ann, race is not something we resolve. It's an issue in our country that we live with. Yes, education and discourse is essential, but I don't think my spending a weekend in upstate New York is going to make it easier for your kids in the day to day." *Dammit.*

"So what do I do?" She told me to focus on the day to day: "Bring African American culture into your home—music, art, literature, politics, religion. Celebrate it, talk about it, live it."

* * *

Dan's father passed away two years after we got the kids. Our neighbors were shocked as they watched us load up the van. *You're driving? To South Dakota?* We'd come across this attitude before. In Manhattan, people thought "out west" meant western New Jersey. In the real west, where Dan and I grew up, cities are far apart. You have to drive if you want to go anywhere. My family used to drive 800 miles in a day to visit our Grandma. Dan's hometown was a hundred miles from an interstate highway. Road trips were a part of life.

The funeral was beautiful. At the beginning of this whole process, someone had told me that kids suffering from PTSD know better than anyone when it's really important to behave. Our kids were perfect. We talked them through viewing the body and gave them an out if they didn't want to. They were all interested and respectful. They met Dan's side of the family looking absolutely precious in their Sunday best. They sang and played piano at the potluck in the basement of the Trinity Lutheran Church, the whole time acting nothing less than adorable and well-behaved. We spent the next day driving around Dan's hometown, Mobridge, South Dakota.

The Plains have a very special vast, dreamy calm about them. You can see weather systems from fifty miles away, storms moving slowly left or right, nearer, farther. The clouds have names like "Hammerhead" or "Table Top." The horizon is the only thing blocking your view. At the elementary school playground, we frolicked on the same seesaws and merry-go-rounds, the same twister slide Dan had played on as a youngster. It all felt idyllic in the moment.

But while being a multi-racial family in upstate New York was hard, it was harder in South Dakota. One afternoon, we parked on the campground across from the Black Hawk Indian Reservation and walked down to the river. The water was too low and the wind too high for swimming, so we walked to a playground with picnic tables and benches. Three or four families were picnicking, lots of kids playing and climbing on the jungle gym. Our children ran, tearing down the hill screaming, excited to play with their new friends. Dan and I walked slowly after them with our picnic fixings. By the time Dan and I arrived, the other families were packing up their lunches and putting little ones in strollers. We sat down on a bench as the mini-exodus began: strollers and coolers like a wagon train stretching up the hill and out of sight. Dan leaned over to me and said, "White flight."

Our kids didn't seem to notice. With five of them, they are their own play-date, their own party in a box. Still, we all felt relieved when we pulled up to our motel outside of Detroit. There were more African American kids in the pool than white kids. Ruby looked over at me, smiling and nodding as if to say, "finally."

21

RUBY

Skinny and scared, little Ruby had been a target growing up in the foster home. She'd laid low the first two years she lived with us—there were occasional aggressions towards the smaller kids, and some talking back now and then, but for the most part she was compliant. Then Ruby grew six inches in four months and wasn't little anymore. She was big, bigger than her siblings, bigger than me, and the biggest kid by far on the playground. It was payback time. Throwing her newly gained weight around, her behavior was bullying and intimidating, yelling at the tutors, "You're not the boss of me!" She was right. The tutors weren't the boss of her; I was. I would intervene, talk her down, get her in her room, and shut the door. But the aggression was escalating and with the other kids watching, how we handled Ruby's behavior would set the bar for the rest of our teenage-parenting career.

Ruby had a date playing cards with the residents at the assisted living center near our house as part of her community service unit for homeschool. During the session, the tutor called. "Ruby freaked out, she started screaming and stormed off, I tried to help her turn it around, nothing worked, I have no idea where she is . . ." The tutor was stressing out.

"No problem," I said, "you head home. I'm on it." I was taking Anthony to his swimming lesson. "Sorry, Pal," I said, turning the car around, "your sis is having a day." I found Ruby stomping down the bike path and stopped the car. I left Anthony in the car with his seat belt on and walked over to Ruby. She was agitated, throwing her arms around trying to wave me away. I said, "Hey, Babe. How're you doing?" She ran towards me, fists up, then stopped and shouted, "She disrespected me! Nobody gonna disrespect me! I don't take that shit from nobody!" I nodded to her, "Why don't you walk on home, Sweetie? We'll cool it down, and talk it through when we get back." She screamed, "You always take her side! You don't care about me! I want you out of my life! You're not my real mom, I HATE YOU!" I got her back to the house and in her room using my crisis line voice, calm and non-escalating. "We're having hamburgers for dinner, I'll call you down soon." I had to feed the other kids first and then clear the deck.

Dan was working late that night. I called him to debrief on the Ruby situation. "Maintain control of the house. Shut her down if she tries to bully or threaten." I fed the other kids then called up to Ruby, "Time to eat." She didn't answer. I went upstairs and knocked. She opened the door, still hostile, her eyebrows up near her hairline, baiting me. I said, "It's time to eat, Honey, and please answer me when I call you." She looked past me, "FINE!" then pushed me into the hallway, body-checking me with her shoulder. I was so not ready for that. *She's so strong!* I grabbed her forearms and forced her back into the room. She was screaming now: "Let go, let go, stop it!" as I yelled, "IT STOPS NOW!" She was crying and screaming, more shocked than combative. I let go of her arms, walked to the door, and shouted over her screaming, "STAY IN THIS ROOM! DOOR CLOSED!" I shut the door behind me and slid to the floor. My heart was pounding in my throat and my hands were shaking. That did not go well.

I could hear Ruby crying in her room. I called Dan and briefed him, speaking quietly, my eyes fixed on Ruby's door, fearful. He said, "I'm on my way."

Half an hour later, Dan came up the stairs and smiled at me, sitting on the floor in the hallway. He opened Ruby's door and addressed her softly, "Hey, what happened here?" Dan let her tell her side of the story, listening respectfully. When she was done, he said calmly, "You live in this house, Honey. This is your home. We love you and we want you here. You need to find a way to get along." He gently closed the door. I stood up and followed him down the hall towards our room. "You okay?" he asked. "I screwed it up," I said, shaking my head. He hugged me. "Don't worry. You'll have another chance. This isn't over."

The next day. I called a meeting with the tutors to lay out a protocol for dealing with Ruby. "If I am not here and she behaves in a threatening way, leave the room, go into another room, close the door, and call Dan. If he does not answer, call the police. If I am home, get the other kids out of the house and I will handle it. I hope I don't have to, but I will. We cannot allow her to intimidate, bully, or run this house. Show no fear."

That night I went over the details of "handling it" with Dan. He went over it with grim efficiency: "First, grab her arm, pull her forward and off balance, tangle up her feet and get her on the floor. Lay across her until she stops struggling, then ask her if she is ready and have her sit on a chair for twenty minutes. If she lands a punch, you have to shut her down." I felt sick. "Dan, I'm not trained." He said, "She's not going to expect it, especially from you." I lay in bed rehearsing the sequence over in my mind, left hand here, right hand there. "You'll be fine," he said, "but it's going to happen and it's going to be you. You

have to control the situation or it will send the wrong message."
Copy that.

* * *

Ruby had not liked the foster home. She was teased for having a stutter, was called "stupid" by the other kids, "dunce" by the foster mom, and everyone in the foster home had made fun of her for being held back in school. But Ruby wasn't stupid—not in the slightest. When she felt safe, it seemed Ruby could learn and retain information at a very high level. When we were still a family of four in the city, I met with her teacher to discuss the possibility that Ruby's learning disability was not cognitive.

Ruby and Jimmy had their own chalkboards and would play school in their room for hours on end, working with their make-believe students and disciplining them. I was the principal. We'd discuss the behavior issues of certain students at our faculty meetings. The kids were ruthless. They would send a student to the office for any disruptive behavior, including talking back. "How's everything going?" I would ask, poking my head in their door. They had laid out twelve short stacks of books in a circle on their rug. Ruby said, "Reading time." I nodded, "Do you mind if I sit in back and watch?" "Yes, that would be fine, Principal Fox."

After our move upstate, we had a weekly winter knitting session in our kitchen aptly named "Stitchin' in the Kitchen." The neighbors would come over, adults and kids. We met every Thursday night and everyone had a knitting name: Ruby was "Purl," Jason, "Slip," Susie "Loopy," and Jimmy named himself, "Mistah B-Knittin'!" One night the conversation turned to spelling. While we slipped and purled, Ruby confessed she always wanted to be in a spelling bee. "I can help her," said one of the tutors, "I used to spell competitively." Some of the neighbor kids also expressed interest, "We could meet in the basement!" Ruby was excited, "Please, Mom, please!" I said, "Hmm. We could call it, 'Speller in the Cellar.' If you can spell 'cellar' we will do it." I thought she'd spell it "seller." She thought a minute, "C-E-L-L-A-R. Cellar." *Wow*.

"How do you know that word, Honey? Did you have a cellar in the Bronx?" No. It was a basement. Hmm. I didn't use the word "cellar" at home and I was keeping pretty close track of what she was reading. Lucky? Curious, I tossed her some more words at random and she caught them all. The tutor said, "She's a natural speller!" The boost to her confidence was like an energy surge in the room. Ruby was spelling things Jimmy couldn't spell, spelling words that Jason hadn't heard of, words that she hadn't heard before, but could spell somehow. I was always looking for these rogue strengths we could build upon.

Within a month of Ruby's spelling victory, she failed a social studies test and tried to hide it from me. "I was afraid you would give me a punishment." I told her I would never be angry at her for failing, only for lying about it or trying to hide it. "I can't help you if I don't know what you are struggling with. This is difficult material, Sweetie! When you fail a test, it shows me is that you need more support."

I told her to stay in her room and correct the test: "I'll come check on you soon." Half an hour later, I stopped outside her door and listened. She was teaching her make-believe class. I knocked gently and stuck my head in. I used my principal voice, "Excuse me, Ms. Fox, am I interrupting?" Ruby stayed in character, "Not at all, please come in, Principal Fox." I sat on her bed in the back of the classroom while she went over the continents, countries, and capitals that had been on her social studies test. She had made lists with colored markers on her dry-erase board. She turned to me and said, "I'm playing school." I smiled, "I see. How are your students doing?" Ruby said seriously, "This is very difficult material. These children need a lot of support."

Basement?" Ruby was excited. "Please, Mom, please?" I said, "Hmm. We could all fit. Stella in the cellar. Bon Bon can sniff

When we first met Ruby, her behavior around adult males was consistently inappropriate. Actually, her behavior was entirely appropriate for a child who had been raised inappropriately. None of this was her fault, but we still had to deal with it. I did a lot of redirecting, "Hop down, Sweetie," I'd say. If her behavior escalated, "Come with me, Miss Ruby," I'd say gently, "let's take a minute."

One in four girls are sexually abused before they turn eighteen. My friends who had been sexually abused recognized her as one of their own, "That was me, I know that look." I couldn't be sure, I wasn't there. But I wished what was done had never happened or could be undone. I wished I could be her undoing.

We started working on her body confidence by playing catch, standing so close that I could reach out and place the softball in her mitt. As soon as the ball was in the air, she would look away to see if anyone was watching her. We shot baskets, swam, biked, and kicked the soccer ball around. Six months after moving upstate, Ruby announced, "Mom! Did you notice I don't walk like that anymore? All bent over? Remember when I used to walk like that?" She mimicked her former posture: birdlike and fearful, bent forward from the hips, shoulders hunching over, her beautiful little face tipped back, staring up and out, like a question mark.

"I did notice, Sweetie! How does it feel?"

"It feels good. I walk like regular now, you know, like normal kids."

I put my arm around her, "Yeah, except you're still so gorgeous. What are we going to do about that?"

Ruby laughed, "Mom!"

I was huggy and affectionate with her, holding her hand, providing piggyback rides, wrestling, snuggling, and putting my arm around her when we walked. Dan was not touchy at all.

He would wrestle with her, but only when the other kids were also in the dog pile, limbs flailing, child's play, non-sexual by association. Any approach she'd make towards him, he would turn into a joke, stiff-arming her, stepping back, or running away. No contact—just fun and love as she'd chase him around the house.

When issues came up, I would encourage her to talk about it and normalize the experience by sharing stories about my one in four friends, many of whom she knew. "It's not on you, babe. It shouldn't happen but it does." She always said nothing happened and I let it go. One time I brought it up and she started crying, "I know . . . I know . . . it's just . . . I don't know." She was flustered and angry. She started to cry and I put my arm around her, "Thanks for telling me that, Miss R. We can leave it for now unless you want to say any more." She shook her head.

"Do you want to play Crazy Eights?" I took out the cards and shuffled. "You deal." We played a few games and had some laughs. She was quiet a minute and then said, "Oh, Mom. All I can say is that there are too many men in this world." I smiled at her. "I hear that, girlfriend. Tell you what, Ruby. Until you are ready, I'm going to keep all those men away from you and keep you right here next to me." She softened and slumped back in her chair. She looked at me with those gorgeous, melty eyes and said quietly, relieved, "Thanks, Mom."

* * *

Although she was only twelve years old, Ruby looked more like sixteen. I upgraded her training bras to some fabulous striped and polka-dotted bras on the condition that no one would ever know how fabulous her new bras were. "Your underclothes are your business. If I can see them, I will take them." She left for school the next day all buttoned up, but came home that afternoon more bra than shirt. Without a trace of anger in my voice I said, "Up you go. You're showing me you are not ready." I told her to go to the bathroom and swap out her new bra for a sports bra. I emptied her drawers of the new bras and Ruby was not upset. In fact, she seemed relieved. I encouraged her sporty side for the time being, buying her hip sweatpants, athletic, but feminine, T-shirts. She went with it, no complaints. "Thanks, Mom."

In a parent meeting with Ruby's feeling doctor, the therapist shared some insights she'd gained: "Ruby has the emotional maturity of a nine- or ten-year-old child." Suddenly everything made sense. Of course! I had mistaken her size for maturity. Dan and I started talking to Ruby as if she were much younger, dressing her younger. We were not lowering, but rather, changing our expectations. She relaxed immediately, was more open and less defensive. I bought her stuffed animals, we played board games, and we went to the playground. I watched her play in the dirt with a yellow plastic shovel for hours, filling little pails and dumping them out. One afternoon Ruby told me, "I feel like I'm a little too old to be playing at a playground, but I really like it. I like the swings the best." I said, "You just keep swinging, Miss R, playgrounds are super fun."

She flew with me to Washington DC for work. Even sitting next to each other, people didn't assume we were traveling together. On the bus, the plane, and the metro, three different men tried to hit on her. "She's with me," I would say, smiling. "I'm her mother." One of them didn't take the hint. I stood up and addressed him, "I'm going to ask you to leave her alone." He looked surprised, "Sorry! I was just being friendly! I thought she might like some gum." I stared him down. He didn't move. I said softly, "Back it off." He turned and took his seat.

Ruby didn't say anything at the time, but she brought the incident up later when we got home, again and again, "And then you stood up and you told him to leave me alone." She loved this story.

I nodded. "I'm your mother, Ruby. I will deal with the men in this world until you are ready. Take your time, I got you."

22

SEE YA SUCKER

*T*he first time Jason "ran away" from home, he locked himself in the downstairs bathroom for over two hours. This was fine with me—he was contained, I knew where he was and didn't have to give him bathroom breaks. Other times, he would hide somewhere in the house, sometimes he'd run outside. But in every scenario, I had four other kids in the house, and it wasn't safe to leave them for a game of hide-and-seek with Jason. He always came back eventually, and usually sooner when I didn't give chase.

Once he ran in the middle of the day when he was the only child at home. I had gone up to his room to check on him and pick up his laundry basket when he bolted past me and took off down the hall. *Ugh, not in the mood.* He was in a lock-down grounding that needed enforcing, so I dropped the basket and ran after him. He heard me behind him as he tore down the stairs and yelled, "See ya, Sucker!"

Charlie started barking as my phone rang. It was Dan. I answered it on my way down the stairs. "He's running ..." Dan asked, "Do you know where he is?" I landed on the first floor, no kid in sight. "No idea." Dan said he would come by and sweep the house, "Watch the exit points until I arrive."

When he got home, Dan asked, "Could Jason have left the house?" We have three exits on the first floor. "Yes." I stood in the kitchen doorway, watching the front and back doors while Dan started in the basement. Three minutes later, Dan and Jason walked past me on their way up to the timeout room. Dan came into the kitchen and set the timer for ten minutes. "We just have to watch him." I was pissed. "That kid's making an ass of me and I'm bloody sick of it." Dan smiled, "He's just a boy. He's in a tough spot. Think about the world he's coming from. We just have to watch him."

*   *   *

In one of the books I had read on adoption of abused children, the author shared a story about a child who was up all night terrorizing the house. He could not be contained, and as the parents became sleep deprived, their decision making became impaired. They needed a break, a temporary solution while they worked on a permanent one. They put a bed for the child on the far side of their bedroom—which is probably a childcare violation—and then put their own bed against the door at night so he could not escape, which is definitely a fire department violation. If they were under investigation, they would have been shut down. They slept this way for two weeks, as they regained their brain function and were able to meet this child's needs in a more creative, productive way. Of course, the book forgot to mention what their creative, productive solution was. Was their method questionable? Yes. Was it illegal? Maybe. But the better question is was it more or less harmful for that child to sleep in his parents' bedroom for two weeks, or to be taken from that home and put who knows where?

BRRRRRING! I went upstairs to check on him. "How are you doing, buddy? Do you need to use the bathroom? You good?" I didn't open the door, he didn't answer but I could hear him moving around. I went back downstairs and set the timer for another ten minutes. If I could not control this child, someone else would. Someone else would restrain him, lock his door, strap him to his bed, medicate him till he wets himself, or maybe get sick of his big fat mouth and decide to teach him a lesson and back-hand him across the face. I was weighing Jason's freedom against the safety of our other children. He needed to get past some of his issues and we needed to supervise him until he did. *BRRRRRING*. Time to check on him again.

* * *

We grounded Jason to his room indefinitely, or "until he was ready." In addition to the tutor who lived on the third floor in the room next to him, I told Jason I would come check on him every forty minutes, whether he wanted me to or not. I accompanied his bathroom visits, standing in the open doorway with my back to him. He would make sudden jerking, fake-out moves, like he was going to run. There was no piano, no swim, no library, and no chess club. Meals were eaten on a timer and he had zero access to the other children. I would tuck him in at bedtime and put the tutor in the neighboring room on notice, then wake him the next morning. For two days straight he would not look me in the eye or speak to me. I woke him on the third day, the same as I always did, gently rubbing his back and whispering, "Jason? Jason? Let's get up, Buddy." He rolled over and looked at me, smiling. "Hi, Mom." *What?* I smiled back, "Hi, Jason. How did you sleep?" He yawned and stretched, "I slept well, thank you. I love you, Mom." *What the?!?!* "I love you, too, Sweetheart." I walked him to the bathroom and back to his room. "Mom, before you go, can I have a hug?" I said of course. I knelt down and we embraced, his head resting on my shoulder. Something had changed. His hug was neutral and boyish. Normal.

He was gentle, open even talkative. Over breakfast together he asked, "Mom? If you have time, I am ready for the second book in the Tolkien series, the third book in the Lemony Snicket series, and I am looking for a book about city planning. I have an idea for a new project." He never asked for his grounding to end, never asked for his privileges back.

"Mom? Can you bring me up some more scotch tape when you have a chance and also, could you get me a sewing tutor? I want to make a costume that is half human, half tiger." Jason thrived in his room. "Maybe he needed a break as well," Dan speculated, "Think about it. He's safe up there and he doesn't have to do his tough guy show for the other kids. He can just be himself."

* * *

Within a week, Jason was back down for piano practice, going to swim, taking his lessons and library trips. We reinstated his beloved "Cindy units," his weekly meeting with our neighbor, Cindy, for reading aloud and then "chatting," as Jason called it. Together they would talk about architecture, hybrid cars, and the looming worldwide, freshwater crisis, a particular concern of Jason's. He never saw his siblings except for Friday night movies or the rare unscripted, but supervised, passing in the kitchen.

During my visits to his room, Jason started opening up to me, telling me about the foster home, things he remembered from his biological home. He told me about his worries, things he had done, things he was ashamed of, things that haunted him. "I think something is wrong with me, Mom. When I see a little animal, I want to kill it. Squirrels, birds, frogs. I throw rocks at them." We talked and I asked questions. He He wanted to hurt the animals and he knew it was wrong. "Thanks for telling me, buddy. There's nothing wrong with you, Jason. Those impulses are there for a reason. We're going to talk this through with the feelings doctor and make a safety plan. You don't have to do this alone. I love you, Bud." He hugged me, "Thanks, Mom. I love you, too." I told Dan about the animal problem. "Control his access, give him no opportunity, no temptation. We need to stop this before it begins." Returning veterans with PTSD can have similar impulses; left unchecked, they can grow into violence against humans.

Dan and I discussed introducing a deity into Jason's life, a God or Christ figure. We had discussed practicing a religion at some point so the kids would know how to pray and worship, two very powerful coping mechanisms. I brought up God in conversation with Jason as it related to a history unit. After a week of studying different belief systems, Jason told me he thought God was talking to him through other people. "Like if I ask you to go outside and play and you say yes, I think that's God saying yes." I smiled, "Does that mean I'm God?" Jason said, "Mom! I'm serious!" I asked him what it would mean if I said no, that he couldn't go out and play. "Then that's you." *Wow.* Jason believed in a benevolent God! It didn't really fit his profile, but I was happy for him. I briefed Dan on our talk: "That's not going to work. We don't need a higher power trumping our authority. God speaking through you? Shut it down." Copy that.

Our goal was to reintegrate Jason back into the family, get him back to public school, and help him create as normal a life as he could manage. It was a long-term goal. Twenty minutes of being around his siblings, even supervised, he would become emboldened and obnoxious. We let Jason play softball with the family and ten minutes into the game he was screaming at Dan, "Go to hell!" Dan took him inside for a timeout. I checked in on them periodically over the next few hours, Jason screaming, "You want to fight with me, bitch? I'm taking you to the hospital! I'm going to kick your ass! Do you hear me, bitch? You want to fight? I'm ready!" Dan was giving him every opportunity for an out, "I never want to control your body. As soon as you're ready, I'll let you go." Jason's face was beet red, "Fuck you, bitch!" Rehabilitation takes time.

As summer came to a close and brightly colored lists of school supplies covered the refrigerator, Jason surprised me. "Mom," he said, "this was the best summer ever!" I told Dan later. "Can you believe that? Being grounded to his room was the best summer ever." Dan said, "Think about it. He could only make good choices, and he knew he would see you every forty minutes. You were predictable, safe, and consistent." I put my head down on the kitchen table. I was exhausted. Dan put his hand on my back. "Good work," he said. "Thanks," I said and started crying.

I had never had so much power and so little influence, so much responsibility and so little control or worked so hard with so little hope. I had never been happier in my life.

23

THE STATE OF THE UNION

*a*s word of our family made its way through the local schools and social services, other adoptive mothers would stop me in the hall or lobby and introduce themselves, "I heard you adopted five children through foster care. I don't know how you do it! My husband and I adopted two special-needs kids through foster care." They shared their experiences, stories about their kids, how hard it was. About five minutes into our conversation I would realize they were warning me about my marriage. "But we're not married anymore. I think it was just too much, you know, too much stress on the relationship." I paid attention.

After my first marriage failed, my sister told me, "Be the husband you always wanted and marry someone you like." So, I made a home for myself, paid attention to and supported the one person I had to live with for the rest of my life: me. I had been dependent as a child, codependent as a young adult, and was excelling at independence as a fully adult. Dan had been married before as well. Both of us knew how to live alone, neither of us had made a marriage work.

When dating, Dan introduced me to the concept of

"interdependence." This was a new one and Dan was pitching it as a viable model for our future together. It sounded good in theory but I had no idea what it looked like. "Tell me more." He talked about the mutual reliance through harsh winters of small town South Dakotans. He spoke of the Marine Corps, *esprit de corps*, stronger together than apart. I still couldn't see it. I had a pretty sweet setup, not a lot of needing going on, and I sure as hell wasn't moving to South Dakota. "So how do we get there?" Dan said, "We need to do something together, something that neither one of us could do alone." Now, I am not suggesting adopting five kids as a way of improving your relationship, but in our case, it brought us closer in ways I could not have imagined. When you are struggling to hold up half the sky and your partner is struggling with the other half, you let the little things go. Dan and I have bigger fish to fry. Five, actually. Piranhas, all of them.

Parenting these children had opened up a whole new world of emotions for me, not all of them life sustaining. For example, my children taught me firsthand about stress and what that can do your body. Before children, I thought I had a stressful job. I was so wrong. I was mistaking pressure for stress. Pressure is external, an expectation of doing well which I personally find exhilarating. My body may clench under pressure but once the pressure stops, I relax. Stress, on the other hand, is more like drinking a cup of bleach: even after the drinking has stopped, you still have that warm feeling inside of your organs dissolving.

Dan has a stressful job. I can see that now, I understand. Back then, when he would get stressed, I just thought he was being an asshole: moody, emotionally absent, chronically fatigued and irritated. He couldn't talk about his work which made it hard to tie his behavior to external events or stresses. It was on me to investigate his work post facto. I would read up on his cases after they had closed, pouring over harmless individual words describing his work that when put together were terrifying. Words like, "shallow" and "grave," "child" and "traffic," "human" and "remains." As a couple, our respective fields were the extremes on the spectrum of human behaviors: art music the pinnacle, crime the nadir.

There is no comparison between Dan's work and the work I do with the children at home, but I like to make one anyway. Like Dan, I follow strict protocols, stay level-headed and professional. As I enforce our consequences, I read them their rights as children: "You have the right to be respected! Anything you say will not be held against you by your mother who loves you no matter what! You have the right to be angry! You have the right to your feelings! You have the right to a consistent and loving parent!"

Like Dan, I am a target, the long arm of the law, taking names and keeping order. Unlike Dan, I can't wait for him to get home at the end of the day. I need a break. Coming in the door he asks, "How'd it go?" I tell him everything, every gory detail in bitter specificity, on and on, but enough about me, "How about you? How was your day?" He says, "Busy." That's it. A one-word bitch session. Dan doesn't get to go off. He too needs a break, but guess what? He's home now: same shit, new shift. Family man and fierce, in it to win it. It's a long haul. We tell jokes, go running, work out, make love— anything to keep ourselves cool and under control, always under control.

* * *

As a double-income, no-kids couple, Dan and I used to enjoy a good argument now and then, a little power struggle here and there. All that stopped when we got the kids. As parents, we fought twice, maybe three times, and each time was horrible. When I got overtired and depleted, I would look at

Dan and all I could see was someone I could rip on, someone strong enough to take it, the adult most likely to forgive. When Dan started looking at me the same way, it did not take much—a word, a look, or an off-handed remark—and we would combust.

We never ever engaged each other physically. He would win. Instead, both human, we'd circle the table slowly, teeth bared, then explode in a botulism of insults, profanities and sarcasm, undeserved and undeserving. We'd cannibalize each other, isometric losers, evil twins, nobody wins. He'd leave the house, the door behind him slamming. I'd observe a moment of silence before going to each child's room.

"Hey there, how are you doing?" I sit beside them, checking in, "Did you hear your Dad and me down there?" I wait for a little yes and make a tired smile. "Well, I'm here to tell you everything is okay. Are you okay?" I'd get a nod. "How did it make you feel to hear all that yelling?" Tiny answer, "Scared." Big arm around a little person, "I'll bet. It's scary when grown-ups yell. We just let ourselves get too tired. What did you think was going to happen?" Pause. "I don't know, maybe hitting." I say, "That would be super scary. Nope, no hitting in this house, just tired grown-ups." I wait, my silence drawing them out. "I thought maybe you were going to get a divorce." I shake my head, "No, no divorce. Your Dad and I really love each other, we are just very different." Finally a smile from the kid and, "That's for sure!" I laugh, "Okay, so you noticed? That's good. So, because we are different, sometimes we have different ideas about stuff, which is usually a good thing. Unless we are too tired. Then those differences make us frustrated. Are you going to be okay?" Smiles, nods, "Good. When you're in a family, stuff like this happens but we get through it and move on. It's hard to live with other people. Any worries? Questions?"

"What's for breakfast?" Nice—an easy one.

But even worse was the whispered fight: soft voices, searing words on open nerves, insinuation striking my ear like a hot mic in a feedback loop. I bite back my scream, my muscles seizing. It is the sound of one Ann snapping, this is the sound of me flipping my shit: dinner's dishes crashing to the floor, silver scraping in clang tone landings, cups and glasses pitch the walls, windows, everything ringing. I throw a chair, knock the pans off the stove, cranberry juice sprays from an airborne pitcher. Slaked and smiling, I leave the room. I have thrown the kitchen table on its side and don't even have the decency to leave the house. Thirty minutes later I return from the basement. The kitchen is clean, the walls are wiped, and the table is righted, but broken. Two clamps are holding it together.

We go about our business as if nothing has happened, our shoes make tiny *smooch, smooch* kissing sounds as we walk back and forth on a sticky cranberry film. We speak of everything but my melt-down. Days pass. I see him standing at the kitchen sink doing dishes. I walk over to him, my gaze low. I can't look him in the eye. I whisper, "I'm, uh . . . I'm sorry about . . ." He interrupts, "No, I'm sorry. I shouldn't have said what I did. You didn't deserve it." I smile, "Thanks, but I'm thinking maybe I could have handled it a little better . . ." He smiles, dries his hands. "Let's get out of here."

We went to the Monopole, a tiny cozy little wood paneled bar tucked in an alley off our main street. The kids were in bed, the tutor on call as we took the short drive through our sleepy town. Sometimes Dan would stop there for a beer after work with my blessing, so they knew him there. Before we had even sat down, someone had bought him a beer. A young man came over, "Someone would have been hurt if you hadn't broken it up the other night. You're the man." Dan said, "No problem." The guy left and Dan explained, "Stupid bar fight. Rolled into the alley." I hung my head. "Oh, Dan. I'm going to be nicer to you."

He sipped his beer. "It's okay, Ann. It's a stressful time. We'll get through it." Oh, Dan. "I love you, Dan."

* * *

A few years after our move, I played a concert in New York with a friend from college. I got home late and woke Dan up, "We had so much fun, just like old times. But our lives are so different now, we have nothing to talk about. All we have are the old times. I miss my friend." Dan said, "I'm sure she misses you, too. We're the ones who moved away, she didn't. We are isolating ourselves. We have to. We're building a cocoon."

The image was as terrifying as it was beautiful. I lay awake in the dark while Dan drifted back to sleep. He was right. We weren't breaking eggs to make an omelet: we were building a shell to put the broken eggs in. Dan breathed slowly, lying on his side, his massive back radiating heat. I reached my arm over his shoulder and found his hand. Silent tears ran down my nose and cheeks.

My love for this man is elemental, every atom exactly the same. Smashed to bits, hammered into endless shapes, my love cannot be reduced—there is no simpler substance. Above and beneath the compound clusters that frame my life; my atoms choose his, choose him. It is difficult for me to describe him, like something I know but have no words to say. My understanding of who he is lives in the quiet of my best and truest self, where words feel false and even music pales. It is easier for me to live my love than explain it, easier to take his name, give up my heart and gamble my life, "I'll see your good and raise you five."

A week later, I found Dan downstairs in the middle of the night listening to the country song "Little Black Pony" on the computer. He looked at me, eyes tearing, no tears. We listened together to the end of the song. Then he smiled and started it over, turned up the volume and, taking my hand, started two stepping me down the hall, through the living room, his eyes plotting our course, his mouth smiling his pleasure. He flew me backwards past Anthony's door, into the kitchen, a too tight turn, I didn't want the song to end.

24

LATE NIGHT THOUGHTS

I feel heavy, like I'm sinking into the bed. My arms are lead, my chest depressed beneath a metal plate. My legs are massive, like downed trees. I'm staring at the ceiling, sucking wind. Dan rolls over, "How're you doing?" I tell him I feel like shit. "It's hard to breathe." He asks me if I'm sick. I say I wish. "I don't know what the hell's wrong with me." He rolls back. "There is mass where lives intersect," he says. "Relationships have weight."

I have a lot of relationships. And they don't always work out. Our kids weren't the first foster kids that were placed with us. Our first match failed. It was our first call from an agency. We were told there were two sisters in an emergency situation, there was a problem with the foster mom and they needed the girls out and placed within three weeks. Normally the matching process takes about six to eight months, but emergencies happen, right? We met with the social worker and child psychiatrist to go over their history, and brought our advocate from the foster parent training class to ask the questions we might forget in our excitement.

Crystel and Yvonne, ages eight and ten, had no health issues, mental or physical. Amazing. Sure, Yvonne was diagnosed with ADHD, but who wasn't? We met the girls and fell in love. We met twice more and bought matching beds with green and pink covers: our first sleepover was a week later. The foster mom sent new pajamas with them, Yvonne's meds, teddy bears, and a note with her phone number, "just in case." I said to Dan, "This does not look like the handiwork of a negligent caregiver." We went to a sports store for a basketball and Yvonne started screaming and pulling stuff off the shelves, over-stimulated, running and throwing things. I led her outside and tried to calm her. Once home, we had lunch and gave Yvonne her medication.

Within minutes she was drooling, her head nodding forward. I asked Crystel if this was normal. "Yeah, she gets like that after her meds." As Yvonne's eyelids lowered to half-mast, Dan researched the medication online. I called my dad who confirmed I had given her the maximum dose of an adult anti-psychotic. "She'll be wiped out for a while. You gave her enough to kill a horse." We called the foster mom. She confirmed it was the correct dose and was surprised that we didn't know about the medication. "I think we should meet," she said, "I'd be very interested to learn what they have told you about these girls." Against agency policy, we met with the foster mom on the Manhattan side of the South Ferry Terminal.

The foster mom had a degree in childhood education and further training in early intervention. There had been some political turnover in the agency and she'd gotten on the wrong side of the wrong person; that was the emergency. Knowing full well they faced a family history of psychiatric issues, the foster mom had worked with the girls since Yvonne was a baby. The girls had two older brothers with mental health issues who had been placed separately, and were so heavily medicated, they wet themselves. The foster mom had chosen not to adopt the girls, "because one of them has repeatedly accused my fourteen-year-old son of sexual abuse." Her son was arrested, handcuffed and led from the house. The allegations were proved ungrounded, "but when I heard they were putting the girls in a home with a male, I thought you should know."

We requested access to the case files and a meeting with the agency as a condition of proceeding with the placement. They put Dan and me in a conference room with a stack of evaluations from teachers, social workers, doctors, and psychiatrists. The words were damning

". . . cannot be contained in the home . . ."

". . . strongly recommend placement in a residential treatment center . . ."

". . . exhibits familial pattern of disruptive behavior and unspecified mental illness . . ."

". . . multiple calls to 911 leading to the arrest of foster brother, unsubstantiated . . ."

The medication we had given Yvonne was for schizophrenia and bipolar disorder.

We met with six representatives from the agency and our advocate. Dan used the word "misrepresented," and the child psychiatrist countered with, "I think you heard what you wanted to hear." Our advocate said, "I was taking notes at the initial meeting. You said nothing about mental illness and there was no allusion to any disruptive behavior whatsoever." Voices were rising, fingers were pointing. The psychiatrist came back with, "Serequel is commonly used as an off-label sleeping aid." Our advocate responded, "If 400 milligrams of Serequel is required to help a child sleep, that should have been disclosed." The tone was getting defensive. I put my head in my hands and started crying. Dan said, "We're sorry. We will not be able to proceed with the placement. This meeting is over."

It was suddenly quiet but for my crying. The psychiatrist said, "It's not your fault." Dan helped me up and we left the room. A social worker from the agency followed us out, "Don't give up. There are more kids out there. I am thinking of a sibling group that might work . . ." A voice boomed from the conference room, authoritative and pissed off, "You're not at liberty to discuss individual cases with prospective parents." The social worker rolled her eyes. "Sorry. Don't give up!" Too late.

Oh, Crystel and Yvonne. What had we done? What did we do to those girls? Our advocate called this "bad case work"; we should not have been matched with them. We can point fingers, assign blame, say we didn't know. Nothing changes the fact that we met with these girls as pre-adoptive parents, talked with them about our future, promised them a future. It caused so many doubts about who I am and who we are as parents. Many tears about what we've done, I'm so sorry. So, so sorry. Oh God.

In foster care they say it is better to be abused than neglected, that it's better to stay in one home, even if it's bad, than to be bounced around from home to home. Worst of all is being placed for adoption, and having it not work out.

Mormons believe in a pre-existence where we, as spirits, choose the families we want to be born into on earth. I think it's great to take responsibility for your life, but really? When your earthly parents have free will and there's no script? Spirit children, Mormon or not, are of the responsibility of adults. We have the frontal lobe, we know right from wrong, and we can reason and plan ahead.

Mormons believe that humans can become gods and create our own worlds. But as parents, we're already gods in the eyes of a child. We create their worlds, the worlds they grow up in, are taken from, and adopted into.

Mormons don't believe in hell. The worst you can get in the afterlife is a place called "outer-darkness," a realm devoid of love, far away from the presence of God. Outer-darkness is reserved for people who have known love and then betrayed it.

25

BIO MOM

*I*n the adoption sub-culture, "Bio mom" or "Biological mom" is another name for "birth mother." Makes sense. But let's be clear. I don't care what kind of mom you are, part of raising children is dealing with the anatomy, physiology, behavior, and vital processes of your living organisms. As an adoptive mom, I'm as bio as the next.

* * *

At the start of our third year together, Jimmy had started acting strange. His teachers and coaches concurred. "He seems out of it." They described him as "spacey," and "not with it." I crunched the data: *what had changed?* I went through his backpack with him when he got home, followed him at school, and went through his locker for clues. Nothing. I woke with a start in the middle of the night with a possible answer. "Dan! I bet Jimmy's whacking off. He's twelve and he's big for his age. It's entirely possible." Dan said, "Could be." I offered, "Is this a man-to-man, or do you want me to take it?" Dan said sleepily, "Take it." My dad was professor of anatomy and physiology so I knew how things worked. I had also been playing in the brass section since fourth grade band, so I knew what things were called.

The next day, I took a deck of cards to Jimmy's room, "Hey buddy, I'm going to teach you how to play Crazy Eights." I figured if we had an engaging parallel activity, we could easily change the subject if he felt uncomfortable. Jimmy was excited—with four other kids, we never had enough time together. "I'll shuffle, you deal."

I taught him the rules and then went for it. "Do you know what the strongest drive in the human body is? The thing humans need more than anything else?" He thought about it, "Air?" I played a card. "Good guess, but breathing is a reflex. I'm talking about a drive, an action we have control over. Diamonds." He shrugged and drew. I answered for him. "Thirst. If you are thirsty, you are driven to find water at the expense of all your other needs. Hearts. A human will die without water; the thirst drive is a survival mechanism for individuals. The second strongest drive in humans is a survival mechanism for the human race, it keeps the species alive. Any ideas? Diamonds." Jimmy drew some cards and shrugged. I said, "The sex drive, the drive to reproduce. Without it, humans would have no children and the species would die out. Spades. So the body grows and then when you get big enough— not necessarily old enough—you wake up one day and you're all hairy and stinky and the same girls that were giving you cooties, or boys that were chasing and teasing you, are suddenly looking good. Like, 'I want that.'" Jimmy looked up and smiled.

"You gettin' hairy?" Jimmy grimaced and nodded. I go on: "Hairy, stinky, voice drops . . . these are called secondary sex characteristics. Let's name them for boys: testicles get big . . ." Jimmy announces, "I have testicles." He smiles. "That's good, Jimmy. Next, penis. You wake up one morning and it's not just bigger, it is big. What are the names for that? Erection, wood, hard-on, you name some . . ." Jimmy said, "Boner?" I nod, "Good call." We play for a little while.

"Now Jimmy, this is all good. That penis can help keep the human race going. You may have had a hard-on already, maybe not. You don't have to tell me, it's not my business. The problem is the human body is able to reproduce before the brain is ready to be a parent and make good choices. And as your mother, that lag time is my business." He replies, "Spades." I draw.

"Jimmy, the sex drive is like the thirst drive; it's strong, but voluntary. You have a choice about what you drink and you have a choice about where you put your privates, and some places are better than others. Until you are ready, I'm going to suggest you keep matters well in hand. Do you understand what I am saying?" He looks at me and shakes his head no.

"If you have sex with someone before you both are ready, you can have all kinds of issues: medical, emotional, diseases, babies. So you're going to have to deal with it yourself for a while." Jimmy looked at me inquisitively, "I don't know what you mean." *He's playing dumb. He's testing you.* So what? Whether he knows or not, he knows I'm down to talk about anything. *Proceed.* "J, you are a smart young man. What do you do if you have an itch?" He says, "Scratch it." I smile. "It's like that. Instinct. You'll know what to do."

Jimmy asked, "How does it feel?" I told him the truth. "Jimmy, it feels great. That's one reason people do it." He said, "Does this mean I'll stop wetting the bed?" I pause. "Maybe, but something else comes out which is also wet. It's the stuff the sperm are swimming in: cum, wad, jizz. Do you know any?" Jimmy smiles, "Uh, semen?" I laugh. "You got it. So are we playing cards or what? Hearts." We kept playing. "Any questions?" Nope. Diamonds. I play a diamond and Jimmy goes out. "Mom, I won." *Oh, I hope so.*

* * *

Before Ruby's twelfth birthday, I gave her some options for

discussing puberty. "So, normally a mother and a daughter sit down, and the mother talks about really embarrassing things, and the daughter feels really uncomfortable and completely weirded out. Or, if you want we can make a list of all the girls and women you like that have started their periods, go out for ice cream, and have everyone tell you their most embarrassing moments during puberty." She picked the latter option.

We made a list: Aunt Marie, cousin Lucy, neighbor moms and daughters. Soon the women gathered around a big table at the ice cream place. We had a great time, everyone laughing, sharing our stories, how old, how awkward, where were we. We put plans in place: "What if you're at school? Who are you going to tell?" We talked over what to expect: cramping, mood swings, feminine supplies, and their failings. Ruby, the center of attention, sat quietly and smiling the whole time. Any questions? She shook her head, still smiling.

A few months later, the big day arrived. Ruby gave me the secret coded wink and nod, and we excused ourselves. It was a rough few days and messy, but we got through it together. *Phew.* "And don't worry, Babe. We'll work on our containment skills next time." She stared at me. "What do you mean next time?" I tipped my head, "The next time you get your period, Sweetie." She smiled, relieved. "It's okay, Mom. I'm all done. It stopped." *What? How did she miss that?* I didn't know if I should laugh or cry.

"Ruby, you better sit down. It's over for this month, but it's going to happen again next month. And again and again, every month." Her jaw hit the floor. "Ruby, I still have a period every month. It lasts until you're around fifty." Disbelief, "You?" I nodded. "Yes, me. Most women. I'm sorry, Lovey. It's just the way it is." She was in shock. I sat with her a minute. "I'll check on you later." I smiled in empathy as I stood up to leave. "Every month?" Ruby cried out mournfully as I walked down the hall. "Sorry, Sweetie," I said walking away, "God was a man. It can't be helped."

26

OPPOSITE HOUSE

*M*y friend Nina from the matching meetings in Manhattan had adopted an eight-year-old boy from Georgia about the same time that Jimmy and Ruby moved in with us. We all got together that first Christmas, our new little families, played basketball, and went out to the neighborhood diner. Brendon had been bumped around a lot in foster care, placed for adoption a few times, only to have it not work out. When Nina got him, he was in a residential treatment home, the place for children who cannot be contained in a private home.

After we moved upstate, Nina and I kept in touch, checking in with each other and comparing notes. When a whole month went by and she didn't return my calls, I figured either something really good or really bad was happening. When she finally called, I could hear her manically laughing on the phone, even before I said hello. "Ha ha, I just dropped Brendon off at the hospital, where he's starting school. I am sitting in my car in the parking lot. This is the first time in thirty days that I am alone!"

She gave me the rundown: kicked out of two different therapeutic schools, ran away twice, and pulled a kitchen knife on her. "I took him to a baseball game, turned to buy a hot dog for him, turn back to hand it to him and he's walking down the stadium stairs holding the hand of a total stranger. Can you believe that? He told the man that his mother had run away."

Brendon told the social worker three different times he wanted to kill himself, "just to piss me off, because he knows I'll have to spend the next seven hours with him in the emergency room waiting for another psych eval!" He had smashed a glass coffee table, had to be restrained by a police officer in the park. "It's too much."

I could hear the exhaustion in Nina's voice. I said, "Girl, you need a break." She said, "This is my break! He's living at the hospital for now and I hope it works. I'll have dinner with him every night and bring him home on the weekends but for now, they've got him. They're the professionals. I can't keep going like this. Who would have thought sixty-five pounds could turn my life completely upside down? I just wanted to share my life with someone. But this. This is too much." We stopped laughing and were quiet for a minute. I felt for her. Then I felt for Brendon and wanted to cry. "You're saving that boy's life, Nina, you're a hero." She laughed, "One kid is nothing—you've got five!" Not true. "You're a single mom. You never get a break. I'd take twenty with Dan before I'd take one by myself." She laughed, "Yeah, you're right." *Don't take twenty.* "Part of the problem is," she said, "I can't talk to anyone about this. If I tell my friends that Brendon ran off, they think I'm a bad mother! They tell me he just needs love, they give me advice, tell me to how to parent him. Really? Like I haven't tried everything in this whole damn world? Who understands what I am going through?" I did. I understood exactly what she was going through.

*   *   *

Parenting special-needs kids is not always normal or intuitive.

Without a backstory or context, our parenting can look extreme, unkind, even inappropriate. For example, in a therapeutic home—which ours is—you don't use a soothing voice to soothe an abused child. It can sound like the voice of choice of a sexual abuser, and can trigger more anxiety in the child. Studies say that yelling at a child can be as damaging as hitting. I believe it. But when dealing with abused children, studies say that if you don't lose your shit and yell from time to time, the child's anxiety and bad behavior will increase as they wait for you to beat them. Some recommend yelling for about sixty seconds—"Unacceptable! This stops right now! You may not hit in this house! You may not call names or threaten"—then immediately repair the relationship in a normal voice, and move on. Then the child learns, *Okay, that's what happens when this adult loses it.* If you never get mad, they keep waiting anxiously for the belt or the back of your hand.

No one wants to see a child being restrained. Guess what? No one wants to restrain a child. If they do, that's another problem. I understand why people feel they must say something, but when I have a child in a non-escalating restraint, that child is taking my full attention; criticism from onlookers enters my consciousness like tiny rocks being thrown at a sheet of aluminum foil. Critics say, "There has to be a better way!" That may be true, but when a chair has been thrown by a child at another child, I follow the protocol laid out to me by the professionals in the field, and I stop the behavior.

People want to feel sorry for our kids, be sweet to them, and explain their behavior to me. Explaining is the easy part, and pity the last thing our kids need. We're trying to correct behavior and teach them coping mechanisms that will allow them to function in the world. My friends cringe and turn away when I hold a screaming child down on the floor, speak harshly or take privileges away from underprivileged kids. We had one tutor, a biology major, who defended me to a critical friend, a nurse by profession, who was upset to see me restraining a child. She said, "Stop! You cannot treat a child like this!" The tutor said, "How is this any different than you restraining a patient who is pulling out his IVs or tearing out his stitches? Ann is making a choice for him because he is a danger to himself and others." The guest persisted, "Screaming and talking back is not a danger." The tutor said, "It will be if she lets it escalate. He will become violent. We work with these children every day. We're doing what's best for them."

* * *

Our tutors are amazing. They have authority to count the kids to three and put them in timeout. If the child resists, they call me. Dan and I are the only ones who restrain them. We have tutor meetings every week or so, after the kids were asleep. We order Indian food, close the kitchen doors, and debrief. One of the tutors confided, "I think I'm losing it. I counted a guy at the bar the other night." Another tutor laughed, "It worked, right?" Yep. "I only got to two and he backed off." I heard some of the early tutors were forming a Fox family tutor survivor support group to help in their recovery. The experience is too different, no one else can understand.

It's easy to feel isolated. The tutors, Dan, the dog, and me share a different reality. Our neighbors say time is flying by while the clocks in our house tick backwards, hours grinding by like sand in your molars, days passing like kidney stones. "It's only 4? It feels like midnight!" We are the land that time forgot. The neighbors say, "Can you believe it's already been two years since your family moved here? It feels like yesterday!" Are you kidding. It feels like thirty years. Outside our house, time is relative. In our house, time is a relative that comes to visit and never leaves.

Our neighbor's children are learning to drive while our kids are gunning in reverse, tires peeling, rubber burning as we push them forward in a cloud of smoke and fumes. Our neighbors teach their children not to judge a book by its cover. In our house, we couldn't judge if we tried because Anthony has torn all the book covers off. In most households, blood is thicker than water. Maybe so. I can say for sure it's harder to clean up.

In our house love is thicker than blood. In our house, the children grow in reverse, from autonomy into dependence, from differentiation into attachment. Little cynics now longing for Santa, street-smart urchins looking for snuggles, deconstructing, reconstructing, reforming their formative years. Sing to me! Read to me! Watch me, Mom! Love me! They are twenty year olds in ten-year-old bodies, five year olds in twelve-year-old bodies, at once sophisticated and immature. We race to catch up intellectually and behaviorally. We brake to catch up spiritually and emotionally.

27

AUDREY

*W*e were going on two years as a family and still needed help. At first it looked like we were following the cycle of a natural disaster: first responders rushing to the scene, followed by rescue teams, then the aid workers and the construction crews. Only our disaster never stopped. We just kept erupting, spewing lava, chucking and heaving with no sign of slowing. Technically we were no longer a family in crisis because a crisis, by definition, resolves. If a crisis never resolves, you have to call it something else.

There is a popular saying in the adoption subculture: "When a child is adopted, a mother is born." I would like to add: "When five, high-risk children are adopted, an institution is born." It was hard to accept that we still needed help but harder still to find the help that we needed. We'd exhausted our friends and relatives, the friends of our relatives, and the relatives of our friends. We were alone and outnumbered. I was terrified. When Dan was traveling, I timed my showers during the REM phase of the children's sleep. I was taking no chances. Any disruption or break in our rhythm could spawn an algae bloom of bad behavior. Charlie lay awake with me at night, ears up in solidarity.

When searching for hired help, I labored over a job description that was honest but not off-putting, a tall order as there are only so many ways one can say "five kids." We joined online childcare websites, advertised on Craigslist and social media, and put flyers up at the YMCA and colleges. Working with our family was a great calling, but a shitty job. We got one response from a junior at Penn State. Her name was Audrey. "I am very interested in your ad. I have a lot experience working with children and feel I have something to bring to your situation having spent time in foster care myself as a child."

Interesting. Dan and I agreed the foster care factor had potential for good, but an even greater potential for bad. Audrey came to the house for an interview. We talked for three hours out on the porch, while our kids rode back and forth on their bikes. She was like no one I had ever met before. When she left, I looked at Dan, "Who *was* that?" He nodded. I waited five minutes before texting her, "When can you start?" Audrey texted back, "I've already written up a schedule."

* * *

The kids loved her. She was fun, easy-going, and a total hard ass when need be. Jason tried to argue with her about his research project on architecture in Dubai. I heard Audrey say softly, "You know, Buddy, life is going to be a lot easier for you if you can stay relaxed instead of getting so angry." Jason raised his voice, "Oh yeah? Well, I had a hard childhood!" She whispered, "So did I. Go to your room." He went. She had street cred. She could empathize. If a new behavior problem caught me off guard, she'd take me aside, "I did that, too. Try this . . ."

Three days after she moved in, I woke Dan in the middle of the night, manically worried. "What the hell? She has no parents! She has no safety net, no health insurance, and no place to put her crap, Life doesn't get easier when you graduate college," Dan rolled over, "New York is one of nine states which allows for the adoption of an adult." I bolted up, incredulous. "How long have you been thinking about this? She's only been here three days." Dan went on, "She could get on our health insurance until she's twenty-six."

I laughed, "Awesome! Let's do it!" Dan slowed me down, "She may not want to. She's self-made. We have to be careful about how we approach this." I asked him what he meant exactly. "First, she has to get used to us. It could take a month." *How does he know all this?* "Then she needs to tell us her story. That's the most important thing. For now, we wait."

I waited. And watched. Audrey was a scanner, reading the room, running contingencies. As a tutor she was amazing, always one step ahead of me. Dan was traveling a lot that summer. After the kids were in bed, Audrey and I would play Scrabble at the kitchen table. One night I broke out a bar of dark chocolate to share. Audrey said, "I don't like dark chocolate." I smiled, towing the line, "They say dark chocolate over 72 percent has medicinal properties." Audrey nodded, "I think you prefer milk chocolate, too. You just tell yourself you like dark chocolate because it's good for you." Did I mention she was perceptive? "You're right," I said.

This was our third summer as a family, and the kids were doing well, memorizing poems, practicing piano, working on their secondary instruments, singing and writing songs. We held a poetry slam in our living room with Susie as master of ceremonies. She stood in front of the neighborhood crowd and said, "We'd like to welcome you to our first poetry slam of the summer." My eyebrows shot up. *The first?* I looked over at Audrey and she smiled back. Indeed, it was the first of many.

Then one night, Audrey and I were in the kitchen making sushi, while Dan was sitting at the computer. "Hey Audrey, come check this out." Audrey came out and sat beside him. He had satellite pictures of his hometown in South Dakota on the screen. He zoomed in on his elementary school, the house he grew up in, "Trinity Lutheran Church . . . Missouri River . . . there's the bridge the town is named after." Zoom. "That was my Dad's airplane hangar."

He said, "Did you say you grew up in Western Pennsylvania?" I listened from the kitchen. He pulled up her neighborhood from when she was six, rural threads of lonely roads hemming through fields and fields, "Wait, turn here . . . I think that was the house, they had a circular driveway. Wait. That's not right." It was happening. I came out from the kitchen and stood behind them. "I remember there was an old school bus in the woods . . ." Dan found a rectangular outline beneath some trees just off the property. "Is that it?" She said, "Wow, I wouldn't have even seen that." Silence. "Wait, go back, go back. See that road there? Yeah, down that road." I stood listening, eyes tearing for the beauty of it, while Audrey told us her story.

At two years old, Audrey was taken from her alcoholic mother and put into foster care. For eight years, she floated through the system, quietly moving from home to home, some of them better than others, some as bad as they get. She was sickly and thin, a blessing in disguise, as the foster dad pitied her over the healthy girl in the basement. Audrey was bright and loved learning, excelled in school though she hated to go— her foster parents made her wear sweatpants two sizes too big, as if her classmates weren't staring already. She asked for a pair that fit and was denied and told to be grateful. For what and to whom?

When she was ten, her grandmother came forward and claimed her. But four years later, Grandma's boyfriend kicked her out; Grandma was sorry but there was nothing to do but cry. The state sent Audrey back to her mom, who was following the path of addicts, going from drinking, to painkillers, to meth. She would beat her daughter to break her fall, so Audrey withdrew from her mother's withdrawal, stayed in her room, and locked the door. She fought her way through it and stayed in school. God bless that girl who wanted more.

* * *

It was a sticky afternoon, the air moist and heavy. A high-pitched insect drone hung in the air. Dan stopped me in the kitchen. "It's time." Audrey had been with us for a month. He put a movie on for the kids while I found Audrey. "Do you have a minute? Dan and I want to talk to you."

She followed us to the porch, looking concerned. Dan began, his voice cracking slightly. "First., we'd like to say how wonderful it is having you here. It's been great . . ." Audrey cut him off, "Am I being fired?" Dan shook his head, "No, no, it's nothing like that. Um, well . . ."

Dan looked at me and I jumped in, my voice shaky, almost shy, "Audrey, we'd like to be your parents." Her eyes went wide. "We know you may not need parents or even want parents, but if you ever do, we would like to be your parents." She was shocked, "Are you serious?" Dan nodded, "Yes, we've thought about it a lot and you don't have to say yes and you never have to say no, but you will always have a home here." Audrey started crying and nodding, "Yes!" she said, "Yes! Yes!" Her hands fanned reflexively at the air in front of her eyes that were swelling with tears. "You can think about it," Dan said, "this can be as much or as little of a family as you want but we are ready to do this." Audrey, crying and nodding said, "Yes . . ." her hands were still fanning and wiping at her tears, "This is what I always wanted."

She cried while we talked her through the legalities, hugged her as she tried to pull it together, "Thank you, thank you." I said, "No, thank you, Audrey. This way we can say that at least one of our children went to college." We all laughed.

Audrey went inside to get a sweater, I slipped around the porch, out of sight, and stopped myself from crying. This was her moment, not mine. She was an adult, of course, but we were adopting a whole person, a whole life, including the child that had always wanted this. I wanted to be a screen for her, neutral and still, onto which she could project while she sorted all of this out.

The next day I stayed with the kids while Dan and Audrey went to see the lawyer. Audrey was visibly subdued when they returned, pensive and quiet. I looked at Dan. "How did it go?" which was code for, "How much is this going to cost?" In the land of adoption, legal parenting can run you anything from completely free, as in adoption through the foster-care system, to tens of thousands of dollars for a domestic or foreign adoption. Once a parent has decided on a child, or in this case an adult, there are no deal breakers, but financial planning is often necessary. Dan smiled, "Seven hundred dollars!" I was shocked, "Wow, that's all? Incredible! I was getting 10,000 together, just in case." Audrey looked up at me, touched. I winked at her, "Whatever it takes."

I checked in on Audrey before going to bed. It had been a big day and she was quieter than usual. I knocked on her door and she invited me in. "Hey, I wanted to see how you're doing." She started crying.

"Oh, Audrey," I said, "this has got to be so weird. I'm surprised you're not more freaked out than you are. Super scary, super weird." She nodded. "Do you want to talk it through? Is there anything specific? Any questions?" No questions, just tears.

"It's going to be okay, Audrey, I know this is crazy. If you want to back it off, take some time, there's no rush. You can change your mind, change it back, we're always going be here. No pressure." Audrey shook her head, "It's not that. I am afraid you guys are going to change your mind."

I down sat next to her and took her hand. "We would never change our minds. We would never jerk you around, I promise." Audrey was still crying.

I put my arm around her. "Audrey, you don't have to trust us. We trust ourselves enough for everybody. We know exactly what we are doing, and we would never suggest anything like this unless we were absolutely sure." Audrey started to calm down. I stroked her hair with my hand.

Audrey spoke. "When I look ahead, I feel fine. I'm excited. It's just looking back. That's when I get scared." I nodded and stopped talking. Audrey spoke at length. She spoke about looking back and all the things that had happened to her. When she was done, I hugged her. "Thanks for telling me, Audrey. I didn't know. I understand now. This whole trust thing takes time, but as a family, we have time, we have our whole lives. Just stick with us, give us a chance." She smiled. "Okay."

She's amazing. *Yes, she is. But she's not twenty-three.* She's fourteen and thirty-five at the same time. It's not always clear which is which.

* * *

When an adult child is adopted, a middle-aged mother is born. In the instant that Audrey agreed to be my daughter, I became forty-five. This was not a bad thing and I only mention it because up until then, my perception of my own age had always been pretty fluid. Music is a non-linear field; talent transcends chronology. Before moving upstate, my two best buds in my band were sixty-five and nineteen; I knew I fell somewhere in the middle, age-wise, but exactly where was neither relevant nor interesting. I called my friend Sue, also teaching performance at the college level. I asked her if as a teacher she sometimes forgot she was old enough to be the mother of her students. "Oh yeah, totally," she said. I broke the news. "We're adopting a twenty-three year old. I am going to have a twenty-three year old daughter." Silence. "Wow," said Sue, "I see what you mean."

Audrey and I met Dan at the lawyer's office to fill out our petition for adoption including a name change, legal affiliation, severing of legal ties with biological parents, etc. Audrey was nervous. Of course she was. This was her choice, but it was a huge choice nevertheless. She would receive a new birth certificate with her new name on it. It would list the original place and time of her birth, but Dan and I would be listed as her biological parents. In the eyes of the law, it would be as if she had always been our child. Dan gave Audrey a hug, "Welcome to the family . . . such as it is." We all started laughing and then couldn't stop.

Audrey was adopted the day before Thanksgiving. Uncle John came up from New York City and we all got dressed up in our new clothes. The judge spoke to us briefly and thanked us for providing one of the few happy proceedings he was required to perform as a judge in family court. "Adult adoptions are unusual, but most have a very sweet story behind them. I don't know your story, but I see that it is sweet."

The kids were ecstatic; they loved their new big sister, and the new addition made them greedy for even more, "Can we adopt Tommy? Can we adopt Kelsey?" I had to break it to them that our other tutors already had families. "You can't adopt someone who has parents."

Dan and I got an email from Audrey, who was back at college that month, thanking us for adopting her. "My stress level has dropped 1,000 percent." I gave Dan a high five. Finally! We'd been able to give something to someone and have them receive it, happy even!

Over one of the breaks, Audrey told me she wished we could have adopted her when she was younger, "but in a way, I'm glad you didn't know me then. I would have terrorized you." I had no doubt. I laughed, "It's a hard time for our kids, we get it, but they're all going to grow up and leave, get their own lives going ..."

Audrey looked at me seriously, "They're not going to leave. People are nice here, the food is good. Why would they leave?" I swallowed hard. "Don't say that." Audrey said, "It's true." *Holy shit.* I said, "But you're leaving, right?" Audrey laughed, "You think I'd stay here with these crazy kids? I mean, it's fine now, but what about when they're teenagers?"

I didn't go out of my way to tell people about adopting Audrey; the five kid thing was already so over the top. People either assumed Audrey was my biological daughter, or they had a lot of questions. "So, is she going to call you Mom? How does that work?" *No idea.* A young friend asked me, "What happens if after a few years, it turns out you don't like her?" Fact: mothers and daughters don't have to like each other. An older friend asked, "So you adopted her to help you take care of the younger kids?" I shook my head, "Oh, no. Audrey's got big plans. I don't know what her plans are but no, she's not living with us." My friend looked confused. "I don't get it.

* * *

Audrey came home for her first summer after college. Her room was next to ours, and I could tell she was struggling. There was stress in the way she moved, the way she spoke. I could feel it. I told Dan, "Something's wrong. I want to go knock on her door and ask her what the fuck is going on." Dan said no, "You can't do that. She's a grown-up." So what? My mom would have done it, barged in on me like that. *Yeah, and how's that working out for you? She drives you crazy.* It's what loving moms do.

But I deferred to Dan. He said, "It's a rough patch, she'll get through it. We just have to wait it out and let her come to you. We'll survive."

I drove Audrey down to New York City at the end of the summer to help her move into our old apartment in Hell's Kitchen. I was hoping the one-on-one road trip might break the tension. I reached out, "How are you doing, Audrey?" We weren't even two miles from the house and she told me everything: every worry, stress, trust issue, and twisted take on what had been happening with her. "Oh, girl, I wish I'd known. I am so sorry you had to go through that alone." Audrey said, "I wanted to tell you but I just couldn't. I was afraid." She hadn't felt comfortable talking to me. *You need to work on that.*

"Oh, Audrey," I said, "I knew something wasn't right. I kept wanting to barge into your room and say, 'What the fuck is going on?'" She stared at me. "You did? You wanted to say that? Because that's I wanted! I was waiting for you." I looked over at her then and quickly back to the road.

"I'm so sorry, I've never done anything like this before. We need to get to know each other. Don't give up on me, Audrey. Promise me you won't give up on me."

We were quiet for a minute before I asked her, "How'd you do it, Audrey? How did you survive all that and turn out so great?" She had an answer, as I knew she would. When she was eleven she asked a friend to go play with her on a pile of broken concrete from a demolished overpass. Her friend said she couldn't, that her mom wouldn't let her. Audrey asked why not and the friend said, "Because my mom cares about me." That's what mothers do who care about their children. They protect them, set limits. Audrey realized she would have to do that for herself.

* * *

I worry that Audrey is going to wander off. She's not like the younger ones. There is nothing I can do for her. I can't chase, snuggle, or ground her to her room. She has to come to me, and I don't know if she will. She may even want to and not know how. I tell myself, *She's smart, she'll figure it out*. But trust is no more a function of intelligence than happiness is. I leave the Scrabble out on the kitchen table. She needs to attach. "Scrabble. How about a game?" I need time to wear her down. If Audrey could trust me, she could argue with me, sharpen her claws and define herself. A strong middle-aged woman is a great asset to a young woman. It's a mother who will never leave you, a teacher or mentor who understands you, forgives your youthful hubris and directs your vitriol as part of your learning.

Sometimes Audrey leaves the Scrabble board out on her table in New York. We talk while we play, about nothing at all, about flossing or that English major who had interesting, if not attractive qualities, student loans and payment options. A lot of people think Scrabble is a word game. It's not. Scrabble is about points. People who are loyal to words, even good and important words, lose at Scrabble. A word like "trust," for example, is not rewarded in Scrabble. It's a five letter word, no counters. I would skip it, save the "s" for the big money. But in the game of life, trust is why I'm playing Scrabble. Trust is what I'm hoping to win at this kitchen table, with this benign conversation, this fussing with the tiles and scribbling scores on the backs of envelopes. But it's not enough. I need longer games and a bigger board.

28

MORTAL COIL

*D*riving down I-87, Jason was stewing in the passenger seat. We'd overheard the doctors talking to each other in the elevator about a cancer patient. Jason said, "Some people die from cancer." I said, "Yes. Some people do." He paused. "Mom? Am I going to die from . . . you know . . . this?" He pointed to his legs, poking his quads with his index fingers. I glanced over at him and then trained my eyes back on the road. "It's hard to say, Jason. Hard to say."

I wasn't lying. It was very hard to say, "Yes, you are going to die," to an eleven-year-old boy. "You're going to die young, and immobile at the very moment that your life becomes truly yours and you should be falling in love, getting laid, and reaching out for what you want in this life and making it yours." That is impossible to say. Most of the time, it was easier to just pretend that it didn't exist.

The social workers told us before placement that Jason had multiple sclerosis. We researched it, grieved it, came to terms with it, and committed to seeing him through it. Multiple sclerosis is horrible and, like every illness, worse in children. A few weeks later, the social worker called back, "I know I told you guys it was multiple sclerosis, but it's not. It's Duchenne muscular dystrophy. I always get those mixed up, sorry about that." *Interesting.* "Okay, well, thanks for calling." We researched Duchenne muscular dystrophy. I groaned, sickened. An insidious disease: assisted walking at eight to ten years, wheelchair at twelve, and mortality at twenty to twenty-five. The wasting begins in the legs and pelvic region, then arms and neck, and then general loss of muscle mass, resulting in paralysis. Most patients die of respiratory failure. If they can maintain lung function, the heart is next and last. Eyes moist, Dan shook his head, "It's a kick in the gut." I started crying.

As soon as we moved upstate, we took Jason to the pediatric neurologist and pulmonary cardiologist who would be tracking his illness. They did a battery of tests to establish his "baseline." I still couldn't really believe it, he seemed so healthy. "And you're pretty sure he has it?" The neurologist stared at me. I explained, "There was some confusion when we got him. I was just hoping there might be a mistake, you know, maybe a misdiagnosis. He seems so healthy." The doctor lowered his head, the bearer of bad news. "Jason has a moderate case of Duchenne's. He will follow the average trajectory."

We researched clinical trials, looked for breaking news in the journals and online forums. We had friends scouring the internet and sending us links. Jason was either too advanced or too old to qualify. He couldn't be helped. Even if the answer came today, it was too late. We got on muscular dystrophy parenting sites for advice on how to stay positive, how to keep the hope alive. Most kids give up once they get in the wheelchair and realize they are never getting back out. I asked the doctors, "What should I do?" They told me to watch for signs of deterioration: coughs that aren't productive, widening gait, fatigue, falling, toe walking. I watched.

Six months into our care, Jason and I went outside for batting practice and when I pitched him the ball, he missed and spun around, falling to the ground. He was unable to stop the momentum from his swing. Second pitch, same thing. "Mom, what's happening? Why am I falling?" I called the doctors. Within days he had to crawl on his knees up the stairs. He couldn't lift his dinner plate. He stared at me, scared, "It's too heavy." I tried to hide my shock, "I gotcha, Buddy," grabbed his plate and helped him upstairs to bed.

The doctors put him on steroids and explained the side effects: sleeplessness, weight gain, the moon shaped face, "but the worst effects are from long term use, loss of bone density, increased aggression when a patient is coming off the steroids . . ." his voice kind of trailed off. "I guess we don't need to worry about that . . ." *Shit!* We weren't long term and we were never coming off them. "Keep watching."

And then what? There is no cure. Doctors can increase his prednisone, and in the advanced stages give him oxygen at night and antibiotics for infections. Swimming becomes the exercise of choice and stretching will prolong comfort and mobility. We were cautioned not to let him work his muscles to exhaustion.

That was the hardest part for me: telling him not to run. When I was a kid, I remember running as fast as I could across sloping fields in the cool dusk, sweat wicking off my skin as I flew back and forth, happiness in motion. I want him to be able to run as fast as he can, fast, faster, so he can remember it forever: the burning cool in his lungs, his heart hammering in his chest, tingling and alive. "Mom, can you hold my sweatshirt?" Off he goes, running faster, faster, then smack into some weird, invisible force field. Mid-stride, his legs buckle and he crumples to the ground, laying where he falls and doesn't move. He shakes off his surprise, sits up and waits, his legs out straight. I walk over to him, "How're you doing?" He sits. "It's weird, Mom, they just stopped working." I ask if it hurts. "Not really, they just stopped working." I rub his hair, "Well, let's give 'em a rest, maybe take it a little easy, huh?" I give him a piggyback ride back to the blanket. "Did you see me, Mom? Did you see how fast I was running?" I sure did. "You were awesome, Buddy, superfast. Let's put that sweatshirt on for me." He pulls it on, "Good man."

* * *

We talked about muscular dystrophy in vague terms with all of the kids, providing a forum for discussion and questions. We checked in with Jason one-on-one: "Hey, Bud, how it's going with the MD, any questions?" He wanted to know if there was a cure yet. "Not yet but they're working on it, Pal, new discoveries every day." Jason looked at Dan. "Dad, will I have to be in a wheelchair?" Dan said, "Well, there may come a time when you find it's easier to get around if you have one. We'll trust you to tell us when that is. There are a lot of other things we can do in the meantime to help with your mobility if you need it." Jason was interested. "Like what?" Dan said, "Para-bouncing, rocket ships, personal pack helicopters . . ." Jason smiled.

Dan got a flight simulator for the computer, bought some used radio-controlled airplanes, and got us a family membership to the local radio-controlled aircraft club. He bought a buddy-box with a parental override in case your young pilot got in a tailspin, went for an outside loop, or had trouble landing. We went to air shows and flew radio-control gliders pulled into the air by little radio-controlled tow-planes. On cold or windy days, we flew our fleet of micro helicopters in the living room and stair wells. On the sunny days, we'd tip our heads back, staring into the sun, squinting to catch a flash off a rolling foil or looping tailpiece, climbing, banking, falling, "Dan. You're a genius," I whispered.

In the advanced stages of Duchenne's, a young man will have the use of a few fingers, his eyes, and his voice. As a young radio control pilot, Jason could make his planes do what his limbs couldn't; as his world pulled in, the planes could push it back out. A helicopter with a video feed means he could go anywhere. It meant he could play tag with the neighbor kids, hide and seek, peeking around corners with his remote control helicopter. Genius.

* * *

Twenty minutes into the family movie, it was clear Anthony was not interested. He was squirming and getting into it with the other kids. I told him to get his poem journal and meet me in the kitchen. We were writing a poem a day, on different places, people, events. "Okay, Anthony," I said, totally not in the mood. "Let's do a feeling poem today. Is there a feeling you want to write about?" Anthony thought a minute. "I feel mad." Excellent! "'I feel mad.' Write it down." He wrote laboriously in his marble composition book. He could not have strayed more outside the lines if he had tried. "Why do you feel mad, Anthony?" He said, "Because she hits me with a spoon." I asked Anthony who had hit him with a spoon. He said, "Ms. Smith hits me with a spoon." I whisper to him, "Very good, Anthony. Write it down." He got stuck on "with." We sounded it out together, "wh . . . wh . . . wh . . ." Anthony, excited, shouted "Double you!" I smiled, "Next, Ih . . . ih . . . ih . . ." Anthony was getting it. "I," he said. He paused and looked at me strangely, smiling. "Good, Anthony. Th . . . th . . . th . . ."

He paused again, looking up at me from his work, focused and quiet. This was not like him at all. His cheeks started to flush as he worked, pausing now and then to look at me. He finished his writing, put his pencil down, and smiled. I had never seen him so centered and calm. "Super, Anthony, now read it to me." Haltingly he read, "Anthony feels mad . . . because . . . she hits me . . . with a spoon."

His rounded cheeks were blushing with emotion. He stared

at me, smiling quietly, present and intimate. As I held his gaze, I felt I was seeing him for the first time. "How do you feel, Anthony?" He said, "Feel? Feel? Happy." I asked, "Why do you feel happy, Anthony?" He said, "I don't know."

Anthony was condensing, changing form before my eyes. I watched, breathlessly, as his true self flickered. Something beautiful was happening. I wanted him to know how he got here. "You feel happy because you wrote it down, Buddy, and now everyone can know why Anthony feels mad. Why do you feel mad, Anthony?"

He said, "Because Ms. Smith hits me with a big spoon." I saw a teaching moment and grabbed it, "Ah, a *big* spoon, nice detail!" I point to his composition book, "Let's add 'big' so the reader . . ." He cut me off. "No, no thanks." He held up his hand for me to stop and pulled the book back towards himself.

"No? You like it the way it is? We're good for today?" He nodded. He flipped a few of the pages back and forth in his poetry journal and then stopped. In a lucid, quiet, age appropriate voice he said, "Anthony's . . . feelings . . . is gone." He leaned back in his chair, exhausted and excited. He yelled, "Give me kissy, Mommy!" I embraced him and kissed his cheek.

* * *

"You've got a million dollar baby," his doctor said, pointing to the two-inch scar on Anthony's left thigh. It was the scar of last resort: invasive, painful, and expensive. "By the time they do a muscle biopsy on a two year old, they have run every other possible test and have nothing left to try." Anthony had suffered unexplained seizures as an infant; his eyes would roll back in his head and his lips would turn blue. Even though he was born full-term, tox-negative, the doctors thought maybe he had lesions on his brain, but further testing showed nothing. He was four months old when he was put in foster care, described as listless when not projectile vomiting. The muscle biopsy gave no answers, just more bad news. His muscle tissue had no dystrophin protein; he was a Duchenne's boy. Muscular dystrophy, completely unrelated to Anthony's original symptoms, is an X-linked recessive gene meaning his biological brother was potentially affected as well. That's how they found out Jason had Duchenne's—not that early treatment makes any difference, because there is no treatment. Anthony's Duchenne's was extreme. He was four years younger than Jason but would decline at the same rate as Jason, maybe faster.

I took Anthony to one of his teachers from public school for an informal assessment of his academic progress. After a year of home school and enormous effort trying to wake his potential, would he still be categorized as learning disabled? She asked, "Have you ever considered letting him be, just letting him live his life? I mean, given his medical condition?" It was a fair question. Educating these boys was a huge investment of time, money, patience, and energy for all involved. No one would expect our boys to seek gainful employment, few would even suggest it. But to let him be? Anthony has some pretty serious emotional and behavioral issues, easy enough to manage if he's strapped in a wheelchair. I could pull the plug on his electric wheelchair if he started acting out, but aggression doesn't go away with lack of mobility, just power. It's not moral agency unless you have a choice.

I read about another mother who had two sons with Duchenne's. When she found out, she asked the doctor what she should do. He told her, "Go home and love them up." She wasn't satisfied with that; her maternal instinct demanded she act. She raised her boys, raised awareness of the disease, raised money for research, and raised hope for her boys and muscular dystrophy families everywhere. And when her boys died, she kept fighting, a rare and noble act when your life is devastated by the loss of your personal motivators.

That mother had always loved her boys, from the minute they were born. Those boys were hers, and she was theirs. Their formative years were safe and nurturing, their needs were met, bonds were formed, and trust grew like their long bones in deep, peaceful sleep. They were loved. Unlucky, yes, to have a punishing, fatal disease. But I dream of her boys, their hearts grounded in love as their young bodies ground to a halt.

Our boys are unlucky among unlucky boys. They had no love, no trust to buoy them, no platform on which to discuss their feelings, their fears. They survived behind complex defenses; they fight, but do not trust. That is why I can't just let Anthony live his life. I have to teach him how to love and respect, so he will know he is loved and respected. He must learn the value of all life, so that he can value his. Knowledge is power: over himself, his world, his self-expression, and self-control. Like all MD parents, ours is a race against time, a race for a cure, for Duchenne's, but also our societal ills, a race for love and trust as their little bodies sit in slow setting cement.

Am I dreaming too big? Asking too much of his global delays? All I know is that Anthony feels mad because Ms. Smith hit him with a spoon. He wrote it down, he said it aloud and something changed, he saw himself anew. If we can teach him to write and read, paint, sing, and express himself, he can know who he is. I can't just let him live his life; not until he knows it is his life to live; not until he knows who he is, that he is mine and I am his.

* * *

The boys fare better than expected. The doctors think that it has something to do with them not growing. Tiny bodies have tiny levers, their muscles have less work to do and muscles don't tear if they don't grow. It's a bizarre and double-edged sword.

Anthony is eight and looks like he's three, Jason is twelve and looks like a seven year old. They are spoken down to, overprotected, and unable to go on roller coasters. The police picked Jason up walking home from lap swim, mistaking him for a five year old that had wandered away from home. "I hate this," he said. Of course he does. It doesn't help that Jimmy, also twelve, looks like he's seventeen.

The boys' therapists have told me, "You will need to be careful." What they mean is that when the boys really start to go, our whole house could crumble. They warned me of entire families getting depressed, especially the parents. This disease could redefine us. We may become a muscular dystrophy family, instead of a big, adoptive, multi-racial family. We'll trade in our two canoes and passenger van for a small bus with a lift and two wheelchairs. Our kids may be the survivors of brothers instead of survivors of foster care.

I will not fail. I will be strong and fierce, strong enough for all and the children will take their cue from me. Death is a part of living. I will show them how it's done, how to keep living when our hearts are broken, again and again. I will lead them, take their hands, and walk with them, across five stages of loss for the two we have lost. And if I falter, stumble and fall, I will sell my soul for self-delusion, the devil's denial. I will swear uncontrollably, swear to be strong, swear and swear as I clean our clothes, steep our rooms with fragrant flowers, fruits and melons, hire pianists to play for us, in a major key, in the key of G, reminiscent of our future past.

And if I fail and our grief turns sour, and the tar covered vines of depression crawl beneath our sills and up our walls, I will beat them back, palms up and fleshy, beat them and beat them and hit them with a spoon, "Get out! Get out!" I'll rear up on my hind legs, bare my teeth and roar, my baby's mama bear, "You want this house? Then you go through me! Nobody hurts my kids! Nobody hurts my kids!"

29

QUODLIBET

𝓜y parents have always said that if you do something as a family for three years in a row, then it's a tradition. For the Fox kids, once was enough. After their first Christmas, I overheard the kids talking: ". . . and we always get to open two presents on Christmas Eve, but one is from our parents, and we always know what it is because they always give us feet-y pajamas, and we always get to wear them that night and then all day long on Christmas day . . ."

Our Christmas season begins immediately after Thanksgiving dinner. We surrender our forks and, stuffed, move slowly to the piano. The lodge is cheery, but chilly; the propane heater is working overtime, the roaring fire in the fireplace creating an illusion of warmth. I sit down at the grand piano. Before I became a mother, I used to squander happy, careful hours tuning this piano; it is holding its pitch better than most of my other neglected hobbies. Everyone grabs a songbook, Jimmy opens the lid, and we stand around the piano singing through our Christmas carols. Dan stands behind me, watching the music over my shoulder and singing in his heart-melting baritone.

Is it corny? Hell yes! We're a Norman Rockwell on steroids, singing together as loud as we can and these are carols, mind you, not Christmas songs; no Frosty or Rudolph here. This is straight up "Hark the Herald" and "O Little Town of Bethlehem." No chaser. "Deck the Halls" is the hippest chart we got and the kids love it. They talk about the Christmas carols weeks before Thanksgiving, "Remember, Mom? And then we always sing the Christmas carols before we eat the pie? And then for 'Silent Night,' remember? We always sing the second verse without the piano?" It's appalling, this level of cheer.

Audrey reads in the corner, embarrassed for us, half cringing, half admiring of the kids' willingness to suspend their pasts and be innocents. I understand why she can't join us. She reads, watches, and smiles as we dive head first down a month-long slippery slide of sugar cookies, and careen into a vat of figgy pudding.

It's our first Christmas with their new sister Audrey, we crank the radio to the popular Christmas station as we drive home from the lodge. The kids know all the words. We put Christmas music on the sound system when we get home. Dan buys the biggest tree on the lot and ties it, canoe-like, to the top of the van. He holds the tree upright in the tree holder, while the four oldest kids each grab a stabilizing bolt and start screwing it into the base. The kids remember who put the star on top last year, whose turn it is this year, whose turn it will be next year, and the year after that. We cut out paper snowflakes and tape them to the windows, make red-and-green chains from construction paper to wrap around the tree and down around the banister. The first Christmas upstate, Dan changed the lights in the chandelier, mixing in red and green bulbs with the white ones. We never changed them back. This is a Christmas house, year round.

We have twenty or so plush velvet Santa hats that I bought at the Salvation Army in New York City. We put them on and do not take them off—indoors, outdoors, Santa's is the hat of choice for the month of December. Jason and Jimmy arrange the nativity scene on the upright piano; Anthony hangs the stockings over the fireplace in age order. It takes him a few times, but he gets it. Ruby and Susie untangle the lights and wrap them around the tree, top to bottom. We have our alcohol-free Wassail on the stove, its fragrant aroma adding harmony to our Christmas mix. The mood is calm and friendly.

Before the kids can send Santa their wish list, they have to make a list of gifts to give each other. We call social services and ask for a family that we can help during the holiday, a different family every year, usually a single mom with two or three kids. They give us the first names, ages, and sex of the children, along with a list of things that the kids might like. We put their information on the refrigerator and brainstorm: Toys, sure, but maybe they could also use some food? How about diapers? That's a good idea, they're expensive, and the little one is just two years old. Susie says, "How about some lotion? It gets kind of dry in the winter." Excellent. We write that down.

Jimmy says, "If they don't have any money, maybe we should give them some money. I can give them ten dollars from my savings." Dan agrees it's a good idea. We will match any Fox child donation times three. "So if you give ten dollars, Jimmy, and we donate three times that, how much will the family get?"

There is a pause, "Um, so you give them thirty dollars, and I give them ten dollars, so they have forty dollars." Christmas math.

All the kids donate what they are comfortable giving. We wind up with two hundred dollars for the family. "That's going to help!" Yes it will.

Now the kids can give us their wish lists to Santa. We order most of the stuff online, my tutor-elves help me with the rest. "Dan, are we spoiling them?" He answers quietly, "Not possible." We put out presents from the family under the tree and rearrange the furniture to make room for the slot car track. Dan has the kids assemble the track as a group, then races them, hour after hour, all the while Christmas music playing in the background.

* * *

The Fox family Christmas Party. Show time. The kids make the invitations to our "Holiday Open House," and we photocopy them onto red and green paper. Each kid takes a stack to school, to the YMCA, the library, and to our neighbors. Everyone is welcome.

A few days before the party, I was waiting for Jason in the lobby of his elementary school and one of the teachers came up to me, "You're having an open house, with no RSVP?" I smiled, "That is correct." She said, "Did you know that Jason photocopied one of his invitations when he got here this morning? Every child, teacher, and staff member in this school has an invitation." I laugh at Jason's generosity. "That's awesome," I say. "Bring 'em! We're ready! Are you coming?" She laughed, "Yeah, I'm coming. This I have to see."

The kids place bowls and bowls of clementines in the window sills, on the desks and tables, baskets of mixed nuts in their shells and nutcrackers standing by. We have soups on the stove, English tea rings, plates of cheese and crackers. Guests bring cookies, candy, and sugary goodness to share. We play Christmas music on the sound system and then, at the top of every hour, the kids pass out their hand-decorated caroling books to the guests, "I made this one, I hope you like it . . . It's a manger scene with a snow angel." They gather people to the piano and we kick it up. "Angels we have heard on high, gently singing o'er the plain . . ." I put the piano lid up on full stick. The louder I play the piano, the louder everyone sings.

We have potato soup on Christmas Eve, an advance penance

for our excess the following day. Dan and I leave cookies and milk for Santa, put the kids to bed, and then stay up until the wee hours wrapping gifts. It's our Christmas wish for our kids to feel valued, precious, adored, and indulged. Dan and I wake from our short sleep to the psychic energy of excited children waiting, the house vibrating with anticipation. The rule is, no one leaves his or her room until Dad calls everyone down, which will not happen before 7 a.m. We lie in bed, Dan and I, giggling, torturing them, making them sweat it out until 7:01. Then we release them into the spoils of Christmas morning, a free-fall frenzy of delight, shrieks and superlatives fly about the room like confetti. It's a wrapping paper ticker tape parade, a welcome home for our hero children, brave and strong.

And what's this? Santa brought us seven boxes of sugar cereal? A children's heaven. We eat one box a day until the New Year. On December 26 we go out to dinner at the Jade Buffet, an all-you-can-eat Chinese restaurant. There is a whole table just for fried food, an express train to a heart attack. There is pudding at the dessert table, a dream come true. We lounge. We do nothing. We play with our toys, go sledding, and watch movies. The mood is happy. Happy family.

30

HOW MANY ROADS

*a*nthony lays in the leaves that I'm collecting. Bright orange and red, faking a fire for the sake of October. "Hi, Mama!" Anthony squeals, "Look at me!" He is throwing the leaves in the air. They flutter down around him in brilliant decay. It's our third fall together, and we're spending a weekend at the lodge. I am shivering and raking, talking with Anthony while watching the other children. They are playing well. I drop my threat level to orange, use a soft focus lens for scanning, and stare for a moment into the abyss of the coming summer, still nine months away. Just thinking about it, I feel terrified. Summer is hell. I know what it costs and I know I don't have the energy I need to survive it. I, like the leaves, am burning out.

This is not just a bad day. It is every day. The fatigue is relentless, cumulative, and chronic. It has been a Tour de France-style uphill push since the kids moved in. Everyone sees what's happening to me: "You need to take a break, you can't keep up this pace." The problem is that there can be no break. To stop, or even slow down, is to fall backwards down the hill. I can't get off the bike because my feet are welded to the pedals, and even if I could unclip myself, dismount for one minute, I could never get back on. The hill is too steep, my consequences too great, and the crest too far away.

I dream of that crest, where our hill gives way and flattens and we can stop, finally, stop and rest. In my dreams, we find shade, spread quilts and make sandwiches. We were so not there yet. Not even close. We were still forming as a family. These things take time, but if it didn't happen soon, I was not going to make it. We needed unity, Umoja, trust. It was going to take something epic, something galvanizing to get there. I could still make it, stand on my pedals, get off my seat, and sprint through my death throes. I could do it but only if I truly believed it would work, that we would reach the crest and rest together as a family. I waited for the right moment to bring it up.

One evening the kids were in their rooms and Dan was outside with the dog. I walked out and stood beside him, silent, holding my constant cup of hot Darjeeling. Dan picked up a stick and threw it. I sipped. Charlie bounded like a much younger dog, grabbing it, shaking it, then laying down to chew. Dan and I stood side by side, eyes forward, quiet. I said, "Cross country road trip. They're the perfect age. If we do it this summer, they will look back and think we did it every summer." Dan said nothing but I could see his shift. I waited a minute and said, "We can think about it." I walked back inside and left him to think.

I brought it up again a few days later; I wanted him to know I was committed. "The whole family together, three weeks, round-the-clock, dealing with our issues as they come up. If we break down in Elko, we break down together. Think about your childhood. It's the road trip, am I right? Ask anyone about their childhood. They remember the road trip. It's what families do." We were in the kitchen, the kids were in bed, lights out. Dan said, "Come here, I want to show you something."

He sat down at the computer. "Take a look." He pulled up some routes he had been researching: "Drive south in June, then north in July to avoid the heat." He showed me a few vehicles he was looking at and, by the way, there is nothing hotter than an ex-Marine field engineer talking about diesel engines. RVs were out: our sight lines would be obstructed by bathrooms, kitchen, contours. Lord knows what Susie would try and hide in those cupboards. "We need a visual on hands and feet at all times."

We needed something strong. The United States climbs in elevation east to west, until it reaches the continental divide, then a taxing grind up and over. "It would have to get us across the pass." Dan pulled up a picture of a white Bluebird, flat-nosed, twenty-six-passenger bus. "The largest vehicle you can drive without a commercial license. This would do it." The price was right and it had an enormous rearview mirror in which the driver could see everyone, and everyone could see him. "Nice!" I said, "too bad it's in Texas." Dan turned and smiled at me. "Texas is dry, less rust. Jimmy and I will drive it up." Sold.

When they got back home, Dan tricked it out. He modified the overhead handrails to accommodate military surplus canvas stretchers to use for bunks. He took some seats out, reversed others, and built metal tables between them, like the dining cars in an Amtrak train. He attached three additional stacking stretchers in the far rear of the bus for sleeping at night and any child that needed a timeout during the day. He strapped a five-gallon cold water thermos with a spigot in the back corner and tied a small twelve-volt refrigerator to the floor. He removed the hydraulic lift by the rear cargo door but put it in the garage, "You never know." By each seat he installed a fold up beverage holder and in each holder, a twenty-four-ounce stainless steel water bottle, labeled with every passenger's name on it. He rigged the PA system to support a laptop, which he mounted and used as a screen for movie night.

Each child had a parental-issued pair of color-coded crocs, a duffel for their clothes, a toothbrush, two books, a journal, colored pencils, a sleeping bag, and a pillow. I kept the toiletries in a yellow travel kit, a first-aid in a red travel kit, and towels and swimsuits in a common bag. Dry food, canned food, perishables, and utensils were in duffels. Jimmy made a chess set out of Femo clay with magnets baked into the base of each wild colored piece. Jason made a Femo checkers set, Susie glued magnets to backs of Scrabble tiles, and Ruby drew Scrabble and chess boards onto paper, colored and laminated them. Two full decks of cards were in the emergency first-aid kit. Our journey began the day school let out.

*   *   *

All happy road trips are alike, but each road trip mishap is unique in its own way: the rainstorm at Niagara Falls, the snow at Crater Lake, the windstorm in Iowa shaking the bus through a sleepless night, tumbleweeds battering against our windows, flashes of lightning lighting up the sky. Jason's two hour timeout at Yellowstone Park, miraculously ending seconds before the geyser erupted. Jimmy's canvas stretcher splitting open beneath his butt while he was sleeping, and me buttressing said butt with nylon straps from the dry food duffel, while Jimmy slept soundly through it all. Charlie crashing through my parents' plate glass, floor-to-ceiling window in hot pursuit of a cat teasing him from the outside. We spent more on the emergency vet and custom glaziers for that doggie in the window than we paid for the bus.

After Charlie's, mine was the only other serious injury. I was walking backwards on the Golden Gate Bridge, taking a picture of the family walking behind me. I had Charlie on a leash. There was a bike-a-thon of some kind sharing the pedestrian walkway with us. I got the picture, and Charlie lunged. The kids told me later that I hit my head on a pole. All I remember was running to the bus, I got some ice on it, which helped the swelling and sped the draining of the blood and fluid into my right eye. Within a day or two, I had a shiner so big, it surpassed the perimeter of my sunglasses.

Clogging toilets at every hotel, rest stop, and relative's home became a new family tradition. On my third dripping trip to the front desk to borrow the plunger, one clerk said sweetly, "Why don't you just keep it?" Drawing 5 a.m. stares from the truck stop diner's diners, with our Fox family parade: a line of pajamas, curling through the restaurant to the bathrooms, day clothes, brushed teeth. Plate after plate of home fries, pancakes, sausage and bacon, hot chocolates with whipped cream and, "By the way, one of your toilets is backed up." We woke up one morning outside a Denny's in Bakersfield, still wearing our bandanas around our heads, proud souvenirs from the Grand Canyon. Someone approached me and asked if we were a church group.

Every day the kids wrote in their journals and made drawings. Every day we would set up the electric piano, and had our practice rotation. "Really, Mom? Can't we skip? We're on vacation!" I would answer them, incredulous, "Are you suggesting we shouldn't practice every day? I've never even heard such a thing. Skip piano? That's crazy talk!" They practiced. And when we were at a relative's house, they would practice for their audience, proud and impressive. It's what Fox children do.

Audrey hopped on the bus in Boulder. She'd been waiting for us at her Aunt Michelle's house; another house, another way of living, another family practicing kindness and respect. Michelle's husband, Uncle Bruce, took them rock climbing in Boulder Canyon. Uncle John hopped on the bus and played card games, I Spy, Hangman. I passed out M&Ms as bribes, one for every baby carrot or cherry tomato eaten. We made sandwiches: PB and J for lunch, turkey and cheese for dinner.

The bus was lively, laughing, with two guitars and ten singers, loud and proud.

Then as quickly as were loud, we came to the four corners and into the desert solitude. No singing, no journals, no piano. Desert dispensation. Moab, Arches, Monument Valley, Devil's Peak. The red, rough, ocean floor, serene and severe. We were visitors only, awed by the arid, inhospitable beauty of the desert, pulling us out of our lives and into ourselves. We sit by our windows, breathing dry air, staring in, staring out. Each of us alone, together. I look up at Dan from the back of the bus and watch him drive. He hears my eyes over the tireless pitch of the engine, looks up at me in his enormous rearview mirror, and smiles.

* * *

Ruby was struggling; she needed her alone time. We knew that this trip would challenge her and had hoped for a learning moment. She wanted to share her discomfort, worked the vibe, staring at me, rolling her eyes, not responding, and muttering under her breath. I was feeling for her, but with the younger four taking notes on what behavior would be tolerated, we had to shut it down. She flipped me off in front of everyone and swore at me under her breath. We stopped the bus, and Dan and I had a talk with her, letting her know we understood it was hard to be around everyone all the time, but that she was approaching the limit. She got back on the bus, angry and called me a bitch in a voice for all to hear. We got back off the bus to talk further between the two of us. Dan was firm and crystal clear. "Don't be surprised when it happens." She got back on the bus and walked to her seat without a look or a word.

We arrived midday in Reedley, California at the home of my horn teacher. Dave and his wife, Carol, had invited us to visit, feeling confident their 180 acres of vineyard could accommodate us. His sister lived next door and put up Dan, the kids, and me in her cottage, while Audrey and a tutor stayed with my brother in the guest house. It was California at its best: fresh peaches, oranges hanging from trees, tomatoes on the vine, lizards and hummingbirds, the Kings River reflecting the sun off its swollen, winding back.

The kids practiced piano and then swam hard all afternoon. We had dinner and played games. When we got back to the cottage, Ruby started talking smack to me, making a point of giving attitude behind Dan's back, but in front of the other kids. I tried to help her to cool it down—"Let's take a walk, Ruby"—but she wasn't hearing it. The vibe was escalating. Dan told her to sit in timeout, away from the other kids and as he turned to grab a chair, Ruby threw up her fist at me. She didn't hit me, but got close enough to show me she could. Threatening to hit in our house carried the same consequence as hitting. Together, Dan and I held Ruby in her first ever non-escalating restraint. She started screaming and kicking. I couldn't decide if I wanted to cry or throw up. She was too big for this—some things are much worse when you're older. She was swearing and screaming, "Let go of me, let go!" Dan told her we would let her go as soon as she stopped struggling. "I don't care! I hate you! I hate you!" Anthony started screaming and Jimmy started crying. Dan said, "Go to them, I've got Ruby." I spoke clearly but calmly over the screaming, assuring the kids that this was Ruby's choice, that she was not being hurt, "Come see." I took Jimmy by the arm, "Come on Jimmy, come see," but he didn't budge. He was frozen stiff, his eyes fixed on the corner where the screaming was coming from. "It's okay, Jimmy, no one is hurting her."

Susie was in the bedroom curled up, breathing deeply. "You okay, Susie?" She nodded. Jason was lying in bed, eyes closed. I picked Anthony up, carried him over to where Ruby was struggling. Dan looked at him and said, "This is her choice, buddy. She is free to go as soon as she stops struggling." Anthony stopped crying. Jimmy was sobbing and wouldn't move. I put Anthony on the couch and went back to Ruby. It lasted ten minutes. Finally Ruby was still and Dan asked her if she was ready. "Yes, Dad," she said, and we let her up. Dan got her a chair in view of the other kids and she sat.

I went to Jimmy, led him to bed and told him to lie down. He was still crying, eyes staring blankly. I said, "Hey, Jimmy. I know this was hard for you, I bet it probably brought up bad memories of when you kids were getting hurt. I'm sorry about that. We love Ruby and we are not going to let her behave in a way that is a danger to herself or to the members of this family. Are you okay, Jimmy?" He nodded, still crying. "How can I help you?" He didn't answer. "Would you like me to play the piano?" He nodded.

The practice keyboard was on the kitchen counter. I climbed up on a bar stool with Ruby sitting behind me quietly. I played slow movements from Mozart and Beethoven sonatas. The timeout ended. I turned the piano off, and said to Ruby, "Let's get your PJs on, teeth brushed. I'll make up your bed while you're in the bathroom." She smiled at me, "Thanks, Mom."

A few days later we had an incident in the back of the bus. Ruby was having an issue with me, swearing at me under her breath, not responding. I made a preemptive move to shut it down before the behavior escalated. I stood up. "Dan, we need to stop the bus." He answered, "You got it," and pulled over on the empty Oregon freeway.

I turned to Ruby, "Come with me." We exited the bus and stopped about three feet from the door. With a quietly charged voice, I said, "It seems we're having a problem, Ruby. Do you have something to say?" She shook her head. "Excuse me? I asked you a question. Do you have something to say to me?"

She whispered, "No, Mom."

"Then lose the attitude. If you have something to say, you say it."

She bristled, "But I didn't do anything."

I leaned in close to her face. "Ruby, you and I both know exactly what you were doing and the next time I see it, I will start counting. If I get to three, I will hold you down. Is that clear?"

"Yes, Mom."

I pressed it, "You're better than this, Ruby. Now get on the bus." She complied. "Yes, Mom." Dan closed the door behind us and started driving. My heart was racing. She had backed down.

Next, repair the relationship. I asked her to help me make lunch. We worked together catching apple slices from falling off the table, keeping the cherry tomatoes from rolling away. Ruby on peanut butter, me on jelly, coming together. "Sweetie, this behavior is not the way you want to go. You're fourteen, you're a big girl and you're going to scare people away. It's not you and it's not what you want." She passed me the loaf of bread, "I know, Mom. But I don't know how to do it. I want to be like a normal fourteen year old, but I don't know what to do." *Oh Ruby, my sweet girl. I love this girl.* "It's okay, Babe. It's not as hard as you think."

We made a list of women and girls, females we knew whom everyone respected. We identified the attributes that made them special. They all respected others and they all respected themselves. "Be yourself, Ruby. You don't have to be tough. I won't let you disrespect others and I won't let others disrespect you. If you're having a problem, let me handle it." She relaxed. "Thanks, Mom." I went on. "Honey, these teenage years are the best years for a mother and daughter." *Ha ha ha, as if. You will go to hell for this.*

"Really?" Ruby asked, surprised. I said, "Absolutely!" *You are so full of shit!* "Wow." Ruby was happy, looking forward.

"You're going to have a lot of feelings, even about me, but feelings aren't facts and the truth is, those feelings tell us we're connected, we're a team, we're going to get it going and face those hard times together. I love you, I love hanging out with you. I love being your Mom. I'm so proud of you and you're doing great." Ruby smiled that smile. "I love you too, Mom."

* * *

We entered Idaho, the land of my people, to visit my cousin Melanie and her husband, Max. As we pulled the bus into the driveway, my cousin's family came out to greet us. The girls were in their teens, beautiful and poised. Adam, the oldest boy, was married with a baby, the second oldest was engaged and there was our Jake, seventeen now, a young man. Smiles and hugs, introductions, we met Melanie's new son, a little cutie named Anthony. He was three years old and weighed more than our eight-year-old Anthony.

Melanie and Max had converted a horse barn into their beautiful two-story home. "No way! This was a horse stable?" They showed us the original metal bars from one of the stalls which they used to separate the kitchen from the rest of the house, "in case people don't believe us," Melanie explained. "And so when people ask our children if they were raised in a barn, they can say, 'I was, as a matter of fact.'"

We took a tour of the yard while Charlie rolled around with the other dogs and sniffed at the chickens and the goats with their little kids. Max and Melanie had an improvised outside swimming pool with a tiny, lone goldfish swimming in the middle of it. "That's Carl," Max explained. "He's our guard fish." Max lifted our kids up so they could see the fledglings in a bird's nest and let them collect the chicken eggs from the coop. Anthony was fascinated by Jake's wheelchair, asking questions, wanting to touch it and drive it. Jake let him sit on his lap and took him for a spin. Jason, on the other hand, would not look at Jake or his wheelchair. When introduced to Jake, Jason looked away and mumbled. We didn't press it.

Melanie's eldest daughter took the Anthonys outside to play; Melanie and Ruby made dinner, while Jason fixed a latch on the back door, and Dan and Max lifted heavy things. Melanie called us in when dinner was ready, and we packed around the table and blessed the food. We talked and visited while we ate, laughing and teasing, breaking bread, brothers and sisters, parents and children, and every kind of cousin: first, second, adopted, once removed.

After dinner the children broke off into smaller groups, the adults sat around the table and talked. I could hear Anthony and Jake talking on the other side of the metal bars.

"Why can't you walk, Jake?"

"Because my legs don't work, Anthony."

"How come they don't work, Jake?"

"I was born this way."

"Why were you born this way, Jake?"

"That's a hard question to answer, Anthony. I would have to ask God to find out and to be honest, I'm not sure I want to know the answer."

"Sorry about your legs, Jake."

"Thanks, Anthony."

*   *   *

My brother took over 2,000 photos on our trip. Dan and I chose 500 in which the kids were all happy, and laughing, and engaged. We ran our selection as a slideshow on our computer monitors and movie screen. It was pure propaganda; we were selling them an image of themselves, equal and opposite, their laughs and smiles shouting down the images of themselves as foster kids that still flashed across their psychic screens. Our slideshow was proof that the Smiths were wrong, and we were right: Fox children are happy, healthy, strong, and confident. That's what Fox children are. Or can be. We weren't there yet. These things take a long time.

The trip was over-the-top, yet everything I needed it to be. We were ready to oversee: confront the children less, manage their environments, remove triggers, redirect and avoid. Enjoy them more, correct them less, and provide a calm, safe, individual space for their brains to mature. And if it didn't work, we would try something else. Because that's what the Fox family does.

EPILOGUE

*F*ive and a half years have passed, about fifty years in Fox years. I have been waiting for a really good day where everyone was happy and moving forward to write this epilogue. It took a while to get there.

Dan and I are living on a sailboat in the Puget Sound with our three youngest kids. I haven't been bitten in months. Days go by without me even breaking a sweat. Sometimes I'll ground a kid or count them to three, just to keep my skills up.

Audrey married a German software engineer she met rock climbing. The ceremony took place in 2016 at my parents' home in California. They are currently living outside of Heidelberg and we got some FaceTime tours of the apartment, baking projects, and new cat. There is talk about starting a family soon and we're excited for them.

Ruby graduated high school last June, just before her nineteenth birthday, and moved back to upstate New York where we used to live. My spies tell me she is doing well, singing in the SUNY gospel choir and has had a steady boyfriend now for five months. (Shh! I'm not supposed to know that.) I told the children they could not start dating until they were thirty-five, hoping that would give me some negotiating room as they got older. But my sources all say he's a good guy and you know what? It's hard for anyone to maintain a relationship at that age, so good on her. Ruby started community college this month as a full-time student, and is working towards a degree in criminal justice. It's going well. She is making new friends and catching up with some old ones.

Jimmy celebrated his eighteenth birthday two months ago during boot camp at Pendleton. He is now a private in the US Marine Corp, and spent the last ten days at home on leave. My sister asked him what the hardest part of boot camp was and he said, "Missing my family." I drove him to the airport at 3 a.m. for a flight back to San Diego, where he will train for another month, then get assigned to Lord knows where. I gave him a hug goodbye, "I love you, Jimmy." He hugged me back, big hug, bigger smile. He turned and walked towards security, then stopped, looked back and we waved to each other. I stood there, waving. He looked back three times to wave before disappearing around a corner. One of the airport staff said, "You can walk with him to security if you want." Tears were streaming down my face, "No, it's okay," I said, "he doesn't need me bawling all over him."

Jason is seventeen and a senior in public school. He's getting straight As (except for math), manages the wrestling team, and sings in the choir. He plays piano, writes his own songs, singing beautifully in tune, a core Fox family value. Jason sang at Audrey's wedding, and is available for birthday parties and poetry slams. He opens this weekend as a solo act for a regional battle of the bands called "Rock the Island." After graduation in the spring he is planning to attend a culinary arts school and become a chef.

Susie is sixteen, a sophomore in public school and a promising violinist, performing regularly in recitals, chamber music groups, and regional youth orchestras. She is currently singing one of the lead roles in the school musical and taking a break from running track and field to get her grades up. She wants to go to college and be a social worker.

Anthony is fourteen, growing slowly, but steadily. He's four feet tall and is celebrating his recent growth spurt into size 7 children's clothes! We're still homeschooling him, reading Harry Potter and studying piano. Anthony swims two hours every day and rides his bike when the weather permits. Both he and Jason are healthy, completely mobile with no deterioration in the past three years. The doctors ordered another genetic screening of them to be sure the diagnoses for Duchenne's muscular dystrophy is correct; the disease is not manifesting characteristically. The test confirmed they have Duchenne's, but can't explain why they're doing so well.

It was a rough time getting here and we know there are rough times ahead. We still take it a day at a time, working to build our family even as the kids are growing up and leaving. Some days I succumb to empty nest envy, wishing I could miss all our kids sooner. Dan and I are exhausted, but take heart in knowing the older kids have a home to miss, and the younger ones can see a future ahead. Ruby texted me the other day, "I'm nervous about going to college." I texted back, "It's okay to be nervous, sweetie. We've seen you work hard. We know you can do it." She wrote back, "You're right. I'm a Fox kid. We are strong and confident. We always make it through."

ACKNOWLEDGMENTS

THANK YOU:

FOR MAKING THIS BOOK
Kelsey Sears, for getting up early with the kids so I could stay up late and write

Nina Jeppesen, my first and gentlest reader

Lily Holgate, for helping me find my voice and being a hard ass in the kindest possible way

Lee Cyphers, for making me sound smarterer

Sheila Silver, for her relentless championing of me

Dave and Carol Krehbiel, my tag-team, safe-place, two-part patronus

FOR READING AND GUIDING MY WRITING
Veronica Alvarado, Elizabeth Ballantyne, Sharon Boorstin, Reiko Davies, Kate Elliott, Sabina Thatcher, Elizabeth Flemming, John Gattis, Sue Heineman, Tommy Johnson, Krista Kaufman, Nick Lyons, Laura Marostica, Julie Miesionczek, Anette Naumann, Dan Paget, Gena Rapps, Peggy Fletcher Stack, Laura Weiner, Keve Wilson

TO THE VILLAGE
Mayor and Auntie, Marie Ellsworth
Behavioral Health Services North
Plattsburgh City School District

Plattsburgh YMCA
Plattsburgh Public Library
Seton Catholic
UVM Pediatric Neurology
Pat Cordes, Andrea Ogle, Benn Rymon, Marilyn Reynolds,
and our neighbors on the US Oval

TO ALL OF OUR TUTORS
(in order of appearance)
Tommy J., Leroy B., John M., Marie C., Lucy B., Jen M., Kelsey
S., Jen C., Vicky B., Donna K., Rachel C., Casey C., Amanda
T., Beza W., Eunice O., Monica H., Ally E., Carly C., Lily H.,
Lorenzo K., Owen L., Joelle T., Jessica L., Liam M., John O.,
Erik E., Mariel L., Julian C., Katy R.

TO THOSE WHOSE MUSIC SAVED MY MORTAL SOUL
Renée Allen, Ray Anderson, Andy Bove, Ken Cooper, Lacina
Coulibaly, Stefania DeKennesy, Debra Dine, Rachel Drehmann,
Wayne DuMaine, Suzanne Farrin, Matt Fieldes, Annamae
Goldstein, Marianne Gythfeldt, Sue Heineman, Lily Holgate,
Dan Paget, Lew Soloff, Jo-Anne Sternberg, Sabina Thatcher,
Mark Timmerman, Keve Wilson, Pascal Von Wroblewsky, and
to Brian Pertl and the Lawrentians

TO MY LIFELINE
My family relations, my besties

TO MY HEROES
Ruby, Jimmy, Jason, Susie, Anthony, and Audrey

AND TO D.J.W.
The love of my life